Dr. Powell
Behavioral Sci
W.O.U.

MW00338885

FORENSIC EVALUATION
AND TREATMENT
OF JUVENILES

FORENSIC EVALUATION AND TREATMENT OF JUVENILES

INNOVATION AND BEST PRACTICE

RANDALL T. SALEKIN

American Psychological Association • Washington, DC

Published by
American Psychological Association
750 First Street, NE
Washington, DC 20002
www.apa.org

To order
APA Order Department
P.O. Box 92984
Washington, DC 20090-2984
Tel: (800) 374-2721; Direct: (202) 336-5510
Fax: (202) 336-5502; TDD/TTY: (202) 336-6123
Online: www.apa.org/pubs/books
E-mail: order@apa.org

In the U.K., Europe, Africa, and the Middle East, copies may be ordered from
American Psychological Association
3 Henrietta Street
Covent Garden, London
WC2E 8LU England

Typeset in Goudy by Circle Graphics, Inc., Columbia, MD

Printer: Maple Press, York, PA
Cover Designer: Mercury Publishing Services, Inc., Rockville, MD

The opinions and statements published are the responsibility of the authors, and such opinions and statements do not necessarily represent the policies of the American Psychological Association.

Library of Congress Cataloging-in-Publication Data
Salekin, Randall T.
  Forensic evaluation and treatment of juveniles : innovation and best practice / by Randall T. Salekin.
     pages cm
  Includes bibliographical references and index.
  ISBN 978-1-4338-1934-6 — ISBN 1-4338-1934-1 1. Juvenile delinquents—Rehabilitation. 2. Juvenile justice, Administration of. 3. Restorative justice. I. Title.

  HV9069.S243 2015
  364.36—dc23

                                 2014035188

British Library Cataloguing-in-Publication Data
A CIP record is available from the British Library.

Printed in the United States of America
First Edition

http://dx.doi.org/10.1037/14595-000

To Karen, Tyler, and Alexandra:
The three of you are a terrific source of inspiration.

CONTENTS

ACKNOWLEDGMENTS

In the course of producing this book, I realized there are a great many people to thank for their contributions. I would like to thank my primary mentors, Richard Rogers and Jim Ogloff, for their help in getting me started in the field. Their advice has been invaluable. In addition, I would like to thank Susan Reynolds for her steady support, thoughtful help, and wisdom in helping me find a home for this book. I owe a thank-you to David Becker, Ann Butler, and Eric Ustad for their work on the manuscript. I also owe a lot to my dedicated students as well as students who have worked in the Disruptive Behavior Clinic—Liz Adams, Xinying Ang, Lee Bare, Abby Clark, Sarah Debus, Crystal Dillard, Casey Dillon, Ross Grimes, Natalie Harrison, Karen Hubbard, Anne-Marie Iselin, Franz Kubak, Whitney Lester, Emily MacDougall, Jill Rosenbaum, Meghann Sallee, and Kim Sokowloski. Similarly, I owe gratitude to my many friends in the American Psychology–Law Society, Division 41 of the American Psychological Association. In this regard, I am thankful for the advice and scholarly work of Marc Boccaccini, Stan Brodsky, Elizabeth Cauffman, Rob Cramer, Keith Cruise, Mark Cunningham, Dave DeMatteo, Kevin Douglas, John Edens, Paul Frick, Naomi Goldstein, Tom Grisso, Laura Guy, Stephen Hart, Kirk Heilbrun, Matt Huss, Eva Kimonis, Ivan Kruh, John Monahan, Tonia Nichols, Candice

Odgers, Dustin Pardini, Barry Rosenfeld, Martin Sellbom, Jennifer Skeem, Jodi Viljoen, Gina Vincent, and Patricia Zapf. I also thank Randy Otto, Alan Goldstein, and Richard Frederick, also members of the American Psychology–Law Society, who often provided me the opportunity to conduct workshops on the topic of juvenile forensic evaluations for the American Academy of Forensic Psychology. I also owe thanks to Ted Altar, Eric Chu, Ted DeLaet, and Murray Ferguson for their invitations to provide workshops in their provinces in Australia and Canada and to states not typically covered by the American Academy of Forensic Psychology workshops. Conducting workshops on the topic of forensic assessment and treatment of juvenile offenders and receiving participant feedback has been incredibly valuable. The two-way interchange has helped me think about the complexity of these evaluations and has shaped my thinking and the eventual development of this book. I extend a thank-you to Joel Dvoskin. Through Joel's assistance, I became increasingly involved in the treatment of juvenile offenders in the state of Alabama. I also owe thanks to Walter Wood, Steve Lafreniere, Tim Davis, Alesia Allen, John Faile, and Judge Philip Lisenby for their help with this body of work. I greatly value the friendship, scholarship, and practice of all those who have assisted with the production and publication of this volume.

FORENSIC EVALUATION AND TREATMENT OF JUVENILES

INTRODUCTION

The primary goal of this book is to offer a synthesis of recent research and policy development on adolescent offenders and to provide state-of-the-art guidance to clinicians who want to conduct disposition and transfer evaluations. In the past decade, a large body of literature has accumulated on the risk assessment of young people. In addition, research pertaining to the treatment amenability of adolescent offenders has expanded. An area that has perhaps seen the greatest growth is that of the *developmental maturity* of adolescents. This line of research was sparked by advocates and scientists concerned with the increasingly harsh treatment of children in the legal system. Scholars publishing in the developmental maturity literature have attempted to show the connections between adolescent (im)maturity and criminal behavior. Some of this research has suggested that because of their immaturity, adolescent offenders may be more prone to, and less culpable for, antisocial behavior than adults (Moffitt, 1993; L. Steinberg & Scott, 2003). Developmental maturity has subsequently been considered in recent

http://dx.doi.org/10.1037/14595-001
Forensic Evaluation and Treatment of Juveniles: Innovation and Best Practice, by R. T. Salekin

U.S. Supreme Court rulings and state-level mandates (Bonnie, Johnson, Chemers, & Schuck, 2012; Scott & Steinberg, 2008). Examples include *Roper v. Simmons* (2005), which abolished the death penalty for juveniles; *Graham v. State of Florida* (2010); and *Miller v. State of Alabama* (2012), which held that juveniles cannot be sentenced to life without the possibility of parole for nonhomicide and homicide offenses. (The term *juvenile* generally refers to youth under age 18 years, although legal definitions of the term may vary from state to state.) The wave of change in the manner in which juveniles are treated is also reflected in New York State's movement toward the provision of treatment for young offenders in designated communities rather than in detention centers and residential facilities.

In addition to developmental maturity concerns, recent research has also shown the very high levels of mental health problems and mental disorder in juvenile offenders, especially those in detention (Becker, Kerig, Lim, & Ezechukwu, 2012; Kang, Wood, Eno Louden, & Ricks, 2014; Teplin, Abram, McClelland, Dulcan, & Mericle, 2002; Teplin, Welty, Abram, Dulcan, & Washburn, 2012), underscoring the need for a more developmentally sensitive and psychologically informed approach to the treatment of juveniles. Advancements in the research base for understanding key juvenile concepts, as well as significant changes in policy and law, highlight the pressing need for a book on the very best practice regarding juvenile forensic evaluation and treatment.

It is this confluence of rapid change in research and policy that led to the writing of this monograph. Through science and practical experience, it became increasingly clear to me that five vital factors should be examined in juvenile offenders when conducting disposition and transfer evaluations. These elements include the (a) truthfulness of youth and parent report, (b) youth personality and pathology, (c) risk for dangerous behavior (d) developmental maturity, and (e) treatment amenability. These five broad issues are at the heart of juvenile evaluations because they provide the necessary psychological fuel to write detailed and comprehensive psychological reports for the courts. Because of the high importance of these constructs and what they signify for the developing juvenile, they are covered in considerable detail in this book (*Kent v. United States*, 1966; Rogers, 2008; Salekin & Grimes, 2008).

Although juvenile evaluations are difficult in many respects, this book provides a clear road map for how to conduct them. In these chapters, I demonstrate how tests can be combined to develop a sound psychological battery that will facilitate a better understanding of relevant psycholegal constructs. In the pages that follow, readers will find information on how traditional and structured interviews can facilitate clinical judgment and better guide analysis, report writing, and testimony. Also discussed are various self-report, behavioral rating scales, and even projective tests (e.g., the Thematic

Apperception Test; H. A. Murray, 1937) and their links to pertinent legal concepts. This volume covers specific forensic assessment tools, such as the Risk–Sophistication–Treatment Inventory (Salekin, 2004), the Structured Assessment of Violence Risk for Youth (Borum, Bartel, & Forth, 2005), and the Youth Level of Service/Case Management Inventory (Hoge, 2005), that can facilitate clinical decision making as it pertains to disposition. Using accurate assessment technology leads to increasingly precise information and clearer clinical formulations. Accurate evaluations will have a favorable net effect on the youngest members of U.S. society as well as young people in other countries by directing them toward adequate treatment programs early in their development while their ability to change still holds so much promise.

This book is divided into 10 chapters. In Chapter 1, I define disposition and transfer evaluations, discuss the juvenile justice system and the legal process, and provide an overview of the different potential placements for young people within the system. Forensic clinicians will learn when they might be called on to conduct juvenile evaluations as well as where such evaluations may occur. In the second chapter, I review juvenile characteristics, political climate, and transfer. I highlight the demographic contours of juvenile offenders as well as underscore the need to be cognizant of the political atmosphere in the United States. Next, in Chapter 3, readers will find a review of the forensic mental health concepts that apply to juvenile offenders and their placement. I address issues related to veracity of children's reporting; personality and pathology; and three key constructs that pertain to juvenile evaluation cases: (a) risk, (b) developmental maturity, and (c) treatment amenability. Chapter 4 concerns the science behind the forensic mental health concepts, and in Chapter 5, I discuss factors concerning preparation for evaluations and general practice guidelines with young offenders. In Chapter 5, I also delineate what will be required from clinicians before mental health professionals can ethically and competently conduct juvenile evaluations. In Chapter 6, I cover data collection methods and specify what information is needed for the evaluation itself and how to comprehensively obtain such information. Given that this material is the needed content for the evaluation, I offer details on how to search for, and uncover, key pieces of psychological information that can lead to the very best clinical decisions. The focus of Chapter 7 is on interpretation and on providing readers with further guidelines for both collecting and interpreting their data.

I offer in Chapter 8 information on report writing and testimony, and I delineate how forensic clinicians can collate the psychological material they obtain from multiple sources into a clear and comprehensive report. This chapter also contains information on how to testify in juvenile and adult courts. Further, the chapter details how psychologists can continue to help to shape policy, improve adolescent forensic evaluations, and provide opportunities to rehabilitate young people within the justice system. Chapter 9 covers the topic of treatment and offers new insights into what forensic clinicians can look for in treatment programs in order to make recommendations that facilitate improved youth conduct and well-being. Last, in Chapter 10, I summarize the information covered in the preceding chapters and highlight several new directions for psychological evaluations of young people involved with the legal system.

Over the past 10 years, while conducting workshops on the topic of the assessment and treatment of juvenile offenders, I have become increasingly aware that there existed no one book that specifically provided detailed and focused guidance on disposition and transfer evaluations. This volume is intended to fill that void. The book is designed for use by psychologists, psychiatrists, social workers, and other allied mental health professionals working in the juvenile justice system. It will likely also be of value to upper level undergraduate students wanting to learn about forensic assessment of juveniles for the first time and for graduate students wishing to obtain training in juvenile forensic assessment and treatment. Indeed, many social and behavioral science doctoral programs require a practicum or internship for which it is expected that trainees step out of their offices and conduct live evaluations with young individuals involved with the law.

Although I wrote this book for forensic clinicians at various levels of the profession, it is also meant to be valuable to lawyers, judges, criminologists, and legal scholars who would like an insider's view into the thinking and science behind juvenile psychological evaluations, their interpretation, report writing, and end-point testimony. Such knowledge will likely assist attorneys in the preparation of their cases and will certainly aid juvenile and adult court judges in their construal of psychological reports. In short, this book is intended for those who work with young people within the juvenile justice system and especially for professionals or upcoming professionals who have a keen interest in learning more about forensic clinical practice and who want to promote, wherever possible, the healthy psychological development of young people who have come into contact with the law.

1

LEGAL CONTEXTS AND MORE

The risks associated with being young are well documented in American fiction. Consider Mark Twain's novels depicting the various societal troubles encountered by the exploratory behavior of the youthful Tom Sawyer and Huckleberry Finn. Their conduct is portrayed as investigative, playful, occasionally destructive, and temporary. *Calvin and Hobbes*, a popular comic strip that at its peak was published worldwide in more than 2,400 newspapers, portrayed an even younger child whose spirited attitude bordered on oppositional and whose conduct teetered on dangerous. In the real world, Calvin's daily actions might be considered a risk factor for later life setbacks.

The hazards associated with the adolescent years are also well articulated in the scientific literature, in which developmental pathway research documents the "normality" of mild delinquency but also underscores the ways in which delinquency can be extreme and translate into adult criminality. Pathway research has shown that the bulk of children who engage in delinquency do so temporarily during adolescence and then, fortunately, desist shortly thereafter (Loeber, 1991; Moffitt, 1993, 2003). However, research has

http://dx.doi.org/10.1037/14595-002
Forensic Evaluation and Treatment of Juveniles: Innovation and Best Practice, by R. T. Salekin

also identified a smaller, more enduring class of young offenders whose criminal activity is quite destructive and projects into adulthood. These young people are often identified as *chronic offenders* in antisocial taxonomies. The scientific literature on pathway research also typically describes how an array of risk and protective factors can shape this variation in development, describing, for example, the ways in which youth living in high- and low-risk environments can be set on markedly different life trajectories (Barker, Trentacosta, & Salekin, 2011; Belsky, Bakermans-Kranenburg, & van IJzendoorn, 2007; Belsky, Fearon, Bell, & Bell, 2007; Lahey, Moffitt, & Caspi, 2003; Loeber, 1991; Loeber, Stouthamer-Loeber, & Green, 1991; Moffitt, 2003, 2007).

Variation in several areas—severity (e.g., violence, petty theft), motivation (e.g., play, jealousy, revenge), environment (e.g., nourishing, neglectful), and youth characteristics (e.g., extraverted, adventuresome, mean)—highlights the need for individualized forensic assessment and treatment. This process can be complicated but it is manageable if forensic clinicians are well trained and prepared for the task at hand (see, e.g., Chapter 5, this volume). Equally complex, however, especially at first glance, can be the juvenile and adult court systems themselves. Because forensic clinicians do not operate in a vacuum, knowledge regarding these systems allows for optimal practice. Thus, as a first step toward better understanding juvenile evaluations, forensic clinicians will require an understanding of the legal context and the subsystems that make up the broader juvenile justice system.

Fortunately, learning to navigate the various systems is a matter of familiarity. Acquiring knowledge about forensic evaluation and the juvenile and adult justice systems can be akin to learning a new city subway system. Forensic clinicians will discover that there exist various subsystems, interwoven at various locations, that all underpin the broader juvenile justice system. As with a new subway system, one has to learn the rules of the rail system, including what fees might be charged, what one can carry on the train, and how to act and dress. Likewise, one has to learn the specific subway lines and various subsystems and stations prior to effectively getting to the location to see the city sites. Although the locations within the legal system bring with them abundantly more responsibility than visiting a new city of interest, and they have much more at stake than discovering a new city attraction, they also bring an opportunity to offer one's expertise in ways that can empower youth development, facilitate public safety, and assist with the sculpting of policy and practice.

The current chapter covers four broad topics that help prepare the clinician for forensic practice with young offenders. First, I offer an overview of the development of the juvenile justice system in the United States. This section of the chapter is designed to be a brief introduction to the history of the juvenile justice system and touches on several chief areas, including the initial processing of juveniles in criminal courts, shifts in social life that led to the development of the juvenile court, the adoption of juvenile code across the United States, and the various eras through which the courts have moved. This initial section is meant to provide a succinct rationale for the system's development as well as overview its broad changes over the years. In addition, this section is intended to help the forensic clinician understand why various subsystems are required to effectively operate the juvenile justice system. Additional details on this topic can be garnered from other sources (e.g., Sacks & Reader, 1992; Schetky & Benedek, 1980; Tanenhaus, 2000).

Second, I review the integration of psychology into the juvenile justice system. I highlight how psychology and other allied mental health fields have occupied a place within the juvenile justice system in essence from its inception. This discussion underscores how professionals in the field of psychology continue to work jointly with the juvenile justice system, providing both scientific information and practice guidelines.

Third, I provide definitions for disposition and transfer evaluations, to help readers understand the purpose of each evaluation. Details on the assessments themselves are given throughout the book.

Fourth, I provide an overview of juvenile law and the various points and locations at which forensic clinicians will find themselves conducting evaluations, including preliminary information regarding what is required for best practice in juvenile assessment and intervention, to initiate an understanding of the best way to achieve excellence in this field. Taken together, the various sections of this chapter set the stage for best practice and innovation in the assessment of young people involved with the law.

HISTORY OF THE JUVENILE COURT SYSTEM IN THE UNITED STATES

Public perception of adolescent offenders has changed drastically over the years. These views have ranged from rehabilitative perspectives to crime control outlooks. Young people (i.e., under age 18) historically were processed in a single adult court, and there is some evidence to suggest that, during this time (before 1899), discretion may have been exercised for some, but likely not all, youthful offenders (Feld, 1997, 1999; Zimring, 1998). The processing of youth in a single court had primarily to do with general beliefs that children and adults differed in age and physicality but not necessarily in terms of intellect or culpability. Two key events foreshadowed the development of the juvenile justice system. The first occurred in 1825, when the New York House of Refuge was established, allowing for the separation of young offenders from adult offenders. At the time, philanthropists believed that children could suffer more harm from being treated like adults and being placed in adult jails than if they were provided a developmentally sensitive alternative (Sacks & Reader, 1992; Meng, Segal, & Boden, 2013; Schetky & Benedek, 1980). The second major event was when John Augustus, early in the 1800s, began serving as a "probation officer" for young adult offenders. His laudable goal was to provide young people with an opportunity to reform while allowing them to remain in the community. For his initiatives, Augustus is thought to be the forefather of our formal probation system, given that his actions ignited the ideals of this new way of handling young offenders (Fagan & Zimring, 2000).

Changes in social life continued in the United States over the early and middle part of the 19th century, and novel philosophical views powered many positive societal changes, including the development of a public education system, child labor laws, and the promotion of the intellectual growth of children. The momentum for promoting the nurturance and education of children in broader society eventually set in motion the movement for a separate legal system for youth. In 1899, the state of Illinois adopted the first juvenile code, which established the country's very first juvenile court (Sacks & Reader, 1992; Schetky & Benedek, 1980).

The establishment of the juvenile court changed the way young people were processed from that year forward by imposing an overarching objective of rehabilitation. The concern of this law was the character of the young individual rather than the nature of the offense. The movement was geared toward "saving" children, and this naturally led to the development of proceedings with a rehabilitative aim. Given that the system was designed to protect youth, the proceedings were informal and held behind closed doors. Theoretically, there was no need for the formal protection of due process because all parties were interested in the same overarching goal: the rehabilitation and improved well-being of young people. Given that there was a focus on the healthy development of the young person, records were sealed to avoid stigmatization of children and adolescents who had broken the law.

In the 20 years following the initiation of the first juvenile court, many states officially enacted juvenile court laws in an effort to help, protect, and rehabilitate, rather than punish, young offenders. Dispositions evolved on the basis of the model of examining and diagnosing environmental problems (e.g., social) rather than solely focusing on the young person's offense. Under the rehabilitative model, the juvenile court's two key considerations included (a) who needed treatment (risk, mental health needs, maturity) and (b) who could benefit from it (amenability). This fortunately opened the doors of the courts to psychology, psychiatry, and allied mental health professions. The chief expectation of the mental health field was that professionals would be able to provide information on the psychological, developmental, and environmental needs of the young person. The mental health field was also called on to provide information regarding what could be expected in terms of psychological change in young people, either with or without intervention (Grigorenko, 2012; Sacks & Reader, 1992; Schetky & Benedek, 1980; Tanenhaus, 2000).

Despite the good intentions of the juvenile justice system, there have been critics of the approach, and this has led to different views regarding how to handle juvenile offenders. Indeed, over the years the pendulum regarding the processing of young offenders has swung back and forth between a *rehabilitative model* and a *crime control model*. These shifts in philosophy have been conceptualized into four eras of the juvenile justice system (Grisso, 1998/2013). The first era, described above, was the *parens patriae* era, during which the emphasis was on rehabilitation. This era was followed by the *due process* era, when the rights of juvenile offenders were the main concern. This second era was sparked by what appeared to be arbitrary decision at the juvenile court level (e.g., youth receiving exceedingly stiff sentences that would not be allocated if they were charged as an adult) and concerns about transfer proceedings. Two cases in particular (see *In re Gault*, 1967, and *Kent v. United States*, 1966) made their way to the Supreme Court. In *In re Gault* (1967), Supreme Court Justice Abe Fortas ruled that juveniles should be afforded many of the due process rights as adults (e.g., the right to question witnesses, the right to an attorney), and in *Kent v. United States* (1966), Justice Fortas outlined factors that should be considered in transfer hearings (e.g., whether the offense had been committed in a violent, premeditated, or willful manner). The third era has been referred to as the *get tough* era; it stemmed from unease regarding the rate of violent crime in the mid-1980s. This led to tougher punishments of the juvenile offender. I discuss the due process era and the "get tough" era in greater detail in Chapter 2. Finally, the fourth and emerging era is one that, once again, focuses on developmental differences and is a return, of sorts, to the rehabilitative era. It differs from the first era in that the present-day era has been increasingly inspired by discussions regarding adolescent brain development and neuroscience research (e.g., Aharoni et al., 2013; Aronson, 2007; Glenn & Raine, 2014).

Throughout these periods, psychology has played a key role in better understanding young people involved with the law (e.g., Strasburger, 1989). The recent advances in psychological theory, new forensic test development, insights from juvenile research, and improvements in the ability to measure brain activity have sparked even further interest in the potential to solve the puzzle of juvenile delinquency and redirect youth to prosocial life paths. Recent science has also put psychology and allied mental health fields on the map in a more serious way in terms of being in a better position to provide increasingly empirically based evaluations and interventions for youth who come into contact with the law (Eyal et al., 2007; Glenn & Raine, 2014; May, Osmond, & Billick, 2014). As a consequence, mental health professionals are in a position to write progressively more clear and instructive psychological reports that will be powered by increasingly sophisticated science. In the following section, I describe several chief historical psychological contributions to the juvenile justice system that led to the better integration of the two fields (psychology and juvenile justice) in modern-day practice.

PSYCHOLOGY AND THE JUVENILE JUSTICE SYSTEM

American psychologist G. Stanley Hall, who had previously worked under William James at Harvard University, first began his study of adolescence at Clark University in the early 1900s. His research on adolescence roughly coincided with the establishment of the first juvenile court. At the time, the study of adolescence was brand new and very little was known regarding the nature of this human developmental stage. It was in fact Hall who coined the term *adolescence*. Through his studies and writings, Hall (1904) helped promote the idea of adolescence as a discrete category of human development and stimulated research on the topic that is still being realized today. The early contributions of Hall and the psychologists who followed in his footsteps, such as Erik Erikson (1968) and James Marcia (1966, 1980), provided an initial foundation for understanding this specific developmental stage as one that differed in meaningful ways from both childhood and adulthood. As one specific example, Hall's early contributions subsequently helped facilitate our understanding of adolescence by suggesting that both biological and environmental factors likely explained why some adolescents test societal rules whereas others do not.

Subsequent work on adolescence and the law, including work by present-day scientists such as Thomas Grisso and Laurence Steinberg, have paved the way for research and clinical work with adolescent offenders. Their scientific efforts moved the field of adolescent psychology and the law even farther forward by underscoring developmental differences between children and adults. For instance, their work has demonstrated that there are potential disparities regarding what juveniles are capable of understanding in court proceedings in comparison to adults (Grisso et al., 2003). This research has hinted that a specific minimum age may signal threshold levels of competence to stand trial. Moreover, their work suggests that there may be concerns regarding decision-making capacity during the adolescent years that could affect culpability. For instance, using simulation designs, this research has examined the risks youth take when driving a car that may also pertain to the risks they take in other settings. These findings may eventually illuminate what requisite abilities (e.g., foresight, emotion regulation) are necessary for adult-like decision making (Gardner & Steinberg, 2005). Other contributions, such as those by Loeber (1991) and Moffitt (1993), have facilitated a better understanding of the various life tracks youth can take based on risk and protective factors that sculpt development. Also, of course, legal scholars have provided an increasing amount of detail regarding how psychological material can be presented in order to assist with disposition decisions (Feld, 1997, 1999; Zimring, 1998). This two-way interchange between psychology and the law has advanced what forensic clinicians have been able to offer in their psychological evaluations and interventions.

PSYCHOLOGICAL EVALUATIONS FOR JUVENILE AND ADULT COURT: TWO PRIMARY TYPES OF EVALUATION

There are two commonly requested and highly important evaluations related to young persons involved in the legal system. These evaluations have historically been the means by which professionals in psychology and allied mental health fields have assisted the courts. Evaluations and resultant psychological reports are geared toward answering the question of what should be done to help a specific young person who has come before the juvenile court. These two primary evaluations are (a) *disposition evaluations* and (b) *transfer evaluations*. Disposition evaluations can occur at various stages in the process, such as at preadjudication, postadjudication, and sometimes when the young person is already in a treatment program. Transfer evaluations can be requested by juvenile court judges, attorneys, and criminal court judges. Requests from the latter occur when youth have been automatically transferred to adult court and are being considered for reverse transfer. Because of the importance of these evaluations, in the next two sections I provide greater detail on them.

Disposition Evaluations

Disposition evaluations are the most common type of evaluation used in the juvenile justice system and fit very well with the historical roots of the court. They are typically requested by a judge and are usually tailored toward assessing intellectual functioning, behavior, personality, and mental health. The risk, developmental maturity, and amenability to treatment of the young person also are assessed, all with the primary aim of informing rehabilitation. The evaluation, aside from describing the young person, is expected to provide a road map for change. As such, a disposition evaluation report provides specific information as to how a young individual can regain mental health and to continue to develop in a social manner. Because of their stated purpose, these evaluations are also referred to as *rehabilitation evaluations*. The various statutory decision points and locations for evaluating youth are covered in more detail later in this chapter.

Transfer Evaluations

Transfer evaluations, on the other hand, are used by the courts to determine whether a particular child or adolescent is better suited for juvenile or adult court. In judicial waiver hearings, the juvenile court judge requests the evaluation, and the same factors—such as the personality, pathology, behavior, intellectual functioning and mental health of the young person, as well as his or her potential danger to the community, his or her developmental maturity, and his or her amenability to treatment—are considered. If the young person is being processed in adult court because he or she was automatically transferred to criminal court, the evaluation is requested by a criminal court judge (or an attorney) rather than a juvenile court judge. In either of these locations—criminal or juvenile court—the evaluation does not need to express an opinion regarding within which system the young person would be better processed; instead, the report and testimony are designed to provide relevant psychological information that can facilitate the legal decision. Readers should keep in mind, however, that judges often look for this type of information from psychologists and other mental health professionals and may want the mental health professional to weigh in on the legal issue. Whether it is appropriate to provide one's ultimate opinion information is a matter of debate (Melton, Petrila, Poythress, & Slobogin, 1997; Rogers & Ewing, 1989, 2003). It is recommended that, when it comes to transfer, psychologists and other mental health professionals be cautious and to not make with ease specific recommendations regarding transfer. I address this topic, including the various mechanisms for juvenile transfer, in greater detail in Chapter 2.

One important difference between disposition and transfer evaluations is that in transfer evaluations there may be greater emphasis placed on the young person's risk, developmental maturity, and amenability to treatment. It is the judge who decides how she or he will balance these constructs based on the nature of the crime and other relevant legal information. For instance, after considering all pertinent legal issues, if there is a concern about public safety a judge may place greater weight on risk and less weight on treatment amenability factors. Alternatively, if a judge believes that the risk to the public is not excessive, he or she may place less weight on risk variables and more weight on amenability factors in deciding whether to assign a young person to the juvenile or the adult system. In these and other instances, transfer evaluations can be quite helpful in identifying positive amenability characteristics as well as developmental maturity issues, if they exist, that may allow the judge to put greater weight on these dynamic factors. In such cases, judges may conclude that the child is simply too young and developmentally immature to be transferred to adult court. In addition, the judge may see the young person as showing a reasonable degree of preparedness for treatment, resulting in a less restrictive placement determination. Psychological reports and testimony can be quite valuable in shedding light on these psycholegal factors as they relate to each young person's case (Brannen et al., 2006; Salekin, Rogers, & Ustad, 2001; Salekin, Yff, Neumann, Leistico, & Zalot, 2002).

LAW, LEGAL PROCESSING, AND RELEVANT SYSTEMS

Forensic clinicians may be asked to evaluate young people at a variety of legal decision points. Because of this, a good working knowledge of relevant juvenile law, legal processing, and relevant systems is necessary for competent practice. As I mentioned earlier in this chapter, the juvenile justice system can be compared to major world subway systems (e.g., London, New York City, Paris): There is a level of knowledge necessary to successfully navigate them. Therefore, here I briefly describe the legal system, how youth are processed at various stages of the legal course, and where evaluations can occur. Also provided is information on the court system, probation system, court evaluation units, detention centers, and the various state departments of youth services. I also discuss secure residential treatment, where some young offenders are sent for rehabilitation. Familiarity with the system, including laws, allows for better connections to relevant people and places in the system and for more effective assessment and treatment of juvenile offenders.

Local Laws

Forensic clinicians working within the juvenile justice and adult legal systems will need to familiarize themselves with the law. Laws, of course, provide order and structure and outline such factors as the age at which young people are subject to the juvenile justice system, and what constitutes status versus nonstatus offenses, as well as who is subject to transfer to adult court. For most states, children under a certain age, usually 18, are processed within a juvenile justice system. There also exist laws governing the procedures for detention and transfer, which allow for the movement of youth between the juvenile and adult criminal justice systems. For example, to transfer a young person to adult court in the state of Alabama, he or she must be at least age 14 years. In other states, however, the minimum age can be significantly lower, such as, for example, Colorado, Missouri, and Montana, where the minimum age is 12, or, in Kansas, Vermont, and Wisconsin, where the threshold age for transfer is 10.

Knowledge of the specific state laws is a necessary first step in the evaluation. This familiarity is a direct link to the types of information that the court is considering in its decision making. Because, as noted earlier, the laws are different in each state, it is best practice to examine the specific statutes for the state in which the evaluation is being conducted. Discussed in greater detail below is the manner in which youth can advance in different legal directions within the system and at what points forensic clinicians' psychological knowledge may be requested and used by the court.

Statutory Decision Points for Assessment of Young People

Because of efforts to prevent loss of liberty, legal and court personnel include *intake probation officers*, who are often the first point of contact for youth and can divert young people in a variety of ways prior to adjudication. Many cases in which youth are referred to the court are never actually tried in a juvenile court, and thus young individuals can avoid delinquency adjudication altogether. This can be a positive outcome for the young person and the community as long as the young person's delinquency is not a cause for large-scale societal concern. According to the most recent statistics available as of this writing, of the 1.5 million delinquency cases that receive a juvenile court sanction each year, almost two thirds of those youth (60%) will be placed on probation, nearly one third of the youth (27%) will receive a residential placement, and a small minority will receive some other sanction (13%; see Livsey, 2012).

Once young individuals enter the system, there are a number of stages, called *statutory decision points*, through which they can pass. Youth can be diverted back home; diverted to treatment programs; required to go on probation; required to pay restitution; required to pay a fine; sent to secure residential facilities, or, in more serious cases, transferred to adult court. The options are quite wide ranging. These primary statutory decision points within the juvenile justice system are outlined in Table 1.1. Essential to many of these evaluation points is the question of the juvenile's risk for dangerous behavior, his or her developmental maturity, and his or her treatment amenability. Other issues are also very critical in the assessment, such as the young person's truthfulness (i.e., reporting) and mental health status (e.g., Swanson, Borum, Swartz, & Monahan, 1996). Evaluations may be used to aid in decisions regarding civil commitments, institutional placements, or appropriate treatment strategies, all components of disposition and transfer evaluations.

MORE ON CONTEXT AND LOCATIONS FOR JUVENILE EVALUATIONS

As shown in Table 1.1, the juvenile justice system has a variety of social institutions and agencies with interlinking functions. A few of the systems require further discussion. For instance, key systems within the juvenile

TABLE 1.1
Major Statutory Decision Points and Options
Within the Juvenile Justice System

Decision point	Options
	Precharge
Release	Youth in these cases are dismissed by the police and will typically receive a warning. In addition, the parent(s) may also receive a warning. The decision to release the youth is usually based on the severity of the offense and the officer's informal assessment of immediate risk to public safety.
Diversion	Youth in these cases are not charged but are directed to intervention programs. Programs typically involve an accountability component whereby the youth admits to the transgression and may have to engage in some form of compensatory action (e.g., community service). Successful completion of the program typically terminates the youth's involvement with the system. These decisions, depending on the jurisdiction, can be made by police, probation officers, and intake probation officers. Mental health evaluations, centering on risk, maturity, and treatment amenability, might be helpful here because they help identify which youth are better suited to such diversionary programs. However, because of time restraints and training these decisions are often made without formal evaluations.
Arrest	Once the youth is arrested, there are many opportunities for the forensic assessment, including indexing his or her risk, developmental maturity, and treatment amenability and needs.
	Postcharge–preadjudication
Pretrial detention	Youth are detained until their trial. Mental health, risk, maturity, and treatment needs and amenability are pertinent to varying degrees. Determining the length of detention might be based on the youth's level of risk to the community.
Dismissal of charges	The charges are dismissed against the youth at this phase.
Referral to mental health system	Youth are referred to a mental health facility for needed mental health treatment.
Referral to adult system	Transfer to adult court is an option in all states. As part of such a transfer, or reverse transfer (i.e., from adult to juvenile court), judges consider the youth's developmental status, risk, and treatment amenability as well as other factors. Mental health professionals are key here and very much needed to provide information on these relevant constructs.
Diversion to alternative program	Youth are diverted to alternative programs to receive treatment and education. Treatment outcome evaluations can be requested by the judge.

(continues)

TABLE 1.1
Major Statutory Decision Points and Options
Within the Juvenile Justice System   *(Continued)*

Decision point	Options
	Adjudication
Dismissal	Cases are dismissed by a judge. A psychological report may facilitate this decision process.
Referral to mental health system	Youth are referred to mental health systems on the basis of an assessment (screening or full assessment) or someone's noticing that a young person is having mental health problems.
Adjudication of delinquency	Youth are adjudicated delinquent if determined culpable for offenses. If they are not adjudicated delinquent, youth are released; if adjudicated, they receive some form of disposition sentencing.
Disposition sentencing	At sentencing, the court decision makers decide what to do with given youth (i.e., placement). Mental health assessment and evaluation of risk, developmental maturity, and amenability to treatment are key here and obviously a place where evaluations are often sought and taken into account when placing youth.
Adjudicative discharge	Youth are discharged from court jurisdiction following adjudication of delinquency.
Warning reprimand	Youth are given a reprimand and warned following delinquency adjudication.
Fine/restitution	Youth are charged a fine or must provide some restitution to the community following delinquency adjudication.
Alternative program	Youth voluntarily enter treatment programs before being subjected to further judicial processing. Successful completion of the program generally ends the processing. Sometimes evaluations are used at entry level or to determine progress.
Probation	Youth are placed on probation and required to report to a probation officer. This is a mandatory supervision period in which a youth is returned to the community. This requires that the probation officer keep checking on the young person. This is the most common disposition used and one in which risk, developmental maturity, and treatment amenability assessments are helpful. Youth at higher risk require closer supervision. Also, developmental maturity and treatment amenability could inform the types of checks and/or treatment required. All three constructs are useful in monitoring progress.
Secure custody	Youth are detained and provided rehabilitation (treatment, training, and education) during detention. Evaluations can be helpful to determine progress in the program.

justice system include those under the purview of judges; attorneys (prosecuting and defense); and probation, detention, and rehabilitation professionals. Knowledge of the various systems and facilities where youth might be processed and temporarily located helps to keep the evaluation focused, legally relevant, and maximally effective. In the following subsections, I provide information regarding the court system as well as additional detail on potential disposition decisions and then discuss the probation system and the other various systems and locations within the juvenile justice system.

The Court System

In line with the *parens patriae* model, the juvenile and family courts are located in cities across the United States. Juvenile and family courts process a wide range of legal cases involving the welfare of children and adolescents (Grisso, 1998/2013). Although this book is focused on delinquency cases, juvenile and family courts hear both delinquency cases and dependency cases (e.g., neglect, abuse). Many metropolitan areas combine their juvenile and family court systems, and terminology varies. Some courts across the nation have single court systems that process only "delinquency" cases. Others may process "dependency" or "domestic" cases. In some states, these courts are separate but conveniently located in the same building. Having the two courts located within the same facility assists with communication. Legal personnel and mental health professionals working in these modern court settings can easily transport themselves between the two courts rather than having to travel to separate city locations when youth have cases in both courts.

Juvenile Court Judges and Referees

Juvenile court judges control a number of important issues regarding the evaluation. Specifically, the juvenile court judge decides whether evaluations are sought as well as whether young people are detained prior to adjudication. They also decide whether youth are to be adjudicated with delinquency charges and determine the disposition that is to occur in delinquency cases. Juvenile court judges can also be involved in providing rehabilitative services (Grisso, 1998/2013), and in some states the judge will have a "referee" who takes the place of the judge in the proceedings even though judges make the final ruling. The judge can perform all his or her functions without recourse to a psychological evaluation; however, in many cases juvenile court judges will seek psychological input to facilitate their decision making. Attorneys can also request psychological evaluations in order to better inform their cases and strategic legal planning.

Specifics Regarding the Court Cases

When youth are not diverted by probation officers, *adjudicatory hearings* will occur to determine whether the young person should be judged delinquent. Adjudicatory cases are increasingly similar to adult court cases. Like adult court cases, adjudicatory hearings provide the opportunity for the presentation of evidence by the prosecution and defense, including the cross-examination of any witnesses, including expert witnesses. The judge then bases his or her decision regarding the young person's delinquency on this evidence. Although the presentation of evidence and other procedures in juvenile court have become increasingly similar to those used in criminal courts, the level of formality with which the proceedings are conducted can vary across jurisdictions (Grigorenko, 2012; Grisso, 1998/2013; Sacks & Reader, 1992).

With respect to making decisions in juvenile cases, judges often produce their findings in writing. Within their written findings judges will describe the evidence relevant to their decisions, taking into consideration the information provided by forensic clinicians. As outlined in Table 1.1, in many states, when juveniles are adjudicated delinquent there is a follow-up disposition hearing to consider evidence regarding the proper legal action to the young person's delinquency. In some courts, the judge may ask to have the psychological report prepared for the adjudication hearing. This requires caution, given that the youth has not yet been adjudicated delinquent. Evidence is provided from both sides, including information from probation officers and mental health professionals. Best practice regarding evaluations requires knowing what the potential options are for young people after the adjudication hearing. In the next few sections I provide brief examples of the thinking that may go into disposition decision making based on mental health issues and a young person's potential risk, level of developmental maturity, and treatment amenability.

Potential Outcomes of a Disposition Evaluation

If a young person is viewed as being of low to moderate risk, shows signs of developing prosocial maturity, and is amenable to treatment, this may signify that he or she should be handled by the juvenile court system, evaluated and likely put on probation with a specific rehabilitation plan in the community. Conversely, if the young person is deemed to be of high risk, high in developmental maturity, and low in amenability to treatment, the report could delineate that the risk, maturity, and needs of the young person are such that he or she would be more appropriately placed in a secure residential facility. If it is discovered that the young person has experienced serious mental health problems (e.g., a psychotic or mood disorder), commitment to a mental health facility may be warranted. Finally, if a young person is viewed to be of very high risk, the judge may make a decision to transfer the young person to adult court. Although disposition decisions are legal ones, a forensic clinician's psychological evaluation can have a significant impact on the judge's decision.

Where Are the Evaluations Conducted?

Psychological evaluations can be conducted in a variety of locations, including the evaluator's private office, a community health setting, an attorney's office, or other location, even the family's home. Some courts in larger cities even have court clinics specifically designated for the evaluation of youthful offenders. University settings, such as the University of Alabama, are becoming increasingly common sites for evaluations.

Private Practice and Community Mental Health Centers

At the request of the judge or an attorney, forensic clinicians are assigned the case and subsequently contact the child's parents to set up a meeting time for the evaluation. Alternatively, the family may be asked to contact the clinician to set up an appointment for the assessment. Initial meetings usually take place in the forensic mental health clinician's private office or an attorney's office. The evaluation might also be conducted at a community mental health facility, juvenile court location, university setting, a juvenile court evaluation unit (in a separate building from the juvenile court), or a detention center (Chapman, 2012; Grisso & Quinlan, 2005). At the University of Alabama, some juvenile court evaluations have been conducted with doctoral students and supervising psychologists cowriting reports. Because of their historical importance, court evaluation units are discussed further next.

Court Evaluation Units. In 1909, William Healy and Grace Fernald established the first United States court clinic designed for youthful offenders (Schetky & Benedek, 1980). They named their clinic the *Juvenile Psychopathic Institute*. This court clinic was developed to serve the newly established Juvenile Court of Chicago. Healy and Fernald's clinic offered psychological assessment and treatment services for children who had come into contact with the justice system. Their contribution regarding the integration of psychology into the juvenile justice system might be considered one of the most important contributions to the field of juvenile assessment and treatment. Not only did

Healy and Fernald open the first court clinic specifically for assessing youth involved with the law, but they also made two other important contributions: They (a) developed psychological measures specific to juvenile offenders and (b) developed the notion of using offender-specific information from interviews and psychological measures to inform their clinical opinions regarding intervention. This assessment guided intervention is fortunately more common practice in juvenile justice settings today.

Larger cities, such as Chicago and Philadelphia, have newer versions of the Healy and Fernald court clinic. These modern clinics have on-site psychologists who regularly provide the juvenile and/or family courts with psychological evaluations. In previous years, the city of Miami, Florida, offered an excellent example of this hybrid system, in which the family courts and juvenile courts were housed in the same building. The assessment center was adjacent to both court buildings and employed six to seven psychologists at any given time. These mental health professionals carried regular caseloads consisting of five to six juvenile or family court cases. If the caseload exceeded a level at which the evaluations could be competently completed, then outside private practitioners were contracted to handle excess evaluations. Although the Miami evaluation unit was eventually closed because of budgetary constraints, in its time it represented what many consider to be the ideal court and assessment setting (Salekin, 1998).

Related to these above-mentioned models, the Office of Juvenile Justice and Delinquency Prevention developed the community assessment center concept as part of the larger comprehensive strategy for serious, violent, and chronic juvenile offenders (Oldenettel & Wordes, 2000; Wilson & Howell, 1995). This concept is similar to the one used in the Miami court system in that its main features include a single point of entry for all juveniles who come into contact with the juvenile justice system, an immediate and comprehensive assessment, a management information system to monitor the young person's needs and progress, and an integrated case management system that uses information from the management system to develop recommendations (Oldenettel & Wordes, 2000). Because many cities do not have such integrated systems, forensic clinicians may have to work even more industriously to accomplish this same type of integration, independently. In this regard, clinicians may need to be especially diligent in their efforts to create their own professional networks, connecting with other clinicians, attorneys, court personnel, and staff at treatment facilities whenever possible.

As an aside, it is worth mentioning that the hybrid systems such as those discussed in the preceding paragraphs tend to be more technologically advanced and allow for young offender education. For example, within some modern assessment and court waiting areas, videos are used to instruct youth regarding the juvenile and family court systems and the legal process.

These videos describe the respective roles of defendants, attorneys, judges, and probation officers, and the information is thought to improve, or assist, with young individuals' competency to stand trial. To my knowledge, these educational videos do not yet provide information on the philosophy of the juvenile courts or the role of the mental health professional and the nature of assessment and treatment in the context of these cases; however, this might be a very important next step in the educational process. The aforementioned systems represent the ideal, but of course, not all cities have such facilities.

Probation System. As can be deciphered from Table 1.1, many youth are placed on probation after some contact with the law. Most cities are equipped with a probation office where a chief probation officer manages the work of a fleet of probation officers who are charged with overseeing the progress of youth who have come into contact with the juvenile justice system. Ideally, the probation system—and, more specifically, probation officers—provide the monitoring and guidance necessary to see that each youth effectively completes a period of probation and successfully returns to the community where they can continue to thrive. As documented in Table 1.1, aside from being on their best behavior, youth may also be asked to complete some treatment and adhere to other specified conditions while they are on probation. Judges can order psychologists to conduct progress–outcome evaluations to determine a young person's level of advancement. In these cases, forensic clinicians assess a young person before and after his or her treatment.

Research is beginning to emerge showing the types of factors that affect successful completion of probation. For example, ample time availability, active monitoring, and the warmth of the probation office staff can positively affect youth outcomes (Rettig, 1980; Trotter & Evans, 2012; Umamaheswar, 2013). When considering probation recommendations in disposition evaluations, it can be helpful to obtain an estimate of the average caseload of the probation officers in one's location and learn what they typically do to manage young people. This helps when considering the benefit a youth might receive from being on probation alone versus having some other form of intervention. If interested, mental health professionals may also consider accepting a few paid (or pro bono) treatment cases to help with a young person's recovery while on probation. This can be ethically accomplished so long as the cases accepted are not the same cases for which one is providing the psychological assessment.

Detention Centers. All states have detention centers where youth may be placed temporarily. The goal or purpose of the detention center is to provide safety to the public but also to ensure that detention is kept to a minimum amount of time. If forensic clinicians provide an assessment early in the process, one consideration might be temporary detention. The typical time limitation for temporary placement in Alabama detention centers is 72 hours, inclusive of weekdays and holidays. Within this window a hearing must be held to determine whether there is a probable cause to believe that the child committed an offense and to determine whether continued detention is required. Some states have shorter or longer stays for temporary placement. Forensic clinicians are more commonly consulted after a young person has been detained but can also be asked to evaluate a young individual while that individual is detained. Detention centers differ widely in their provision of mental health services, and thus the case files could be quite thin in some facilities but relatively rich in other facilities. If a forensic clinician is called in to conduct an evaluation following a detention, he or she will want to collect file information from the young person's detention period, specifically, gathering information on how long he or she was in detention, what was reported on his or her mental health, and how his or her conduct was noted to be while in detention.

Time in Detention/Custody

Statistical reports on detention provide information on time in custody for two groups: (a) *committed youth* and (b) *detained youth*. Committed youth include those placed in a facility as part of a court-ordered disposition. Committed juveniles may have been adjudicated and disposed in juvenile court or convicted and sentenced in criminal court. Detained youth, on the other hand, include juveniles held prior to adjudication while awaiting an adjudication hearing in juvenile court as well as juveniles held after adjudication while awaiting disposition or after adjudication while awaiting placement elsewhere. Therefore, there are a variety of reasons why a young person might be detained or committed for a certain period. The Office of Juvenile Justice and Delinquency Prevention offers recent statistics regarding the percentage of youth who are detained as well as those who are committed by the number of days they are detained (see e.g., http://www.ojjdp.gov/ojstatbb/corrections/).

Department of Youth Services

Each state has a government agency responsible for promoting the welfare, rehabilitation, and correction of juveniles committed to their custody after being adjudicated delinquent. These ideals of promoting the welfare of young people harken back to the new philosophical views mentioned earlier in the chapter regarding the promotion of young people's intellectual growth and promoting well-being. These state government agencies have a variety of names. For instance, they are called *Department of Youth Services* in Alabama and Florida, *Division of Youth Services* in Alaska, *Juvenile Division* in Illinois, *Office of Youth Development* in Louisiana, *Department of Youth Authority* in California, and *Department of Juvenile Justice* in Virginia. An Internet search will yield the name and location for any state facility. Regardless of the specific name, forensic clinicians aiming for best practice in this area will want to know that these state departments typically manage several secure facilities for the incarceration and rehabilitation of juvenile offenders. These facilities have also been referred to as *training schools*, and this term may still be used in some states. Residential facilities or training schools typically have a program handbook that is provided to each young person on entry into the facility. The handbook outlines how the child or adolescent can advance in the program, progressing through various levels (usually labeled *Level 1–4*, with 4 indicating that they are getting near discharge). Residential facilities are discussed in greater detail below.

Departments of youth services may also oversee a variety of community programs, which may include group residential facilities, substance abuse treatment programs, halfway houses, and probation services for young people who do not require the highest level of secure treatment. The treatment of youth in these facilities may be contracted out to private companies that offer some specialty in treating juvenile offenders. In the state of Alabama, residential treatment occurs at three primary campuses: (a) one that houses boys adjudicated delinquent, (b) another that houses girls adjudicated delinquent, and (c) another that handles more serious offenders as well as young people who have committed a sex offense. A working knowledge of the juvenile system in one's jurisdiction can help facilitate the evaluation and eventual writing of the report because the recommendations are based on knowledge regarding the availability of programs both in the community and in residential settings. This knowledge also helps one communicate with attorneys, courts, and other juvenile justice personnel. On occasion, forensic clinicians are involved in progress–outcome evaluations. With respect to progress–outcome evaluations, the mental health professional would likely need to personally go to the facility to conduct one or more of the multiple-time-point evaluations.

More on the Treatment and Services Available at Secure Residential Facilities

Facilities across the United States range from small programs with more intensive clinical emphases to very large training schools (see Grigorenko, 2012). All programs must offer some basic services to youth, including education, medical services, and recreational activities. In addition, programs must include individual and, possibly, group counseling services. The aim of these programs is for the youth's eventual reentry into the community. Unfortunately, a chronic problem of the juvenile justice system has involved little to no follow-up with youth once adolescents reenter the community (Ashford, Sales, & Reid, 2007; James, Stams, Asscher, De Roo, & der Laan, 2013). Thus, even when youth receive what might be effective treatment in a residential facility, there is no guarantee that these gains will be maintained in the community. This underscores the need for strengthening mentorship and transition programs and highlights the need for psychological reports and testimony to emphasize the importance of aftercare. Mental health professionals should use their knowledge and skill to help with the advancement of existing programs or even participate in the development of new programs.

The funds available to states' departments of youth services affect the resources that are available to treat youth. If a department has a reasonable degree of funding, it can hire additional staff, employ more mental health professions, use psychology interns to deliver psychological treatments, and bolster mentorship programs. When funds are limited, many of these facilities operate with minimal services, although, of course, the basic requirements must legally be met. As I discuss in Chapter 8, the recommendations section of a psychological report should outline what will be required for successful treatment and a successful transition. It is reassuring that the back-and-forth flow of information among mental health professionals, juvenile court judges and personnel, as well as treatment facility staff, offers the opportunity to further improve and shape change in the juvenile justice system.

CONCLUDING COMMENTS

In this chapter, I briefly discussed the history of the juvenile justice system and psychology's emergence onto the juvenile justice system scene. I also reviewed where clinicians are expected to conduct such evaluations, the routes by which juveniles travel through the juvenile justice system, the locations in which forensic clinicians and young people may find themselves, and the importance of being knowledgeable about the various juvenile and adult systems. I used the analogy of a subway system to illustrate the intricacies and complexity of the juvenile justice system because in many ways their structures are similar, with many routes and locations with which one must be familiar to navigate successfully. Obtaining information on the processing of youth and the facilities young people may encounter is one of the first steps toward best practice in child and adolescent forensic psychology. In Chapter 2, I focus to a larger extent on juvenile characteristics, political climate, and, in particular, transfer, because transfer evaluations are key to understanding juvenile evaluations more broadly.

2

JUVENILE CHARACTERISTICS, POLITICAL AND SOCIAL CLIMATE, AND TRANSFER

Best practice with regard to juvenile evaluations involves being familiar with recent data on youth characteristics, crime trends, and how to best treat juvenile offenders. Two related topics, societal views and the political climate, are important because these factors can affect such matters as detention rates, whether youth are treated in the community versus in juvenile justice settings, how frequently transfer mechanisms are used, the age at which young people may be considered for this legal alternative, and whether reverse transfer (i.e., from adult to juvenile court) is available as an option. Youth characteristics can also affect assessment and intervention foci. These subjects are included in a single chapter because youth statistics and political and social climate are interlinked in meaningful ways. The social and political climate affects how juveniles might be treated within a system (rehabilitation vs. punishment) and can drive legislative and policy change. Because of the significance of these topics and how they relate to policy, they are covered in some detail in this chapter.

http://dx.doi.org/10.1037/14595-003
Forensic Evaluation and Treatment of Juveniles: Innovation and Best Practice, by R. T. Salekin

JUVENILE CHARACTERISTICS

Fortunately, statistics on juvenile offending and youth characteristics can be readily obtained, from rich sources. A list of some of the primary fountains of knowledge for forensic clinicians is provided in Exhibit 2.1. With respect to juvenile offenders, there is now considerable information on such characteristics as age, race, and gender and how such characteristics relate to delinquency. Moreover, information exists on a variety of mental health problems, reported substance use issues (e.g., frequency), and offense characteristics. The topography of youth characteristics can differ over time and across geographic locations, and demographic changes can occur quite quickly. For instance, in some states an increase in Latino and Asian youth in the juvenile justice system has been seen; also, the proportion of girls in the system has grown at a faster rate than expected. These major changes have affected the statistical contours of youth within the juvenile justice system (Puzzanchera, 2003, 2013a, 2013b; Snyder & Sickmund, 2006). Moreover, further changes are expected in the years ahead as the demographics of the U.S. population change, meaning that forensic clinicians will need to constantly refresh the statistical information they have regarding the characteristics of juveniles today by keeping an eye toward the characteristics of juveniles tomorrow.

Information on the types, and frequency, of the referral offense separated by age and race, victimization, and other important statistics can be easily located at the website of the Office of Juvenile Justice and Delinquency Prevention (OJJDP; http://www.ojjdp.gov/). This resource is effortless to access and provides extensive information regarding young people who have come into contact with the law. Mental health professionals can run live Internet searches obtaining information at the OJJDP and other sites to answer many questions they may have regarding juvenile offenders (see Exhibit 2.1). Mental

---

EXHIBIT 2.1
Sources of Information on Juvenile Characteristics

Juvenile Court Statistics Report, OJJDP[a]
Juvenile Offenders and Victims, OJJDP[a]
Juvenile Transfer, OJJDP[a]
National Juvenile Court Data Archive, OJJDP[a]
National Council of Juvenile and Family Court Judges (http://www.ncjfcj.org)
U.S. Department of Justice (http://www.justice.gov)
Uniform Crime Report, Federal Bureau of Investigation (http://www.fbi.gov)
Youth Risk Behavior Survey, Centers for Disease Control and Prevention
  (http://www.cdc.gov)

Note. These reports can be located by searching each group's website or by cutting and pasting the information into an Internet search engine. OJJDP = Office of Juvenile Justice and Delinquency Prevention. [a]Main URL: http://www.ojjdp.gov/

health professionals, legal personnel, students, and others interested in this information can sign up to have briefs mailed via regular ground mail or have reports sent electronically.

The OJJDP can provide specified information regarding mental illness in a specific location, such as the prevalence rate for depression in a detained population. Similarly, information can be obtained on the nationwide rate of transfer of youth for all age groups or even more specific information, for example, regarding those youth who are transferred and are below age 12. Although there is a lag from the time data are collected to the time they are published, at present the OJJDP website, reports, and newsletters may be the most important ways to stay current with juvenile offender characteristics and processing.

POLITICAL CLIMATE

It is important to be aware of societal views toward youth offending. Although it is crucial to be objective in one's evaluations and to remain unaffected by current political views, it also is also important to avoid being completely oblivious to the current climate and how that might affect one's own view, a colleague's view, a judge's view, or legislative decision making. Although the juvenile justice system was founded on the *parens patriae* model of rehabilitation (see Chapter 1), perspectives on juvenile offenders vary over time. Perspectives typically sway from a rehabilitative model to a crime control model and perhaps even a punitive model, depending on the political and social climate. As an example, although the aims of the juvenile court were initially rehabilitative in nature, these views changed over time, as history has shown. Specifically, although the juvenile courts began with a rehabilitative model in 1899, in the first quarter of the 20th century critics of the juvenile justice movement suggested that the juvenile court system was failing. Many individuals believed that the system was not able to control crime (e.g., Champion & Mays, 1991; Grisso, 1998/2013; Sanborn, 1994). Critics argued that this was especially true with regard to serious young violent criminals. In the late 1980s to late 1990s, there was an overall spike in violent crime, with an increase of 70% in the number of youthful offenders arrested for violent offenses (K. L. Jordan & Myers, 2007). As a consequence, there was a public perception regarding the enhanced dangerousness of youthful offenders and, according to some writers, society demanded even greater crime control and harsher treatment, in particular, of young violent offenders (Fagan & Zimring, 2000; Feld, 1997, 1999).

In newspaper articles of the 1990s, youth were referred to as "super predators" (DiIulio, 1995) and even as a "new breed of vicious kids" (Annin,

1996, DiIulio, 1995, 1996; Fields, 1996; Koprowski, 1996; J. Miller, 1998). During this period, the general contention was that youth did not represent the typical errant adolescent for which the juvenile justice system was originally designed—the Tom Sawyers and Huckleberry Finns of the world. Instead, the view held by some was that the ranks of juvenile super predators were on the rise and the recent wave of violence was simply the "lull before the storm" (Brownstein, 2000, p. 11). When these types of societal views and political outlooks prevail, it is even more important for forensic clinicians' reports to reflect the true nature of the young person's character and to be constructive with respect to the best possible routes for rehabilitating youth while at the same time considering public safety. This is also where statistical information from the OJJDP and other sources, even when there are fluctuations in crime rates, may help minimize dramatic viewpoints and provide countering evidence to overly sensational news stories. In the sections that follow, I delineate some of the legislative changes that resulted from concerns about the rise in violence experienced in the 1980s.

NEW LAWS FOR JUVENILES

During the early 1990s, the number of mechanisms for transferring juveniles to adult court increased. At present, every state allows for the transfer of youth to adult court (Redding, 2010). As many as 250,000 youthful offenders are processed as adults on a yearly basis (Bechtold & Cauffman, 2014; L. Steinberg & Scott, 2003; Woolard, Odgers, Lanza-Kaduce, & Daglis, 2005) and of those, approximately 10,000 are processed by judicial waiver (B. Adams & Addie, 2010). This indicates that the majority of youth are transferred by some other mechanism.

Legislative changes also resulted in a significant increase in the number of youthful offenders held in prisons (Austin, Dedel Johnson, & Gregoriou, 2000). As of 2008, approximately 3,500 youthful offenders were being held as adults in local jails, and 6,400 youthful offenders were incarcerated in state prisons (West & Sabol, 2009). Preliminary empirical evidence shows that this captivity in some secure residential treatment facilities may result in delays in psychosocial maturity, suggesting that residential housing may not be the healthiest manner in which to handle young people who have broken the law (Dmitrieva, Monahan, Cauffman, & Steinberg, 2012). Occasional program upgrades and the staff training can help counter this potential problem. Fortunately, there has been a move away from transferring and incarcerating youth in recent years (B. Adams & Addie, 2010), although a recent *New York Times* article noted that many youth are still imprisoned for long periods of time (Eckholm, 2014). This is not to say that transfer and incarceration are unnecessary but only that these mechanisms should be considered as a last option rather than a first one (e.g., automatic and prosecutorial direct file mechanisms).

THE PENDULUM SWINGS BACK TO REHABILITATION

In the past decade, views have again changed, and there has been a return to a rehabilitative focus. Part of this momentum was initiated by the Annie E. Casey Foundation, which emphasized reducing the number of youth committed to residential facilities and shifted the emphasis toward the provision of treatment in the communities. In addition, the John D. and Catherine T. MacArthur Foundation has funded research that has focused on better understanding the developmental capacities of youth involved with juvenile justice. For instance, the private foundations have already had a major impact on the juvenile justice system with respect to consideration regarding competency to stand trial. These renowned foundations have the potential to further influence changes in practice in this area because they fuel the much-needed research on young people who have become involved in the legal system. Governmental agencies, such as the OJJDP, are also continually working to improve the way youth are handled within the juvenile justice system in all quadrants of the United States, through funding, education, and dissemination of important science.

TRANSFER TO ADULT COURT

Despite the change in focus in recent years to rehabilitation, transfer to adult court continues to be an option for more serious juvenile offenders. Familiarity with the various transfer mechanisms is therefore necessary for conducting juvenile evaluations (either disposition or transfer) for at least three reasons. First, forensic clinicians may be asked to conduct a disposition evaluation, and the report they produce may be subsequently used in a transfer hearing. Second, forensic clinicians may be directly asked to evaluate a young person for transfer, so knowing the statutory language, and hence the functional and legal criteria for that evaluation, will be important. Third, because the hearing can be held in different courts, either juvenile (for juvenile waiver) or criminal (for automatic, prosecutorial direct file, and reverse waiver), it is also necessary to recognize that the location has implications for the rules of evidence applicable to testimony. Having information on the specific court can also be helpful for practical reasons, including, for instance, issues such as how quickly the report may be required by the court.

MECHANISMS FOR TRANSFER TO (OR FROM) ADULT COURT

Four mechanisms exist for transfer from juvenile to adult court or the reverse (see Table 2.1). The first mechanism is *judicial waiver*. In some cases, when the offense is of sufficient magnitude, judges are required to decide whether the crime is serious enough that the young person should face his or her charge(s) in the adult system. This procedure is currently allowed in 45 states and may, at times, be one of the most common ways in which youth make their way to criminal court (D. R. Chen & Salekin, 2012; Grisso, 1998/2013). The second mechanism is *statutory exclusion*, also known as *automatic transfer*. This involves having a statute specify that an offender of a certain age who performed a specific crime (e.g., a 16-year-old who committed first-degree murder) be charged as an adult. Statutory exclusion is currently authorized in 29 states (D. R. Chen & Salekin, 2012). The third mechanism is *prosecutorial discretion*. With this mechanism, prosecutors can choose to file charges in either juvenile or criminal court. Under prosecutorial discretion, which is currently allowed in 14 states, both the juvenile court and criminal court are appropriate jurisdictions. The minimum offender age range

TABLE 2.1
Mechanisms for Transfer

Mechanism	Process
Juvenile waiver	The young person is transferred (waived) by a juvenile court judge to adult court.
Automatic transfer (statutory exclusion)	Because of the nature of the crime and the age of the young person, the young individual is automatically placed in adult court.
Prosecutorial direct file	The prosecutor decides in which court he or she will try the case (juvenile or adult). If the prosecutor decides on adult court, the charges are filed directly into adult court.
Reverse transfer	The young person is in adult court, perhaps because of automatic transfer. An adult court judge transfers the young person back to juvenile court. In six states, youth can be transferred back to juvenile court, even when they are waived upward through judicial waiver.
Blended sentencing	The young person has both juvenile and adult components integrated into the sentence. Depending on how he or she performs within the juvenile component of their sentence will affect the amount of time he or she has to spend time in the adult system.

for transfer by judicial waiver, statutory exclusion, and prosecutorial discretion across the 50 states varies from 10 to 17 years. The fourth transfer mechanism is *blended sentencing statutes*, or *extended jurisdiction statutes*, which integrate a combination of juvenile and adult components into the sentence. The adult component of the sentence is usually enforced only if the offender violates the juvenile component of his or her sentence, or if he or she commits a new crime (Fagan, 2008; Fagan & Zimring, 2000; Salekin & Grimes, 2008).

Twenty-five states also provide for a *reverse waiver option*, also termed *decertification*, by which young offenders can be moved from adult court back to juvenile court. In typical cases, the criminal court judge, after a hearing— and, perhaps in many cases, after looking at the young person's physical development (e.g., young appearance)—determines that it is more appropriate to prosecute the case in juvenile court rather than adult court. In these cases, the young offender is *decertified*, or returned, to the juvenile court for processing. Interestingly, in six states a criminal court judge can oppose a juvenile court judge's ruling and return a young person to juvenile court. This is unlikely to occur, though, because rulings are generally considered final (Salekin & Grimes, 2008).

CRITERIA FOR DISPOSITION DECISION MAKING AND TRANSFER

There are at least five highly relevant U.S. Supreme Court and state cases of which to be aware when working with juvenile offenders: (a) *Kent v. United States* (1966), (b) *In re Gault* (1967), (c) *Roper v. Simmons* (2005), (d) *Graham v. State of Florida* (2010), and (e) *Miller v. State of Alabama* (2012). Both the *Kent* and *Gault* cases, in the late 1960s, changed the way juvenile offenders were processed. Specifically, *Kent* and *Gault* increased due process for youth being administered through the juvenile justice system, but they may have also inadvertently made the system more adversarial in nature and increasingly similar to the adult criminal courts. After these two landmark cases, which occurred 1 year apart, youth had additional procedural rights in preparing for their own defense. Moreover, the standards for transfer became more transparent and structured.

The *Kent* case helped shape juvenile evaluations in general, pointing to the need to assess risk, developmental maturity, and treatment amenability and establishing specific guidelines for the judicial waiver of young offenders to criminal court. The guidelines included the following eight criteria for use in transfer determinations:

> 1) the seriousness of the alleged offense to the community and whether the protection of the community requires waiver; 2) whether the alleged

offense was committed in an aggressive, violent, premeditated or willful manner; 3) whether the alleged offense was against persons or against property, greater weight being given to offenses against persons especially if personal injury resulted; 4) the prosecutorial merit of the complaint, i.e., whether there is evidence upon which a Grand Jury may be expected to return an indictment; 5) the desirability of trial and disposition of the entire offense in one court when the juvenile's associates in the alleged offense are adults who will be charged with a crime; 6) the maturity of the juvenile as determined by consideration of his home, environmental situation, emotional attitude and pattern of living; 7) the record and previous history of the juvenile, including previous contacts with juvenile service programs, other law enforcement agencies, juvenile courts and other jurisdictions, prior periods of probation . . . or prior commitments to juvenile institutions; and 8) the prospects for adequate protection of the public and the likelihood of reasonable rehabilitation of the juvenile (if he is found to have committed the alleged offense) by the use of procedures, services and facilities currently available to the Juvenile Court. (*Kent v. United States*, 1966, pp. 566–567)

Each state was then afforded the opportunity to decide how the criteria should be incorporated into the transfer process. Since the *Kent* Supreme Court decision there has been increasing consensus among the state statutes. Heilbrun, Leheny, Thomas, and Huneycutt (1997) reviewed statutes of the 50 states and the District of Columbia and examined their provisions regarding the transfer of youthful offenders to criminal court. These investigators found that the following five criteria were repeatedly important to the decision to waive a young offender: (a) the offender's treatment needs, (b) risk assessment, (c) characteristics of the offense, (d) sophistication–maturity, and (e) presence of mental illness or intellectual disability. The five concepts can be further narrowed to three: (a) potential risk for dangerous behavior, (b) sophistication–maturity, and (c) amenability to treatment (D. R. Chen & Salekin, 2012; Ewing, 1990; Salekin & Grimes, 2008; Salekin, Rogers, & Ustad, 2001, Salekin, Yff, et al., 2002). This does not eliminate the need to assess issues such as mental illness or intellectual disability, but it reduces the number of higher order constructs to risk, developmental maturity, and treatment amenability and treatment needs. This is because intellectual difficulties can be subsumed under developmental maturity and mental illness under treatment amenability. In the juvenile court guidelines written by the National Council of Juvenile and Family Court Judges (NCJFCJ, 2005) and published by the OJJDP, the NCJFCJ underscored the importance of these three broad constructs, stating that they encapsulate the necessary criteria in the decision to retain or waive jurisdiction of juvenile offenders (NCJFCJ, 2005).

Although risk has always been a factor to consider, developmental maturity and amenability to treatment have more recently been explicitly listed as criteria to weigh in transfer decisions across various states. This was an encouraging step because it allowed a broader consideration of youth characteristics. Instead of solely focusing on risk, issues such as whether the young person was motivated to change his or her conduct, for instance, could be taken into account when making legal decision regarding transfer. As issues became clearer regarding how to think about the youth's "character" for transfer evaluations, it also became apparent that the concepts used for transfer are broadly applicable to general disposition cases as well; that is, risk, developmental maturity and amenability and treatment needs are relevant to all youth within the juvenile justice system. With respect to disposition and transfer cases, the courts are free to weigh youth characteristics differentially. For instance, the courts could allot more weight to dangerousness than they do to the young person's amenability to treatment when making a disposition decision. Some preliminary research using a simulation design for juvenile court judges' decision making regarding transfer indicates that this differential weighting can occur, with some constructs receiving more consideration in transfer cases than others (Brannen et al., 2006).

Three additional cases—(a) *Roper v. Simmons* (2005) and, more recently, (b) *Graham v. State of Florida* (2010) and (c) *Miller v. State of Alabama* (2012)— also changed juvenile justice practice in focal ways. *Roper v. Simmons* removed consideration of the death penalty for juvenile offenders. This effort was led by a number of scholars (legal and psychological) who developed an amicus brief delineating some of the brain differences that appear between adolescents and adults. After deliberating the issues, the U.S. Supreme Court justices voted in favor of removing the death penalty option for adolescent offenders. This brought the United States in line with most countries across the globe where the death penalty is restricted for use with adults or is not used at all. Although this was a fortuitous outcome, the Supreme Court justices were mixed as to whether the death penalty should be removed based on the evidence presented to them. The vote on this case was not a consensus vote; instead, five of the justices were in favor of removal of the death penalty for juveniles and four were against removal of the death penalty for juveniles.

As can be seen from the close results of the vote, the views on the matter were mixed. For instance, Justice Anthony Kennedy cited a body of sociological and scientific research that noted that juveniles have lack of maturity and sense of responsibility compared with adults. Kennedy also noted that a number of other countries had abolished the death penalty for adolescents. Justice Antonin Scalia, in his dissent, wrote a critical opinion of the American Psychological Association's (APA's) "flip flop" presentation regarding adolescents' developmental maturity (*Hodgson v. State of Minnesota*, 1990; *Roper v. Simmons*, 2005; Scalia, 2005). These differing views on how to treat juveniles can also be located in the psychology literature (see Grisso & Vierling, 1978; L. Steinberg & Scott, 2003) where two different views of adolescent decision making were painted.

Scalia (2005) in his dissenting opinion cogently noted that the APA had some 10 years prior argued that adolescents could make mature and thoughtful decisions when the issues pertained to abortion or being able to make decisions regarding entering into psychological therapy (see Grisso & Vierling, 1978; Strauss & Clarke, 1992). Scalia further argued that when the political issue shifted to the death penalty, APA was willing to change its position, presenting information that suggested adolescents, as a class, were quite limited in their decision-making capabilities (*Hodgson v. State of Minnesota*, 1990; *Roper v. Simmons*, 2005; Scalia, 2005; L. Steinberg & Scott, 2003). The conclusions drawn from the science behind adolescent decision making have been generally more mixed than one might expect (e.g., Aronson, 2007, 2010), and it is possible that arguments can be made for and against both increased (decreased) developmental maturity and adequate (inadequate) decision making. Many of these differences likely stem from contextual factors (Fischer, Stein, & Heikkinen, 2009; Mann, Harmoni, & Power, 1989; McCarthy, 1977).

Graham v. State of Florida (2010) and *Miller v. State of Alabama* (2012) further advanced the system by limiting the extent to which young people could be imprisoned without the opportunity for parole. The rationale for these decisions hinged on the notions that juvenile offenders are entering the system at a very young age and that life without parole may be considered excessive punishment. This argument was in part based on the notion that a young person, after a decade or two, could be quite different mentally, physically, and behaviorally. Given that a young individual is likely to make many transformations across his or her life, those potential changes in character should be periodically evaluated to determine whether he or she is prepared to approach the world in a new and constructive way.

Whether the political climate affects evaluations and the nature of conclusions and recommendations offered by forensic clinicians requires further investigation. One would hope that the political climate would not affect clinical opinion (e.g., rhetoric regarding superpredators or the adolescent brain); however, it would be surprising if it did not affect professional behavior to at least some extent. Knowing that these fluctuations occur could be helpful to mental health professionals in providing checks and balances on their impartiality in conducting juvenile evaluations. Again, psychologists' knowledge of the statistics pertaining to juvenile crime, like the information that can be gleaned from science, can be helpful in understanding how they assess and process young people in the juvenile and adult court systems.

THE PURPOSE OF TRANSFER: WHY TRANSFER YOUTH TO ADULT COURTS?

Transfer mechanisms were established for a specific purpose and were not designed solely for punitive goals. The rationale for and juvenile courts' interest in juvenile-to-criminal waiver has historically been fourfold. First, one historical purpose of this route to adult court was to serve as a safety valve whereby the juvenile justice system could avoid the inclusion of young people whose very serious criminality and potential risk might diminish the rehabilitative impact of programs that were intended to benefit children and adolescents in juvenile facilities (Bechtold & Cauffman, 2014). Thus, the waiver mechanism has been used to remove high-risk young people from the juvenile justice system. Second, because youths' time in the juvenile justice system is limited, juvenile court judges consider whether the juvenile system can rehabilitate youth in that time span. If this is believed unlikely, the legal system allows juvenile court judges to waive jurisdiction. This reduces the threat a young person might pose to public safety at the time of their mandatory release at age 17 or 18. Third, in cases in which rehabilitation is very unlikely, it has been argued that the state has an interest in avoiding the use of rehabilitation resources that are in short supply (Grisso, 2000; Mulvey & Iselin, 2008). This is a weak rationale for not treating youth, because the state has an obligation to continually initiate and develop services for youth whose needs exceed the juvenile system's current capacities. Nonetheless, waiver has historically been accepted as a legal mechanism for avoiding the use of existing resources when typically effective treatments are thought to be unlikely to result in rehabilitation (Grisso, 2000; Mulvey, 1984; Mulvey & Iselin, 2008). Although the state should be continually working toward effective treatment for young people, there are times when there is doubt as to whether even intensive interventions will be effective for a particular young person within the time frame permitted. When the best treatments are considered unlikely to work, the judge can make a decision to transfer a youth to the adult court. Fourth, until waiver and transfer laws were passed, it was legally presumed that all juveniles below a certain age (typically 18 years) were insufficiently mature to be held criminally responsible for their anti-social acts or because of their age should be provided an opportunity to correct their course (Bechtold & Cauffman, 2014; Ewing, 1990). Recall that young people below age 18 were automatically treated as juveniles under *parens patriae* (see Chapter 1). This guiding principle, of course, remains, but it can be modified on the basis of the juvenile's level of maturity. Thus, according to the law, juveniles may be transferred if they are viewed as mature participants. Although it is unlikely that a juvenile court judge would ever use this single factor as the sole basis for transfer, it is common for judges to consider developmental maturity in combination with reoffense risk and treatment amenability factors (see Brannen et al., 2006). I cover this issue in greater detail next.

LEGAL STANDARDS FOR TRANSFER TO ADULT COURT

The laws governing waiver require hearings to address whether the statutory criteria for transfer are met (Griffin, Torbet, & Szymanski, 1998). These statutory criteria are generally straightforward. Many states have two to three levels of legal standards for waiver of jurisdiction. The first is a set of basic threshold conditions that need to be met before proceeding further (e.g., age, charged with a serious offense, a special history of prior offenses). If threshold criteria are met, then courts in most states (Grisso, 2002) can proceed to the point of applying one of typically three broad standards referred to as *public safety*, which in different states is also referred to as *danger to others*, *amenability to rehabilitation*, and *the best interest of the child/community*. It appears that many states are increasingly listing all three key *Kent*-like criteria of (a) risk, (b) developmental maturity, and (c) amenability (*Kent v. United States*, 1966) as areas that need to be assessed and considered, rather than simply the broader standard.

Although the legal system uses terms such as *dangerousness* and *amenability*, words such as *risk* and *treatment needs* or *treatment readiness* can be more helpful constructs for mental health professionals to intermittently use to reframe some of the issues that will be of interest in rehabilitation. This is because they may be appraised without the additional values associated with legal constructs. Such terms can also be useful in psychological reports because they also allow for the discussion of treatment targets. Regardless of the specific terms used, it appears that through U.S. Supreme Court decisions (*Kent v. United States*, 1966; *Roper v. Simmons*, 2005) and science and theory (Borum, 1996; Grisso, Tomkins, & Casey, 1988; Salekin, Yff, et al., 2002; Steinberg & Scott, 2003), the concepts of risk, developmental maturity, and treatment amenability are elemental in juvenile transfer cases (*Kent v. United States*, 1966; Paus et al., 2008; Salekin, 2002a, 2002b; Sarata & Provorse, 1989). Moreover, although they are delineated as critical to the transfer evaluation, it is easy to see how relevant the constructs are to both general disposition cases and transfer evaluations. One might say it is difficult to imagine evaluating a young person at any stage within the system and not considering his or her level of risk, developmental maturity, and amenability to treatment, which naturally lead to recommendations regarding treatment needs.

CONCLUDING COMMENTS

In this chapter, I have highlighted how being cognizant of the statistical information on juveniles' characteristics can be helpful in making decisions related to disposition and transfer evaluations. For instance, being aware of the changing demographics and issues associated with those shifting demographics can be of great value (e.g., increasingly high numbers of Hispanic immigrants, increasingly high numbers of girls who engage in delinquency). Websites such as the OJJDP's provide forensic clinicians with statistics needed to further express one's expertise. These resources also allow forensic clinicians to stay current with the latest statistical information on mental health profiles of juvenile offenders (e.g., rates of clinical depression or anxiety). Moreover, mental health professionals can also glean information on the rate of mental illnesses within a particular system within the juvenile justice system (e.g., detained youth). Aside from basic demographics, in the current chapter, I also delineated chief court cases that relate to juvenile justice and provided an overview of the specified purpose of transfer. I also highlighted how being cognizant of the political climate can be important simply because it can help one understand current decisions being made in the courts, and legislative changes that may occur, as well as movements within the mental health fields (e.g., with an emphasis on neuroscience). Such issues may pertain to how frequently transfer mechanisms are used, including prosecutorial direct file, as well as to how juveniles are treated, in general, within the system. Although mental health professionals should operate in an unbiased manner and remain unaffected by these influences, it is important to be cognizant of how the system is being viewed at a specific point in time (e.g., "too lax" or "too punitive"). Regardless of the political climate, it is important for forensic clinicians to operate under the *parens patriae* rehabilitative model whereby the healthy development of the young people is the aim. In Chapter 3, I provide a detailed discussion of forensic mental health constructs and focus on innovative best practice methodology for the assessment of juvenile offenders.

3

FORENSIC MENTAL HEALTH CONCEPTS

Best practice in forensic mental health evaluations with juveniles requires an understanding of the relevant forensic mental health concepts that are directly related to the legal question under consideration. Also vital is an understanding of how these concepts relate to a young person's offense and what is needed to rehabilitate him or her. In essence, it is crucial for mental health professionals who evaluate young people to be familiar with the legal questions and how their answers will be used by the courts.

It is vital to keep in mind that there may well be two perspectives on the young individual's behavior. In typical adult criminal proceedings, the prosecution seeks to establish aggravating factors, and the defense asserts mitigating factors. In juvenile courtrooms this adversarial tone has increasingly become the practice as well. The issues center on whether the young person has limitations with respect to his or her level of developmental maturity, mental health, intellectual functioning, and other influences that may have affected his or her understanding of the actions committed. Other factors

http://dx.doi.org/10.1037/14595-004
Forensic Evaluation and Treatment of Juveniles: Innovation and Best Practice, by R. T. Salekin

come into play as well, such as a young person's values, capacity for caring, risk to the community, and capacity to respond favorably to appropriate rehabilitative interventions.

One side may argue that the young person poses a substantial risk; was well aware of his or her actions; and lacked basic human emotions such as care, empathy, and remorse. The opposing side downplays the young person's responsibility, argues that he or she is developmentally immature, and makes an argument for his or her treatment needs as well as his or her readiness to begin a treatment program. Here attorneys might use psychological reports and testimony to argue for one of the two primary perspectives. In less adversarial cases, the mental health professional simply provides a report to the court, and the judge decides on the best disposition for the young person. Either way, mental health professionals working in this area should conceptualize and write reports that can be helpful to the courts and the child in question.

There are five major forensic mental health constructs in juvenile evaluations. These are the three *Kent v. United States* (1966) concepts discussed in Chapters 1 and 2, namely, risk, developmental maturity, and amenability to treatment. There are also two broad issues that need consideration in any thorough and competent evaluation: veracity of reporting and general mental health issues as measured by personality and pathology. These five concepts should be examined together, and for this reason I discuss them collectively in this chapter. The constructs are not mutually exclusive, but instead overlap, interact with, and inform one another. As such, they provide a clear and effective way to evaluate adolescents who come into contact with the law. The first mental health concept I address is the accuracy of youth and parental report. I cover this topic only briefly, before moving on to general mental health assessment.

VERACITY OF REPORTING

Children and young adolescents have historically been viewed as candid and accurate reporters of their thoughts, emotions, and behavior. The examples of fictional characters mentioned in Chapter 1, including Calvin from the *Calvin and Hobbes* comic strip series, or Tom Sawyer and Huckleberry Finn from the Mark Twain novels, highlight how some deception can take place in a child's youthful years and be considered normative, even playful. It is also easy to recall examples from daily family life that represent somewhat normative deception, like when two parents are trying to decide whether their child who is reporting feeling ill on the day of a big test, is truly ill or is looking for a little reprieve from the daily grind of fifth-grade mathematics. Some deception appears to be part of the process of growing up. However, deception can also become maladaptive and even pathological. Regardless of the degree to which it is normal or abnormal at this developmental stage, inaccurate reporting interferes with the forensic clinician's ability to complete a thorough and accurate assessment of the young person. Because of this, forensic clinicians need to factor into their analyses the accuracy of the information they obtain.

Mental health professionals have become increasingly aware that deceptive behavior may be even more likely to occur in forensic contexts such as juvenile evaluations. However, developmental differences have taught researchers and clinicians alike that deception in adolescents can be both similar and different from that evidenced with adults (McCann, 1998; Salekin, Kubak, & Lee, 2008). Therefore, as a forensic clinician handling juvenile justice cases, being cognizant of both the similarities and developmental differences is essential to make sense of the remaining four forensic concepts.

Several response styles of young people are known to be similar to those of adults, including reliable reporting, defensive reporting, malingering, and random responding. *Reliable reporting* simply means that the responses are consistent. If a young person answers that he or she is "gregarious," he or she does so across tests, interviews, and time points. When youth consistently endorse a trait across tests and time, they are referred to as being a *reliable reporter*. Defensive responding indicates that the individual is presenting him- or herself in too positive of a light. Sometimes tests refer to this as *faking good*. This signifies that the presentation is so positive that it is unlikely to be true. A young person might state that he or she likes everyone that he or she meets and smiles at everyone he or she sees and/or that he or she reads every newspaper, daily. Meanwhile, the young person's behavior in a local detention center may show a considerable cantankerous side.

Presenting oneself in an overly positive manner on a psychological test to create a positive impression may be, to a degree, characteristic of many adolescents; however, as with any psychological assessment, elevations on a scale that signify a concern have to do with the extent to which an individual endorses items geared toward faking good (e.g., "I love all restaurants equally"). After a specified number of items are endorsed—let's say 10—the research will suggest that the child or adolescent has overendorsed. Also, it is unlikely that the young person performs all life activities as specified. For example, reading every newspaper daily would be an impossible feat, and liking all restaurants similarly would not fit with what has been learned about taste variability across age, cultures, and individuals. Moreover, if this same young person has a history of fighting but does not report this specific behavioral problem, this distortion would further misrepresent the self-report by highlighting positive attributes (e.g., reading newspapers daily, enjoying a range of cuisines equally) and lowlighting behavioral problems (e.g., stealing, fighting). This type of reporting is not helpful for the forensic clinician who is attempting to obtain a clear picture of the young person and his or her family's functioning.

Faking bad, on the other hand, means that a young person presents with such a high level of psychopathology that, as a mental health professional, it is especially difficult to believe. Put another way, sometimes the exaggeration is so extreme that it is statistically unlikely that a person would have such a set of symptoms. Moreover, individuals with severe mental health problems characteristically have a degree of coherence to their symptoms; presenting symptoms as part of a syndrome usually breaks down when youth are faking an illness. Thus, bona fide clients typically do not endorse wide-ranging symptomatology that is sometimes seen in the profiles of youth who are faking bad. To detect such exaggerations, psychological tests occasionally use bizarre test items, for example, "I can transport myself electronically to my friend's house" or "My Frisbee is spiritual." These items are unlikely to be endorsed by even those with the most severe psychopathology. Finally, *malingering* involves falsely presenting with a specific psychological disorder (e.g., attention-deficit/ hyperactivity disorder [ADHD], schizophrenia, or major depression). Cases of deception and malingering have been documented in children and adolescents, and forensic clinicians can look to specific case examples for further information (see, e.g., Greenfeld, 1987). This topic is covered in greater detail in Chapter 4.

RISK, DEVELOPMENTAL MATURITY, AND AMENABILITY TO TREATMENT

Specific to youth in the juvenile justice system, examples of actions and motives to deceive include underperforming on Miranda tests in order to have confessions discarded; avoiding placement in detention centers; and attempting to remain, or be placed, in what are viewed as increasingly tolerable settings, such as those in which youth receive special attention. In other words, deception may occur when young people present themselves as more or less knowledgeable and/or more or less mature than they truly are (e.g., Miranda rights, transfer evaluations). For example, a child or adolescent might distort his or her level of maturity or the degree to which he or she knows Miranda material in order to avoid being processed through the court system and/or to avoid responsibility and possible sanctions.

Addressing the three primary constructs of (a) risk, (b) developmental maturity, and (c) prospects for rehabilitation may also pose issues with respect to truthfulness of reporting. Each of these clinical queries raises the issues of social desirability and impression management. For instance, youth may present as being lower in risk and higher in amenability than they actually are. Because a range of response styles may be observed when evaluating young people, knowing how to assess the accuracy of interview information and self-reporting puts clinicians at an optimum vantage point and facilitates the production of valid psychological reports.

Young people may deem it helpful to be "symptom free" when in reality they have a mental illness that requires treatment. Although the young person is unaware of the consequences of his or her deception, acknowledging mental illness symptoms would result in better care. Underreporting may occur more frequently than expected, and it is a complex issue for an evaluator to deal with because some young people are erroneously convinced that the distorted results will help them. Similarly, young people may act overly mature, even though their abilities to think broadly and regulate emotions are quite limited. Here again, they may feel that acting mature could be helpful to their case. On occasion, youth can hide their immaturity by giving short answers to interview questions. This may occur when a young person answers yes to a number of leading or brief ability questions ("Would you say you are mature?" "Are you able to regulate your emotions well?" "Do you weigh the costs and benefits of your decisions?"). If closed-ended questions are asked, they would need to be followed with more detailed interviewing queries and collateral source information to better understand the child's developmental maturity.

Young people may learn that acting "callous" can be adaptive in some environments. As such, they adopt a callous presentation style even with the forensic evaluator. In reality, the young person may have considerable emotional capacity that reflects his or her ability to care for family members, friends, coaches, and teachers. Such a presentation style, although potentially adaptive in the detention center, can be self-defeating in the evaluation and subsequent court proceedings. The developmental differences in presentation of young offenders noted in the above examples further underscore the importance of examining the authenticity of reporting. Inaccurate responding can affect estimates of risk, developmental maturity, and treatment amenability. Presentation styles and motives that are specific to adolescents are summarized in Table 3.1.

TAKE A CONSTRUCTIVE STANCE REGARDING DECEPTION

When conducting juvenile evaluations, it is best to be constructive in written reports and testimony. Using blanket descriptions of youth, such as the adolescent was "defensive," "faking good," "faking bad," or "malingering," may not be as helpful, or accurate, as describing particular aspects of a young

TABLE 3.1
Aspects of Presentation Style and Potential Motives for Deception

Presentation	Potential motives and goals
	Defensive/healthy presentation
Overly self-reliant	Desire for increased autonomy
Overly brave	Desire for increased autonomy and strong self-image
Non-symptomatic	Wanting to be seen as healthy (not ill, different, or weak)
Normal (e.g., IQ)	Avoid being ostracized by peers for too high of an IQ
	Pathological/faking bad
Uncaring	Protect self from other potentially harmful relationships
Highly dependent	Avoid responsibility/seek help from others
Callous	Appear tough and unaffected by environment
Mentally ill	Gain help from mental health or avoid responsibility

person's presentation. For example, it might be more beneficial to look for, and describe, specific areas of reporting that were accurate or inaccurate. For instance, a report might indicate that the young person was protective (even defensive) when talking about his family but appeared to be honest and open when discussing his performance in school. Similarly, a young person may present as brave, self-reliant, tough, uncaring, or disinterested in particular topics covered in an interview while appearing open and engaged when providing rich information regarding the care he or she has for a younger sibling, close friend, or grandparent. Deciphering these contextual details can increase the truthfulness of the overall report. Simply describing the young person as categorically "dishonest" or "callous" would be inaccurate in many cases if the presentation style is more nuanced and specific to certain situations.

Clinical interviewing, testing, document review, and collateral observations, as well as observing the young person in various settings, can facilitate this process; I cover these topics in greater detail in Chapter 6. For now, the point I wish to make is that seeking patterns that recur or desist across sources and settings can be enlightening regarding the accuracy of youth reporting (Heilbrun, Grisso, & Goldstein, 2008; Melton, Petrila, Poythress, & Slobogin, 1997). When the presentation style is, in fact, pervasive that too should be presented, although this is likely to be less common.

PERSONALITY AND PATHOLOGY

Best practice in juvenile forensic assessment involves describing a young person's personality and possible pathology to the courts to ensure that effective decisions can be made regarding management and treatment of the child.

Forensic clinicians may choose from a host of frameworks specific to juvenile offenders so long as they have sufficient data to back their approach (e.g., Jesness & Wedge, 1984, 1985; Megargee, 1984; R. C. Miller, 1958; Moffitt, 1993, 2003; Quay, 1964, 1966, 1987; J. R. Warren, 1966). Brennan, Bradley, Allen, and Perry (2008) summarized the most prevalent typologies and reduced them to five types: (a) *normal or situational offenders* (see Aalsma & Lapsley, 2001; Huizinga et al., 1991; Lykken, 1995; Van Voorhis, 1994); (b) *socialized delinquents, common sociopaths, or subcultural offenders* (e.g., Jesness, 1988; Lykken, 1995; Mealey, 1995; R. C. Miller, 1958; M. Q. Warren, 1971); (c) *adolescent—limited* (Lykken, 1995; Moffitt, 1993; Moffitt, Caspi, Rutter, & Silva, 2001); (d) *neurotic or internalizing delinquents* (P. W. Harris & Jones, 1999; Megargee & Bohn, 1979; Moffitt, 2003); and (e) *undercontrolled serious delinquents who are impulsive and unsocialized* (Lykken, 1995; Moffitt, 1993; Quay, 1987). For detailed descriptions of these types, see Brennan et al. (2008).

Although these classification schemes have added to our knowledge, attempts to validate the typologies have been mixed (see Brennan et al., 2008), and simple descriptions of personality (e.g., extraversion, introversion) and psychopathology (e.g., conduct disorder [CD]) might be more parsimonious and therefore recommended. Other approaches and paradigms, including psychoanalytic theory, have gleaned information about parenting and abuse as well as how those factors can affect delinquency. Some of the recent theories from contemporary models of object relations suggest that internal representations of important figures help to either regulate or disregulate a child's behavior. Social learning paradigms have also been fruitful in demonstrating how modeling, identity, and efficacy can affect delinquency (Bandura, 1999). These groundbreaking explanatory theories, with monumental contributions to the conceptualization of assessment and treatment of young people, should be considered in assessment, especially when thinking about intervention recommendations. However, these theories may need to be augmented and elaborated on to provide relevant conceptualization to the courts. For instance, to be helpful to the courts, discussions of object relations as it pertains to a given child would require considerable elaboration and connection to psycholegal constructs.

Personality

An evaluation of general personality—pick your model, whether it be the two-, three-, four-, or five-factor model of personality—is helpful in appraising a young person's general character and mental health. The two-factor model discusses traits and resultant symptoms in terms of externalizing and internalizing characteristics (Achenbach, 1995; Clark, Watson, & Mineka, 1994; Krueger, Markon, Patrick, Benning, & Kramer, 2007; Krueger

& South, 2009). There is considerable research to support the two-factor model of personality and pathology, and the model is gaining popularity because these metafactors can account for a great deal of the behavior associated with inhibition and disinhibition. Research has also framed these personality constructs in terms of approach motivation (the behavioral activation system) and withdrawal motivation (the behavioral inhibition system; Gray, 1970, 1987).

The three-factor model comprises the Externalizing and Internalizing dimensions mentioned above and has been researched in youth by Achenbach (1995), as has including a young person's level of control (see Markon, Krueger, & Watson, 2005; Watson & Clark, 1993). This structural format originated in the seminal and pioneering work of Eysenck and his colleagues (see, e.g., Eysenck, 1997). Therefore, it has a long history from which to draw and has been replicated in different research laboratories, giving it considerable theoretical and empirical merit. Tellegen (1985) also proposed a similar structure consisting of Negative Emotionality (Neuroticism), Positive Emotionality (Extraversion), and Constraint. Furthermore, Watson and Clark (1993) delineated an analogous model, with factors named Negative Temperament, Positive Temperament, and Disinhibition (disConstraint).

The four-factor model adds Agreeableness as a personality dimension and the five-factor model also adds the domain of Openness. Aside from their replicability, these personality models help describe youth in a non-pathological manner, shed light on the predicaments in which young people may find themselves, and identify strengths as well as deficits related to the personality domain (traits and trade-offs). The five-factor model of personality is highly cited and used as a measure in clinical practice and research (see, e.g., McCrae & Costa, 1996). In fact, the five-factor model—which comprises the factor-based personality traits Agreeableness, Extraversion, Openness, Conscientiousness, and Neuroticism—is so popular that research is now being conducted on it across species, ranging from *Drosophila melanogaster* (i.e., fruit flies), to fish, to chimpanzees, and other animals, to determine whether the model will have the same usefulness in predicting outcomes as it does with humans (Earley, 2010; Earley et al., 2006; Earley & Hsu, 2008). Given the explanatory power of personality models, general models of personality should be considered one way to provide descriptive and predictive information on young people.

Forecasting Behavior With General Models of Personality

One favorable aspect of general personality is that personality traits forecast both positive and negative outcomes (Caspi, Roberts, & Shiner, 2005; Caspi & Shiner, 2006; Funder, Parke, Tomlinson-Keasey, & Widaman,

1993; Lynam, Caspi, Moffitt, Loeber, & Stouthamer-Loeber, 2007; Shiner, 2000; Tackett, 2006). This factoid can be helpful information for forensic clinicians working with juvenile offenders because it provides some evidence regarding the malleability of life outcomes and moves the evaluation away from solely relying on potentially harmful labels (e.g., based on the *Diagnostic and Statistical Manual of Mental Disorders, Fifth Edition* [*DSM–5*], American Psychiatric Association, 2013). This leads to the question of what kind of positive and negative outcomes can result from a single domain, and how this works. Search engines housed in many libraries and medical centers, either for psychology (e.g., PsycINFO) or medicine (e.g., PubMed), can yield copious numbers of research articles that show both positive and negative outcomes for each of the broad personality domains. For instance, Extraversion is associated with delinquency but also with youth being more readily able to socialize with others (Klimstra et al., 2013; Park, 2011; Reichard et al., 2011; Shiner & Masten, 2008). Extraversion is also linked to physical health and participation in sports. High Openness is associated with mostly positive outcomes, such as exploring, friendliness, and academic achievement, but is also associated with unexpected risks (Kanacri, Rosa, & Di Guinta, 2012; Kirshner, Pozzoboni, & Jones, 2011). For instance, taking a walk at 2:00 in the morning in a gang-infested neighborhood, although representing one's openness to experience, would also be considered a high-risk behavior.

Conscientiousness also has positive and negative outcomes. Positive outcomes include good grades in school, better employment opportunities, improved romantic relationships, and the like. Although most outcomes are positive (e.g., Heaven, Ciarrochi, & Vialle, 2007; Krettenauer, Colasante, Buchmann, & Malti, 2014), being three or four standard deviations above the arithmetic mean on Conscientiousness may equate to an excessively obsessive-compulsive personality style. Such an extreme version of conscientiousness could grind effective decision making to a halt due to the impossibility of computing, for example, all the pros and cons of the infinite hypothetical actions individuals can take and the infinite outcomes for any given action.

Furthermore, certain personality traits are linked to lower levels of psychopathology (X. Chen et al., 2002); development of conscience (Kochanska, Gross, Lin, & Nichols, 2002), and protection against the development of externalizing behavior problems; including aggression. For example, research has shown that when certain aspects of Neuroticism are present there can be a reduction in aggression and misbehavior (Laursen, Pulkkinen, & Adams, 2002; Nagin & Tremblay, 1999; Raine, Reynolds, Venables, Mednick, & Farrington, 1998). Conversely, certain personality characteristics also produce risk factors, including social difficulties, occupational difficulties, and even antisocial behavior (see Caspi, Bem, & Elder, 1989; Eisenberg, Fabes, Guthrie, & Reiser, 2000; Judge, Higgins, Thoresen, & Barrick, 1999; Wright, Beaver,

DeLisi, & Vaughn, 2008). With respect to offending, low Agreeableness and low Conscientiousness (and certain aspects of Neuroticism in combination with already-established conduct problems) have been shown to be strong predictors of conduct problems (S. E. Jones, Miller, & Lynam, 2011). Listed in Table 3.2 are several positive and negative outcomes for each personality domain.

Personality and the Connection to Psycholegal Constructs

Personality constructs can be highly informative for another important reason, especially in the evaluation of juvenile offenders. Specifically, personality traits can be connected to the forensic concepts of risk, developmental maturity, and treatment amenability. Although personality domains do not tap these constructs directly, they definitely inform them. For instance, and not surprisingly, a particularly good set of characteristics for young people include such characteristics as attention and control. Children's conscientious attention and self-control, regardless of the method of indexing the trait, appear to promote the development of rule-abiding behavior rather than the less controlled externalizing and antisocial behavior (Ackerman, Brown, & Izard, 2003; Jones, Miller, & Lynam, 2011; Olson, Schilling, & Bates, 1999; Shiner, 2000, 2006). In fact, research has shown that links between early self-control and lower risk of externalizing problems may be mediated in part by more self-controlled children's tendencies to develop stronger consciences (Kochanska & Knaack, 2003). Effortful attention, self-control, and carefulness have predicted children and adolescents' concurrent and later social competence with peers in more than just a few studies (e.g., Lamb, Chuang, Wessels, Broberg, & Hwang, 2002; Shiner, 2000). Positive emotion also appears to help with social functioning (e.g., Lahey, Van Hulle, Singh, Waldman, & Rahouz, 2011; Salekin, Tippey, & Allen, 2012). Thus, the traits underlying both conscientiousness and agreeableness, for example, promote positive adaptation in many different domains, with very limited data to suggest negative outcomes. These two higher order traits may share a common core of self-control, with Conscientiousness focused on task-related behavior and Agreeableness focused on interpersonal behavior (Caprara, Alessandri, Di Giunta, Panerai, & Eisenberg, 2009; Kern et al., 2013; Laursen, Hafen, Rubin, Booth-LaForce, & Rose-Krasnor, 2010). Regardless of the specific common factor, self-control and Agreeableness appear to be very important for social functioning. It is quite possible that a factor such as positive emotion links the two together, which may account for their concomitant favorable outcomes.

These traits are also likely related to developmental maturity, and this further brings forth the reason why general models of personality may be helpful in the assessment of young people involved with the legal system. Youth

TABLE 3.2

Five-Factor Domains and Positive and Negative Outcomes
Associated With Each

Trait	Positive outcome	Negative outcome
Extraversion (positive emotion)	• Social competence • Promotes good health • Healthier relationships • Participation in sports (Shiner, 2000; Shiner et al., 2003)	• Antisocial behavior • Callousness • Substance use (Hampson, Edmonds, Goldberg, Dubankoski, & Hillier, 2013; Hawley, 2003; Krueger, Markon, Patrick, Benning, & Kramer, 2007; Shiner, 2000)
Neuroticism (negative emotion)	• Conscience development • Guilt when expected • Concern (Kokko & Pulkkinen, 2000; Rothbart, Ahadi, & Evans, 2000; Rothbart, Ahadi, Hershey, & Fisher, 2001)	• Poor relationships • Relationship conflict • Relationship abuse • Relationship dissolution • Less competent parenting • Risk for unemployment (Eisenberg, Pidada, & Liew, 2001; Kagan, Snidman, Zentner, & Peterson, 1999; Krueger, 1999; Lahey, 2009; Muris, Schmidt, Merckelbach, & Schouten, 2001; Svansdottir et al., 2013; Uliaszek et al., 2010; Vanhalst et al., 2012)
Conscientiousness (constraint)	• School adjustment\ educational achievement • Occupational attainment • Job performance (Asendorpf & van Aken, 2003a, 2003b; Chen, Li, Li, Li, B, & Liu, 2000; Ferrari & Pychyl, 2012; Gest, 1997; Hill, Turiano, Mroczek, & Roberts, 2012; Israel et al., 2014; Javaras et al., 2012; Lengua, 2002; Sautter, Brown, Littvay, Sautter, & Bearnes, 2008; Shiner, 2000; Shiner, Masten, & Tellegen, 2002; Shiner et al., 2003) • Health	• Obsessive • (Low Conscientious-ness) Antisocial (Brent et al., 1994; Henry, Caspi, Moffitt, & Silva, 1996; Huey & Weisz, 1997; Jensen-Campbell et al., 2003; John et al., 1994; Samuel & Gore, 2012)

(continues)

TABLE 3.2
Five-Factor Domains and Positive and Negative Outcomes
Associated With Each   *(Continued)*

Trait	Positive outcome	Negative outcome
Agreeableness	• Social competence • Positive parenting • Responsible parenting (Hill et al., 2012; Graziano & Eisenberg, 1997; Masten et al., 1995; Newman, Caspi, Moffitt, & Silva, 1997; Shiner, 2000; Wille, De Fruyt, & De Clercq, 2013)	• Exposure to risk without being discerning • Gullible • (Low Agreeableness) Antisocial (Asendorpf & van Aken, 2003a, 2003b; Homant, 2010; John et al., 1994; Lynam, 2012; Maziade et al., 1990; Shiner, 2000)
Openness	• Exploring • Friendliness • Academic achievement (Asendorpf & van Aken, 2003a, 2003b; Graziano et al., 1997)	• Exposure to risk (Homant, 2010; Samuel & Gore, 2012; Seibert, Miller, Few, Zeichner, & Lynam, 2011)

Note. The list above is not an exhaustive list of positive and negative outcomes but instead a sampling of several positive and negative outcomes.

who develop these characteristics (i.e., Conscientiousness) early are likely to demonstrate greater developmental maturity, showing greater autonomy, cognitive control, and emotion regulation. Again, maturity may be considered a broader concept than Conscientiousness, but self-control, at the very least, can inform developmental maturity assessments and thus is one reason to recommend that forensic clinicians assess general personality characteristics in conjunction with the psycholegal constructs in the evaluation of juveniles. This information also serves as an example for why risk assessments alone are insufficient. Risk assessments on their own miss out on key psycholegal and psychological information and consequently miss the opportunity to uncover the potential reasons that a young person might be posing a risk. Moreover, high Conscientiousness, Openness, and Agreeableness in most cases would suggest greater treatment amenability as well as lower risk. Because these characteristics can be altered, as has been noted in the longitudinal research on personality, they offer potential treatment targets. For instance, Conscientiousness training might be an important avenue for intervention, but if it is not assessed it may not come up as a specific target for intervention. This highlights another important point, in that trait personality indexes represent change-sensitive measures because, as mentioned, traits such as Conscientiousness and Agreeableness are thought to be malleable. As such, these traits may be important to index in progress–outcome evaluations.

One other important topic regarding personality measurement that may be relevant to the evaluation of juvenile offenders is the evaluation of stage models, which psychologists may wish to use in their evaluation of juveniles. Central to this topic are the stage models proposed by Erik Erikson (1968) and James Marcia (1966). These psychological stage models can be informative to the psycholegal constructs outlined above given that they introduce the psychological concept of *identity*. With respect to developmental maturity, identity is a critical construct for understanding mental development during adolescence. I describe Erikson's and Marcia's pioneering stage theories more thoroughly in Chapter 4. For the purpose of this chapter, I continue to focus on personality and pathology models to provide a broader understanding of the differential outcomes that can result from a single trait domain (e.g., Extraversion) before I turn to the important psycholegal constructs of risk, developmental maturity, and amenability.

How Can Personality Account for Both Positive and Negative Outcomes in Youth?

Positive and negative outcomes for the same trait domain require further explanation if personality is to be used effectively in the assessment of adolescent offenders. For instance, scholars now know with greater certainty that early emerging personality traits can change (Andershed, 2010; Roberts & DelVecchio, 2000; Salekin, Rosenbaum, & Lee, 2008; Shiner, 2006). At least three factors can affect change in personality: (a) the specific composition, or mix, of characteristics (Allport, 1937; Caspi et al., 2005; Tobin, Graziano, Vanman, & Tassinary, 2000), (b) parental practices (Bøe et al., 2014), and (c) neighborhood or community (Barker & Salekin, 2012; Beaver, Boutwell, & Barnes, 2014; Belsky, Jaffee, Caspi, Moffitt, & Silva, 2003; Cecil et al., 2014; Shiner, 1998, 2000, 2006).

Consider, for example, a young person who works diligently in the community (e.g., a department store, factory, paper route), earns good grades at school (As and Bs), keeps his or her room clean, and pitches in at home when asked by completing household chores. Such a young person will elicit a smile and verbal praise from parents and other adults. This reinforces the young person to continue to be conscientious. Add to those conscientious characteristics that the young person also does all the aforementioned with positive affect (e.g., a smile on his or her face) and addresses adults with respect (e.g., using courtesy titles such as "Mr." or "Mrs."). Such behavior and attitude (agreeable) will bring about even more rewards, such as admiration from adults (e.g., parents' beaming smile, a pat on the back). Conscientiousness and general Agreeableness, if rewarded, will cause the young person to continue to further expand the traits that elicit those rewards. However, if these traits are not rewarded, then there may be little reason to continue or to expand on them.

Consistent, considerate, and warm parenting, as well as a caring community, can serve as a favorable element in the overall environment that elicits social behavior. Thus, as mentioned, positive traits in young people elicit a positive response from adults and increase positive environments (e.g., more positive parenting, such as warmth and monitoring), and as a consequence, maintain positive traits in young people. The two broad sets of traits (Conscientiousness and Agreeableness), in combination, result in the best outcome for youth in a society where education is a major focus and regulation of emotion is seen as a requisite for being able to sit quietly, listen attentively, and earn good grades, for example. However, there are many other factors, such as the composition of the young person's traits, that may include a high level of impulsivity and a low baseline level of Conscientiousness. This set of traits can lead one to risky behavior, but here again much depends on the environment (Deater-Deckard, 2014; Evans & Cassells, 2014; Steinberg, Greenberger, Jacobi, & Garduque, 1981; Sternberg, 2000). For instance, if a young person lives in a high-risk environment, being impulsive (e.g., enjoying doing things at the spur of the moment) is a major risk factor for a number of negative outcomes, and this may have to do with the outlets young people have for the expression of their impulsivity (e.g., playing with peers in unstructured environments after school vs. playing an organized sport that allows the youth to expend energy in a healthy way to help to re-regulate the youth after a busy day at school). Thus, in more regulated and perhaps economically rich neighborhoods, the same set of traits (e.g., impulsivity) might result in a young person initiating involvement in highly active sports such as football, basketball, hockey, or skiing and adventuresome activities such as hiking or rock climbing, and/or even exploring city museums.

These activities are stimulating enough for even youth who are high on impulsivity or on the far outer edge of sensation seeking and Extraversion. In addition, a young person, through the help of his or her caregivers, may engage in prosocial activities in the community, such as volunteering for a good cause early on a Saturday or Sunday morning, if those traits are shaped by the environment (i.e., effective parenting, community involvement). If youth are impulsive and are low in Conscientiousness and Agreeableness (e.g., oppositional), then positive parenting and neighborhood practices are even more critical for effecting change with regard to developing the social aspects of their personality. Favorable parenting and neighborhood characteristics may be absent in many juvenile offenders' lives. Evaluations can highlight these shortfalls, and the evaluator can make recommendations regarding what environmental factors are required to promote change and healthy development for young people.

Psychopathology and Formal Diagnostic Systems

Examining pathology and general mental health is also critical. At present, there are some aspects of young people's functioning that can be better informed by *DSM–5* diagnoses. For instance, psychotic, mood, and autism spectrum disorders are better captured by *DSM* categories. The disruptive behavior disorders such as CD, oppositional defiant disorder, and ADHD have also been helpful in diagnosing and understanding young people's behavior (e.g., Lacourse et al., 2010; Pardini & Fite, 2010). Moreover, formal diagnostic symptoms are likely most recognizable by court personnel, and they have substantial data to back their use. That being said, it is also important to recognize some of the concerns associated with the formal diagnostic systems (Franklin, 2013). One concern regarding the *DSM* (i.e., *DSM–5*) and the *International Classification of Diseases* (11th ed. [*ICD–11*], World Health Organization, 2012), has been the dynamic nature of the systems as evidenced by the most recent revisions of their diagnostic manuals. Part of the concern here has to do with the alterations to disorders that are, on occasion, not always agreed on or consensus based. Another concern regarding the *DSM* and *ICD* diagnostic schemes has been the level of comorbidity that can result when diagnosing individuals based on *DSM* and *ICD* manual criteria (Coghill & Sonuga-Barke, 2012). It is important to recognize that a single symptom can be indicative of more than one disorder. For instance, "deficient affect" (e.g., shallow affect) might be indicative of depression, an autism spectrum disorder, a psychotic disorder, or what is called *limited prosocial emotion*. Professionals at the National Institutes of Health have recently highlighted their concern regarding this symptom overlap by releasing a description of nonoverlapping areas of functioning in what has been named the *research domain criteria* (RDoC). The director of the National Institute of Mental Health, Dr. Thomas Insel, stated that the institutes were not reliant on the *DSM* and called for a focus on RDoC domains, which are now fundable by the National Institute of Mental Health (Insel, 2013). Explicitly listed in the RDoC are the domains of positive emotion (Extraversion, or approach), negative affect (Neuroticism, or withdrawal), and fear (constraint), which are especially recognizable from the description of personality models noted earlier in the chapter.

Combining personality and pathology models might improve descriptions of youth, as well as an understanding of what needs to change, and thus could well be an effective approach for several reasons. First, use of the RDoC and some of the aforementioned personality traits as a method of describing young people not only allows the connection of a number of diagnostic systems, typologies, and disciplines (see Costa & McCrae, 1992c; Frick & Scheffield Morris, 2004; Krueger, McGue, & Iacono, 2001; Krueger & Tackett, 2007; Nigg, 2006) but may also allow for more research to inform forensic practice, help reduce the large degree of comorbidity across *DSM–5* disorders, and provide an explanatory model for a variety of youth behavior problems. DSM and ICD disorders may add precision for specific mental health conditions such as psychotic disorders, mood disorders, and autism spectrum disorders, as well as substance use and dependence disorders. As mentioned, such an approach which combines personality and pathology assessment stands a good chance of increasing the comprehensiveness of the evaluation.

I now provide a brief overview of the ways in which the models can be united and conceptualized together to further illustrate this point. For instance, Achenbach's (1995) two broad factors—Externalizing and Internalizing syndromes—overarch personality models (Conscientiousness and Openness) and DSM–5 diagnoses and can help explain the comorbidity among various disorders. Consider the numerous overlapping diagnoses that co-occur with CD. Specifically, CD is frequently comorbid with oppositional defiant disorder, ADHD, and substance abuse symptoms (Shook, Vaughn, Goodkind, & Johnson, 2011). This overlap may provide support for the notion that some underlying factor (e.g., disinhibition or Extraversion) accounts for all three behavioral manifestations; that is, some other factor accounts for the reasons why a young person displays oppositionality and engages in smoking, drinking, excessively risky sexual behavior, and breaking the law. See Table 3.3 for an illustration of this integration.

Being well versed in the different systems and how they relate to one another may be important for several reasons. First, it allows the forensic clinician to discuss a young person in a variety of ways, including problem areas, personality, and diagnostic schemes. Second, it helps the forensic clinician understand the overlap across various systems, such as the DSM–5 and ICD–11. Even if forensic clinicians primarily endorse one system, it will be

TABLE 3.3
Connecting the Big Five Personality Factors to Specific Childhood Disorders and the Two Broad Concepts of Externalizing and Internalizing

Externalizing	Internalizing
Personality language	
High Extraversion	High Neuroticism
Low Agreeableness	Low Extraversion
Low Conscientiousness (constraint)	High Conscientiousness (constraint)
DSM–5 language	
Oppositional defiant disorder	Separation anxiety
Conduct disorder	Depression
Attention-deficit/hyperactivity disorder	Generalized anxiety
Substance abuse	Obsessive–compulsive disorder, eating disorders

Note. Personality and Diagnostic and Statistical Manual of Mental Disorders (DSM–5) disorders are categorized under the broad domains of Externalizing and Internalizing.

important to be able to frame descriptions and diagnoses in different nomen-clatures and to be able to speak in different diagnostic languages allowing for optimal communication. The last section of this chapter is devoted to concepts that are directly linked to juvenile forensic legal decision making, including risk for dangerous behavior, developmental maturity, and treatment amenability (Brannen et al., 2006; Salekin, Rogers, & Ustad, 2001; Salekin, Yff, et al., 2002).

Risk for Dangerous Behavior

Three risk factors are particularly important in the prediction of risk as identified by numerous research programs, some of which are conducting large-scale scientific studies on typologies (e.g., Farrington, Ullrich, & Salekin, 2010; Frick & Moffitt, 2010; Loeber, 1991; Loeber et al., 2012; Moffitt, 1993, 2003, 2007; Rutter, 2003). The three main risk factors derived from this research include (a) the extensiveness and seriousness of juvenile offending, (b) the extent to which the young person has engaged in prior violence (or serious antisocial conduct), and (c) whether the young person has a character that shows a lack of concern regarding the well-being of others (i.e., interpersonal callous traits; Forth, Kosson, & Hare, 2003; Frick & Moffitt, 2010; Loeber et al., 2012; Moffitt, 2007; Salekin, 2010). For some youth, a stepping-stone pattern may be evidenced whereby a young person begins with perhaps cruelty to animals, which then leads to fighting with peers and subsequently even more severe violent and antisocial behavior. These behaviors are then accompanied by affective cooling toward their antisocial acts (lack of empathy, lack of remorse). As I discuss in Chapter 5, these factors are, to varying degrees, included in risk measures and as such require consideration in risk assessments. Table 3.4 lists the three facets of risk outlined above

TABLE 3.4
Characteristics of Risk for Dangerous Behavior

Violent and aggressive tendencies[a]	Planned and extensive criminality[a]	Psychopathic features[a]
Engages in unprovoked violent behavior	Severe antisocial behavior	Lacks remorse
Violence toward individuals	Premeditated crimes	Lacks empathy
Cruelty toward animals	Leadership role in crimes	Egocentricity
Easily angered and physically aggressive	Frequency of past criminal acts	Manipulative
Generally oppositional and cruel (hurtful/spiteful)	Age of onset of antisocial behavior (early)	Deceitfulness
Bullies others	Delinquent peer group	Social potency

[a]Subscale from the Risk–Sophistication–Treatment Inventory (Salekin, 2004).

and delineated in prototypical analytic studies. As indicated in the table, risk items contain extreme conduct problems; interpersonal callous features; and some legal criteria, including a leadership role in the crime. This table also shows how the *DSM–5* diagnosis of CD with interpersonal callousness and limited prosocial emotion may help with understanding the risk posed by a young individual. Individuals who score high on the risk factors present a higher risk to the community, whereas those who score low on them likely present a low risk to the community. Specialized risk assessment measures can be helpful in showing who is, as well as who is not, a risk to the public.

Two additional points require consideration in the coverage of the risk concept for juvenile evaluations: (a) the varied ways in which youth can pose a risk to the community and (b) whether the alleged index offenses should be considered in the evaluation. With respect to the first concern, there are a variety of ways in which youth can pose a risk in the community. The above-mentioned factors are the most commonly researched ones and probably account for most risk issues in juvenile delinquency cases. However, other conditions and risk factors may be present. For instance, psychotic disorders, when coupled with command hallucinations with violent content, can be cause for concern and have links to antisocial behavior in adults (Douglas, Guy, & Hart, 2009). Mood disorders that prompt violent thoughts also are relevant and worth keeping an eye on via the evaluation. Whether young people are bullied at school (e.g., Barker & Salekin, 2012) or through social media or some other outlet may also be relevant to risk assessment. Young people who feel isolated or not part of the mainstream due to a mental illness or some other factor may also be cause for concern. Some of these risk situations are very specific and bring home the point that risk prediction is difficult. This also highlights the fact that although both static and dynamic factors are predictive of future offending, forensic clinicians should bring to light those factors that are dynamic by informing attorneys and the courts that such factors are often quite amenable to treatment.

The second issue is whether information should be gathered on the index offense. With regard to past behavior, it is likely that the courts will want to know a young person's history and whether he or she has engaged in criminal and/or violent conduct. Whether specific information can be gathered regarding an index crime will depend on whether a legal decision has been made about the index crime. One approach to incorporating an open index crime into risk assessment is to gather information about it but not communicate any incriminating information in either psychological reports or testimony. Some clinicians and attorneys prefer not to touch on issues pertaining to the index crime whatsoever. On the other hand, transfer evaluations may require at least some consideration of the index crime. If the index offense cannot be discussed, past behavior alone will be highly pertinent to the evaluation of juveniles because it provides some description of the individual's tendencies in terms of risk (Loeber, 1991; Moffitt, 1993, 2003, 2007; Salekin, Yff, et al., 2002).

Drawing a conclusion that a young person is a high risk can heavily influence the judge. Such influence is likely to result in more restrictive settings regarding the placement of the young individual. For this reason, it is important to clearly convey the risk estimates and also the limits of their predictive capacity. It is also important to balance these risk estimates with any strengths the young person may possess, including, potentially, a high readiness for treatment. Moreover, it is important to note that many youth with high scores on all three of these risk clusters do not reoffend. Thus, scoring high on such a scale simply means that one is at greater risk for dangerous behavior than young people who score low (see Chapter 8).

DEVELOPMENTAL MATURITY ("SOPHISTICATION–MATURITY")

Developmental maturity is a psychological concept that is highly pertinent to young persons in the juvenile justice system (Savitsky & Karras, 1984). Recall that, as noted in Chapter 1, the assumption that young people are less mature than older individuals was the reason for a separate juvenile justice system in the first place. Nonetheless, there is variation, even within the juvenile population, as to a given young person's level of maturity. *Developmental maturity* is the term I use in this book, because the term *sophistication–maturity*, when used to signify increased criminal sophistication, is likely simply developmental maturity modified by some other factor (e.g., psychopathy, criminal thinking patterns).

What Comprises Developmental Maturity?

Three factors likely underpin the psychological concept of developmental maturity: (a) autonomy, (b) cognitive abilities, and (c) emotional maturity (i.e., emotion regulation skills). Exploration and commitment to values are also important developmental concepts that help distinguish the autonomy of socially mature from socially immature adolescents (Marcia, 1966). These and other related criteria can help clinicians better understand the variability in developmental maturity. As forensic clinicians will recognize, this variability must be taken into account when considering an individual's psychological composition and how young people might be processed through the courts. For instance, a very young and immature child would not be a good candidate for dispositions that entailed placement in settings where other perhaps older youth with more extensive criminal histories reside. The criteria that underpin each subcomponent of developmental maturity are listed in Table 3.5.

TABLE 3.5
Characteristics of Developmental Maturity

Autonomy[a]	Cognitive capacities[a]	Emotional regulation[a]
Autonomy	Aware of what is prosocial	Able to delay gratification
Internal locus of control	Understands behavioral norms	Moral development
Development of self-concept	Able to identify alternative actions	Self-regulation of emotion
Self-reflection	Foresight (future time perspective)	Conflict resolution
Exploration	Cost–benefit analysis in decision making	Interpersonal skills
Commitment to a value/idea	Ability to anticipate consequences	Positive outlook

[a]Subscale from the Risk–Sophistication–Treatment Inventory (Salekin, 2004).

Important Contextual Factors

Assessing any of the three broad constructs requires the consideration of context. Examining a young person's developmental maturity provides a good example of this. For instance, conceptualizations of developmental maturity should consider an individual's developmental status, the environment in which that individual currently lives, any potential psychopathology, and the context or situation in which that person makes choices. This model suggests that developmental status, which includes age, has a two-way interaction with the environment (e.g., parenting practices, family socioeconomic status) that also must be viewed in conjunction with the young person's pathology (e.g., ADHD, depression) or lack of pathology, that may then influence his or her clarity of thought (e.g., broad vs. narrow thinking) and thus decision making. It is likely that decision making has a cumulative effect on maturity and developmental status. Pathology is included because research has shown that a number of juveniles have high levels of psychopathology (Abram, Choe, Washburn, Romero, & Teplin, 2009; Abram et al., 2007; King et al., 2011; Washburn et al., 2007; Wasserman et al., 2008) and mental illness may directly affect decision making and thus developmental maturity (Barbot & Hunter, 2012; Kazdin, 2000). Kazdin (2000) made the cogent point that impairment in adolescent decision making is largely due to the very high level of psychopathology seen in young people who come into contact with the legal system rather than the stage of adolescence per se. In sum, this model serves as an example of a few key factors that should be considered in examining a young individual's level of developmental maturity.

Treatment Amenability

Best practice in disposition and transfer evaluations entails the consideration of treatment needs and amenability. *Treatment amenability* is the consideration of how likely a given youth is to respond favorably to an intervention. Not surprisingly, psychopathology, especially severe psychopathology, can complicate treatment because it creates barriers to prospects of quickly returning youth to a prosocial life. Again, the analogies of Huckleberry Finn from Mark Twain's novels and Calvin from the *Calvin and Hobbes* comic series serve as illustrations of errant youth who arguably did not have "pathologies," or at least not severe psychopathologies, as pointed out by John Richers and Dante Cicchetti (1993). As can be seen from studies conducted by Teplin and her colleagues (e.g., Teplin, Welty, Abram, Dulcan, & Washburn 2012), unlike the Mark Twain characters, many youth in detention facilities do in fact have a number of psychological disorders. Such psychopathology makes treatment more difficult and likely affects amenability ratings. Nonetheless, and fortunately, as a field, mental health professionals have many effective interventions for young people with various forms of psychopathology (Weisz & Kazdin, 2010). Still, it is important to note the levels of complexity involved.

Motivation to change is an important factor, and this personal characteristic can be impactful in the process toward making the young individual's recovery more successful. In fact, it is likely that this factor enhances the prospects for success, in particular with first-time offenders who are treated in the community. Conversely, a lack of motivation to change diminishes treatment amenability. Although there are ways to reboot motivation, low motivation likely affects initial ratings of amenability to treatment and speaks to the extra work that may be needed to gain treatment rapport and adjust treatment readiness.

Family factors also play a role in the number of gains that can be made immediately in psychotherapy. A supportive family provides greater opportunities for a young person's successful recovery from contact with the law. Although some families lack the financial and emotional means to provide strong support, this might become a point of intervention by shoring up such resources or thinking creatively about ways to gain this additional support. Thus, by assessing the risk, maturity, and treatment amenability of youth, the specific treatment needs of a young person become apparent and thus can guide treatment recommendations to the courts. Treatment recommendations may require some follow-up and planning efforts with the people conducting the intervention. Table 3.6 outlines the factors that underlie treatment amenability.

TABLE 3.6
Treatment Amenability

Psychopathology: Degree and type	Responsibility and motivation to change	Consideration and tolerance of others
Degree of psychopathology	Motivated to engage in treatment	Anxiety about the circumstance
Treatability of psychopathology	Takes responsibility for actions	Feels guilt/remorse
Aware of difficulties and problems	Open to change	Considers and generally cares about others
Insight into cause of problems	Expects to change	Has protective factors (sports, hobbies)
Limited police/court/ probation involvement	Positive involvement by parents	Has positive attachments

Note. Based on the Risk–Sophistication–Treatment Inventory (Salekin, 2004).

Severe psychopathology can be treated, as mentioned, but it usually takes more effort. For example, severe CD with interpersonal callousness or, in *DSM–5* terminology, limited prosocial emotion (involving, e.g., severe cruelty to animals, physical fighting, threatening siblings), may be more time consuming to treat than a mild form of CD (e.g., one that involves throwing rocks at passing railway cars, painting graffiti on a building) that does not include a severe lack of emotion toward others. If the young person accepts some responsibility for his or her actions, and reports being motivated to change, this too can further help with treatment readiness and progress. Finally, a young person's degree of consideration of and tolerance for others can be a positive prognostic sign even if this extends to only a certain group (e.g., family). This is because this capacity for a few individuals usually signifies that these human emotions are present and can be extended to others. Assessment of amenability can help one gauge the difficulties one may encounter as well as what will be needed to bring about change, even in the most severe cases.

CONCLUDING COMMENTS

In this chapter, I have stressed that five concepts are essential to the assessment of juvenile offenders: (a) truthfulness of reporting, (b) general personality and pathology, (c) risk for dangerous behavior, (d) developmental maturity, and (e) amenability to treatment. I chose personality as a framework for understanding young people because of its parsimony, predictive power, ability to be integrated with diagnostic systems, and ability to be incorporated into psycholegal constructs. Moreover, personality domains allow for the ability to address their association with positive and negative outcomes. Although this chapter focused on personality as one key factor to assess, forensic clinicians may choose from a variety of systems. Also in this chapter, I highlighted the fact that there are good reasons for evaluators to augment general personality assessment with *DSM–5* and *ICD–11* diagnoses. Regardless of the system primarily being used, forensic clinicians should have a theoretical foundation for their assessment. Also, greater knowledge of the various systems can place forensic clinicians in a better position to handle potential questions in the courtroom. For example, clinicians will be prepared when a developmental psychologist offers expertise on "temperament," a personality psychologist offers expertise on "personality traits," or a judge asks about *DSM–5* or *ICD–11* classifications and diagnoses. In Chapter 4, I discuss the research behind these concepts and describe their scientific foundations and limits.

4

EMPIRICAL FOUNDATIONS AND LIMITS OF JUVENILE FORENSIC EVALUATION

Optimal practice in juvenile evaluation requires that mental health professionals be familiar with the empirical foundation of the areas they are assessing. Juvenile evaluations require groundwork and specialized knowledge that can always be augmented by new literature and data searches (through, e.g., the Office of Juvenile Justice and Delinquency Prevention, PsycINFO, PubMed). This knowledge can be categorized into the five broad mental health concepts detailed in Chapter 3: (a) truthfulness (veracity) of reporting, (b) general personality and pathology, (c) risk for dangerous behavior, (d) developmental maturity, and (e) amenability to treatment. Other areas of knowledge are also important, such as the consequences of placement in certain facilities, substance abuse problems, parental factors, and whether better approaches to juvenile delinquency might be developed. For the purposes of this chapter, I focus on the science behind the five concepts just mentioned

http://dx.doi.org/10.1037/14595-005
Forensic Evaluation and Treatment of Juveniles: Innovation and Best Practice, by R. T. Salekin

with an emphasis on the key constructs of risk, developmental maturity, and amenability to treatment.

Before I discuss these key topics, it is important to provide a brief overview of a few central issues regarding the generalizability of the research behind these concepts. First, although general theories often apply across gender, there clearly are gender differences that should always be investigated in the context of the constructs applied to young people. Some gender issues pertain to the effect of puberty on risk, differential rates of abuse, differences in risk for recidivism, and differences in the presentation of psychopathic-like features (Odgers, Reppucci, & Moretti, 2005; Oudekerk, Burgers, & Reppucci, 2014; Penney, Lee, & Moretti, 2010). For instance, early menarche can be a risk factor for girls with respect to delinquency, but obviously it is not for boys (e.g., Caspi, Lynam, Moffitt, & Silva, 1993; Silverthorn & Frick, 1999). Other differences, such as in prevalence of deception, developmental maturity, and treatment amenability, may also be present across gender. Understanding these chief gender differences is critical to the assessment of both boys and girls who come into contact with the law. Similarly, race and ethnic differences may exist (Fagan & Zimring, 2000; Zimring, 1998), and forensic clinicians ought to look for specific information relevant to the specific case at hand each time they evaluate a young person.

VERACITY OF YOUTH AND PARENT REPORTING

Research on the accuracy of youth reporting, especially youth involved in the justice system, is limited (Fabry, Bertinetti, & Guzman-Cavazos, 2011). Thus, part of the difficulty in assessing the accuracy of adolescent offenders' reporting is that the research base is not as robust as it is in regard to adults. Of course, considerable research on veracity in general does exist, but again, it is limited in what it tells us about the juvenile offender in any comprehensive way. Additional problems include early notions that children's and adolescents' psychological problems are virtually nonexistent. Today U.S. society faces many of the same concerns, although we now know with more certainty that mental illness and psychological problems do exist in young people, including very young children. In fact, rates of mental illness are alarmingly high in juvenile offender populations (Teplin, Welty, Abram, Dulcan, & Washburn, 2012; Washburn et al., 2007; Wasserman, McReynolds, Lucas, Fisher, & Santos, 2002). We also know that youth, perhaps far more often than adults, are not always aware of, or able to describe, the problems they are experiencing. Even if they are aware, adolescents are not always candid reporters regarding their mental or emotional health problems.

Prevalence of Deception in Children and Adolescents

The best information on nonclinical samples stems from two studies conducted in the mid-1980s: (a) Achenbach (1985) noted that a large percentage of normal 4- to 5-year-old children engage in some form of lying, and (b) Stouthamer-Loeber (1986; Stouthamer-Loeber & Loeber, 1986) estimated the prevalence of lying to be 19% in normal children with a gradual decline to 15% in adolescents. Data on malingering and specific response styles are also quite limited; only two studies exist on these topics. First, Rogers, Hinds, and Sewell (1996) conducted a study of 53 dually diagnosed adolescent offenders and found a malingering prevalence rate of 15%, similar to those found with adults (Rogers, 1997, 2008; Yates, Nordquist, & Schultz-Ross, 1996). Second, Zahner (1991) investigated 138 preadolescents, 95 of whom had elevated scale scores on the Child Behavior Checklist (Achenbach, 1991b). Addressing the prevalence of other response styles in children, Zahner examined the quality of the responses to the Diagnostic Interview Schedule for Children (http://www.cdc.gov/nchs/data/nhanes/limited_access/ydq.pdf) and found that 8.3% engaged in acquiescence ("yea saying"), whereas another 10.1% denied any problems ("nay-saying"). Some children were noted to have attempted to please the interviewer (8.0%), and some provided guarded responses (14.0%). In addition, Zahner noted that 12.0% of the younger children (ages 6–8) tended to present themselves in an overly positive light (indicative of a social desirability mind-set).

Age and the Ability to Deceive

Research on developmental abilities to deceive can facilitate an understanding of youth reporting (Bussey, 1992; Peskin, 1992; Polak & Harris, 1999; Ruffman, Olson, Ash, & Keenan, 1993; Sodian, 1991; Talwar, Gordon, & Lee, 2007; Talwar & Lee, 2002). Evidence suggests that the ability to deceive is associated with social skills that develop with maturity (Lewis, 1993). As children develop their verbal and nonverbal skills, they are likely to become increasingly skilled at deception. Research demonstrates that mental health professionals can make rough demarcations regarding the developmental capabilities for dissimulation. A general guideline for age-related deceptive capabilities that may be helpful is provided in Table 4.1. A similar table was first developed for Richard Rogers's (1997, 2008) book on malingering.

An examination of the literature indicates that written accounts of malingering among young people are quite rare. Mental health professionals who feel that malingering may be an issue in a specific case can consult several documented clinical accounts of malingering in late childhood and adolescence (e.g., Faust, Hart, & Guilmette, 1988; Greenfeld, 1987; Stein,

TABLE 4.1
A Developmental Guideline for Examining Deceptive Abilities in Youth

Age (years)	Expected deceptive ability
< 3	Lack of evidence to support deception or dissimulation; lies that are told are likely denials of transgressions; the intention is likely to avoid punishment.
3–4	Capable of telling very basic and unsophisticated lies (i.e., largely denials of transgressions). Perry (1995) noted that although very young children (i.e., about the age of 3) have difficulty understanding the concept of a truth and lie on the basis of beliefs, they can unintentionally deceive others by manipulating their behavior.
5–6	Capable of telling some lies, but they tend to be rather rudimentary (i.e., child is unable to sustain the deception over time).
6–12	Capable of intentional deception (i.e., instilling false beliefs in others and maintaining deception when probed). Increasingly able to tell sophisticated lies.
12–18	Capable of intentional deception and engaging in more sophisticated lies. Possibly malinger psychological problems and disorders; role playing and facial expressions are under adolescents' control, and their ability to do so is increasingly similar to adults.

Graham, & Williams, 1995). To date, the cases that have been written up in psychological research reports vary from a teenage girl malingering psychosis for protection from an abusive parent (e.g., Greenfeld, 1987), to two youth seeking stimulants by faking attention-deficit/hyperactivity disorder in a detention facility (Conti, 2004), to a child and his mother seeking award and compensation for alleged neurological damage subsequent to a car accident (e.g., Boone & Lu, 2003), to school refusal cases in clinical practice (Bools, Foster, Brown, & Berg, 1990; Kearney & Beasley, 1994).

In general, it is best to approach an evaluation assuming that the young person and his or her family will be honest, but it also is best practice to be prepared to deal with aspects of the young person's presentation style that may be distorted and stem from one or more (possibly several) motivational factors. For example, adolescents may lie about substance use to avoid parental disappointment or punishment. Reluctance to disclose information regarding substance use in this instance should not be used against the young person but instead should be used to better understand him or her and his or her treatment needs. In addition to being familiar with response styles, it is also helpful to be acquainted with the research that helps explain discrepancies across sources (see De Los Reyes & Kazdin, 2005).

PSYCHOPATHOLOGY/PERSONALITY

Several models of psychopathology and personality have been proposed, including not only the formal diagnostic guidelines promulgated by the American Psychiatric Association (e.g., the *Diagnostic and Statistical Manual of Mental Disorders, Fifth Edition* [*DSM–5*], 2013) and the World Health Organization (e.g., the *International Classification of Diseases, Eleventh Edition* [*ICD–11*], 2012) but also models put forth by independent researchers.

DSM–5 and *ICD–11* Models

Regardless of the diagnostic system chosen, clinicians should be familiar with the supporting research. For example, if a clinician uses the *DSM–5*, then he or she should be familiar with recent research on *DSM*-based constructs. A good example involves recent research on oppositional defiant disorder (ODD; e.g., Whelan, Stringaris, Maughan, & Barker, 2013), which has helped to explain why ODD has not always been a good predictor of conduct disorder (CD) or antisocial personality disorder in later life (Burke, Hipwell, & Loeber, 2010; Hipwell et al., 2011; Stepp, Burke, Hipwell, & Loeber, 2012; Stringaris & Goodman, 2009a, 2009b; Stringaris, Maughan, & Goodman, 2010). ODD's limited predictive ability is due to its disparate symptomatology. Recent factor analytic work has shown that there are multiple dimensions to ODD and that the various dimensions are connected to different types of comorbid psychopathology (e.g., internalizing and externalizing) and different outcomes (Burke & Loeber, 2010; Stringaris & Goodman, 2009a, 2009b; Stringaris, Maughan, & Goodman, 2010).

The three dimensions of ODD have been named (a) *ODD–irritable*, (b) *ODD–oppositional*, and (c) *ODD–spiteful* (or *hurtful*), terms that better capture the item composition of each dimension. Interestingly, the irritability dimension appears to be linked to internalizing problems and predicts depression and anxiety as far out as 20 years into adulthood but is not strongly linked to CD (Burke & Loeber, 2010). The oppositional dimension is related to mild but not severe CD, and the spiteful dimension is linked to severe CD and to callous–unemotional (CU) traits. Also, these dimensions have connections with temperament (irritable and uneasy) and personality (spiteful and callousness).

Another example relevant to clinicians' familiarity with recent developments within the *DSM–5* includes CD, with its specifier of limited prosocial emotion (LPE). The specifier was initially proposed to be termed the *callous unemotional traits specifier* (Frick & Moffitt, 2010). This is a critical addition to the *DSM–5* because it is purports to capture a more severe form of

CD (Lahey, 2014). The specifier requires that youth meet criteria for only two of a potential four symptoms. The four LPE symptoms outlined in the *DSM–5* are (a) lack of remorse or guilt, (b) lack of concern about performance, (c) callous lack of empathy, and (d) shallow or deficient affect. The four symptoms are designed to assess callous (two items) and unemotional (two items) characteristics. To meet criteria for the specifier, the above-mentioned symptoms have to be present over a 12-month period. If youth meet this threshold, along with meeting criteria for CD, they would receive a diagnosis of CD with the specifier LPE.

There is very little research on the LPE specifier at this point. Also, forensic clinicians should know that although LPE added in some of the characterological aspects of psychopathy for which many researchers and clinicians had hoped, the specifier does not equate to psychopathy, even though this was its conceptual starting point (see Frick & Moffitt, 2010). This is because, as Clark and Watson (1995) put it, it lacks appropriate representation for the broader syndrome of psychopathy (see also Lahey, 2014). Because so few symptoms are necessary to meet the threshold for the LPE specifier, it will be important to know whether the CD + LPE concept will have the same conceptual meaning as its theoretical roots (i.e., psychopathy; Cleckley, 1941; Hare, 1991). Clinicians may also be interested in knowing about a young person's placement on other psychopathy dimensions, including interpersonal features (grandiosity and deceit) and impulsivity features (lack of planning), to complete the psychopathy assessment (Forth, Kosson, & Hare, 2003).

Forensic clinicians will also want to acquaint themselves with research that addresses the incremental contribution of LPE or CU over CD alone to negative outcomes such as recidivism (Lahey, 2014). Clinicians will want to be aware of any contexts in which LPE, without CD, may have positive (or neutral) outcomes for young people. Of note is that research with Romanian orphans who grew up in an environment (e.g., caregiving) that was cold and neglectful has suggested that CU traits can serve to help youngsters survive in emotionally distant and harsh environments (Kumsta, Sonuga-Barke, & Rutter, 2012). Specifically, children in Romanian orphanages developed CU traits but not CD or ODD, illustrating that CU and CD do not always co-occur and demonstrating that CU traits may have adaptive value in some settings.

Other Models of Personality

The scientific study of individual differences can be traced to the seminal work of Thomas and Chess and their colleagues, who initiated the New York Longitudinal Study to examine the significance of biologically based temperament in infancy and childhood (Thomas & Chess, 1977; Thomas, Chess, & Birch, 1968; Thomas, Chess, Birch, Hertzig, & Korn, 1963). These well-known researchers viewed temperament as a style of behavior and abilities. Important about this work, and relevant to juvenile evaluations, is that Thomas et al. (1963) emphasized a two-way interchange between biology and the environment in shaping children's outcomes.

Later, John, Caspi, Robins, Moffitt, and Stouthamer-Loeber (1994) introduced the basic personality dimensions to developmental psychologists and demonstrated that what they called the *Little Five* (Openness, Conscientiousness, Extraversion, Agreeableness, and Neuroticism) were able to predict problem behavior in children. From this study forward, research examining child and adolescent personality and resultant outcomes has proliferated, thereby providing forensic clinicians with an extensive research base (e.g., Digman, 1963, 1990; Digman & Inouye, 1986; Graziano & Ward, 1992; Jang, McCrae, Angleitner, Riemann, & Livesley, 1998; John et al., 1994; Kohnstamm, Halverson, Mervielde, & Havill, 1998; Lamb, Chuang, Wessels, Broberg, & Hwang, 2002; Markey, Markey, & Tinsley, 2004; Martin, Wisenbaker, & Huttunen, 1994).

Although there may be some confusion regarding the terms *temperament* and *personality*, research has increasingly shown that the two are closely related, if not the same thing (Buss & Plomin, 1984; Caspi & Bem, 1990; Goldsmith et al., 1987; Graziano, 2003; Halverson, Kohnstamm, & Martin, 1994). For instance, McCrae and Costa (1992, 1997; Costa & McCrae, 1992a, 1992b; Rothbart & Bates, 1998; Rothbart & Derryberry, 2002) have argued that the defining characteristics of temperament also apply to personality *traits*, and these characteristics include early observability, genetic contribution, and pervasive impact on a range of behavior (McCrae & Costa, 1997; Mervielde, De Clercq, De Fruyt, & Van Leeuwen, 2005; Yamagata et al., 2006). As I delineated in Chapter 3, these traits (e.g., Openness, Conscientiousness) have been connected to *DSM–IV* (American Psychiatric Association, 1994) and *DSM–5* psychopathology models (see Tackett, 2007), making this integration increasingly familiar to clinicians and researchers.

The research also indicates that there is some stability associated with these personality traits (Bernstein, Cohen, Skodol, Bezirganian, & Brook, 1996; Bernstein et al., 1993; Brent, Zelenak, Buckstein, & Brown, 1990; De Fruyt et al., 2006). Roberts and DelVecchio (2000; see also Roberts, Walton, & Viechtbauer, 2006) analyzed 3,217 test–retest correlation coefficients from 152 longitudinal studies and demonstrated an increase in stability from .31 during childhood to .54, in young adulthood, rising to .64 by age 30, with the highest stability of .74 observed between the ages of 50 and 70 years. These findings suggest that there is stability in personality that facilitates prediction. However, the findings also show that personality change is quite possible in young people and occurs further into adulthood than one might expect.

A set of studies conducted over the past few decades, with considerable methodological complexity, have attempted to unravel what accounts for the stability in personality and what accounts for change. Considerable progress has been made on this front, and the best knowledge we have suggests that genes account for stability (Saudino & Plomin, 1996; see also Loehlin, 1992; Saudino & Cherny, 2001), whereas the mix or blend of traits (Allport, 1937), parenting (Bates, Pettit, Dodge, & Ridge, 1998; Belsky, Hsieh, & Crnic, 1998; Hagekull & Bohlin, 2003; Koenig, Cicchetti, & Rogosch, 2004; Murray, Loeber, & Pardini, 2012; Rubin, Bukowski, & Parker, 1998; Rubin, Burgess, Dwyer, & Hastings, 2003; Stoolmiller, 2001) and the neighborhood account for change (Bates & McFadyen-Ketchum, 2000; Chang, 2003; Dodge et al., 2003; Gallagher, 2002; Gazelle & Ladd, 2003; Kernberg, Weiner, & Bardenstein, 2000; Putnam, Sanson, & Rothbart, 2002; Shiner, 2006; Tackett, 2007). Thus, peer relations, teacher warmth, and neighborhood kindness may moderate the links between poor self-control and criminal involvement (Barker, Trentacosta, & Salekin, 2011; Evans & Cassells, 2014; Henry, Caspi, Moffitt, Harrington, & Silva, 1999; Lynam et al., 2000). This is important to be cognizant of when conducting juvenile evaluations because these stability and change factors not only speak to the etiology of conduct problems, for example, but also provide information about key targets for intervention.

Two quick examples illustrate how the research in this area can help with clinical evaluations of young people in the justice system. First, if we consider individual characteristics (the mix or blend of traits), we have learned that children's characteristics, such as intelligence, may change (moderate) the stability and outcomes of their personalities. Brighter children (keep in mind that intelligence is viewed as something that can be altered) may find it easier to handle challenging aspects of their personalities or environment (Asendorpf, 1994). Second, children's relative success or failure in important developmental domains, such as academic achievement and social competence with peers, may influence cognitive skills and personality development (Henry, Caspi, Moffitt, Harrington, & Silva, 1999). The research previously reviewed in this chapter makes clear that childhood personality noticeably shapes later adaptation in school, work, and relationships (Shiner, 2006; Shiner & Masten, 2002). The converse can also occur, whereby life adaptation may influence children's typical ways of feeling, thinking, and behaving and thus change personality.

In the context of discussing youth personality and development, forensic clinicians may prefer to use stage models. Alternatively, they can incorporate stage models into their broader conceptualization of general models of personality and psychopathology (DSM–5 or ICD–11). Either way, stage models may help elaborate on what is known about a young person's character and general developmental status. This information may be highly relevant to juvenile disposition and transfer cases. However, there are a number of different models that require consideration (Freud, 1905/2011; Grotevant, 1998; Piaget, 1970/1983) before I discuss Erikson (1950, 1959, 1968) and Marcia (1966, 1994). In the next paragraphs I review several of these models.

Different developmental theories consider puberty as a significant stage for social and personality development (Grotevant, 1998) because it is a time of changing social interactions with parents and peers. Although I would not recommend using something like Freud's (1905/2011) psychosexual stages (oral, anal, phallic, latency, and genital) of development because of the theory's difficulty and obscurity, puberty and adolescence in general is a key transitional phase, as a number of prominent theorists and researchers have noted. The notion of storm and stress (Arnett, 1999; Hall, 1904), however, is not consistently supported by the scientific literature, and there appears to be greater recognition of the variability in youth development with respect to cognitive and emotion regulation skills. Emotional turbulence (i.e., storm and stress) is no longer believed to be consistently characteristic of adolescent development but instead may depend on a number of other factors (Arnett, 1999).

Erikson (1959, 1968) described adolescence as a critical stage in human development. Erikson considered adolescence to be a second individuation stage in which change is likely to occur. The question adolescents ask themselves during this developmental period is, "Who am I, and where am I going?" Marcia's (1966, 1994) theory elaborated on Erikson's (1963) model and has been important in terms of discussing young people's commitment to social versus antisocial lifestyles. Exploration and commitment are two important concepts in Marcia's model, and these life events further form a young person's personality.

Behavioral theories (e.g., Robin & Foster, 1989) emphasize that during adolescence, learning processes and contingencies are embedded in novel social networks and environments, including changing peer groups that represent an adolescent stage. In addition, Piaget's (1970/1983) theory of cognitive development and subsequent theories regarding brain architecture suggest that newly acquired "cognitive structures" influence the way children and adolescents interact with their environment. According to Piaget, from age 11 onward, young people graduate to relatively adult modes of thinking, including abstract thinking, and may spend hours on abstract issues, such as hypotheses exploration regarding justice, love, and free will. According to Piaget, young people's thoughts are characterized as relatively systematic, logical, and reflective (Piaget, 1926/1929, 1933/1952, 1970/1983).

Vygotsky's (1934/1986) theory proposes that language is primary to helping young people form their thoughts and beliefs about the world, and he believed that language facilitated brain development. His work eventually led to the notion that children eventually develop an internal voice (i.e., self-talk) that guides behavior.

Finally, personality theories such as Cloninger's theory of character development distinguish qualitatively different life strategies that must be mastered before a more advanced developmental level can be achieved (Cloninger, Svrakic, & Przybeck, 1993).

Stage models can bolster personality descriptions by serving as psychologically meaningful conceptualizations of adolescence. Stage theories give the forensic clinician much more to work with in terms of theory and science because they capture difficult life periods and points of potential inflection. These theories clearly also have relevance for psycholegal constructs. Specifically, Marcia's (1966) revision of Erikson's theory can help one understand developmental maturity in adolescents by explaining exploration and commitment that may be indicative of these inflection points (choices of moving in prosocial directions or non-prosocial directions) that also affect risk and treatment amenability (Meeus, van de Schoot, Keijsers, Schwartz, & Branje, 2010). Thus, whether viewed as changing characteristic adaptations (Caspi & Shiner, 2006) or discontinuities (Cloninger et al., 1993), stage theories may well inform psychological reports.

I return now to the two main concepts in Marcia's (1966) theory: (a) exploration and (b) commitment. *Exploration* signifies that, during adolescence, the young person explores his or her environment. This includes traveling either mentally (e.g., reading, imagination) or in real life through different social, educational, occupational, and geographical spaces. Such exploration opens up avenues for educational, occupational, and psychological growth. *Commitment* means that a young person, after a period of exploration, commits to a goal. This is generally meant to be a life goal that would later be reflected by a specific lifestyle. Lifestyles can differ, of course, and can include variations of prosocial, asocial, and antisocial thinking and actions. The extent to which youth commit to these various life goals influences their future development. Youth who explore a number of potential life alternatives (and values) before committing to a goal are better informed about their life choices than are individuals who do little to no exploration. Thus, when it comes to the question of "Who am I, and where I am going?" life exploration helps prepare adolescents for these decisions and the road of life that lies ahead of them. Also, a pledge to social values likely further fuels brain development in a prosocial direction. This might be evidenced by increased neural growth in certain brain regions that may eventually be reflected in physiological measurement studies that use electroencephalography and/or functional magnetic resonance imaging technology.

Although a signature for maturity (i.e., neural structure and function) is likely to incorporate a good portion of the brain, there are already some hints beyond simple myelination and pruning that suggest key circuitry that indicates greater maturity in adolescents. Some of these links include greater neural tracts from the amygdala to the frontal cortex. These neurons are thought to speed the process of down-regulating the system when negative affect (fear or anger) is cued by the amygdala and other regions of the brain. Research has shown that without this brain development the negative emotion produced by the amygdala can prevent the brain's planning centers from effectively doing their job, resulting in poor and impulsive judgment (i.e., low developmental maturity; Davidson, Putnam, & Larson, 2000; van Reekum et al., 2007).

Yet, there is much hope for the capacity for development of pro-social maturity in young people. Research during the past several decades has uncovered considerable knowledge regarding the child's developing personality, including the emergence of a sense of identity, affect modulation, thinking style, and relationship with the external world that has implications for the development of maturity in children and adolescents. With respect to the development of a sense of self, for example, Lewis (1993) found that recognition of oneself by name in a mirror occurs by 3 years of age; a sense of shame, implying self-consciousness, emerges before 2 years of age. Another example is empathy, a basic component of interpersonal functioning. Empathy develops in early childhood, with clear signs evidenced by 2 years of age (Hoffman, 1977). Much of the instillation and shaping of these abilities is steered, of course, by parents and other positive environmental forces. Young people might use self-reflection and evaluate their basic personality characteristics and begin to shape their lives in a social direction. As such, parenting, environment, and improving youth self-reflection are clear targets of intervention.

It is, of course, possible that young people will form their personalities in a less-than-prosocial direction. This also likely reflects a pattern of neural development (e.g., Aharoni et al., 2013; Cauffman, Steinberg, & Piquero, 2005; Decety, Chen, Harenski, & Kiehl, 2013; Glenn & Raine, 2014). Parenting can be a protective factor here. Most forensic clinicians are also aware that the environment affects parenting, and parenting affects child development (Pardini, Lochman, & Powell, 2007; Patterson, 1975; Salihovic, Kerr, Özdemir, & Pakalniskiene, 2012). Many societal difficulties contribute to problems in parenting and a lack of community warmth. For instance, even slight downturns in the economy and subsequent financial insecurity can be major obstacles for positive parenting in families with already low incomes (Bøe et al., 2014; Walper, Kruse, Noack, & Schwarz, 2004).

With respect to the environment, a number of factors, such as socio-economic status, nourishment, prenatal development, parenting, impoverished neighborhoods, and the like, may hamper the developmental maturity of a young person and may even shape brain development in ways that hinder effective decision making (Cecil et al., 2014). Impoverished environments may not facilitate neural growth where it is needed and thereby increase risk because the necessary architecture for broad thinking or regulated processing of emotional information is not in place. This can create patterns of narrow and inflexible thinking (Fredrickson, 2001) as well as potentially impulsive decision making that affect all three of the psycholegal constructs of risk, developmental maturity, and treatment amenability (Salekin, Tippey, & Allen, 2012).

Research conducted with mothers in the United Kingdom has shown that prenatal development is important for the advancement of conduct problems and even CU traits. This research highlighted that prenatal risks predict conduct problems and callousness more than a decade after the prenatal risks were measured (Barker, Oliver, Viding, Salekin, & Maughan, 2011). It also indicated that prenatal risks can lead to the development of a fearless, and bold, temperament at age 2 that subsequently results in harsh parenting, which in turn creates increased oppositionality in young individuals and a lack of commitment to prosocial values. Specifically, more than a decade after the prenatal risks were measured, young people with mothers who had greater prenatal risks demonstrated higher levels of interpersonal callousness and conduct problems. The description of these factors in a developmental frame can be helpful to the courts by linking the developmental risk factors to psycholegal concepts.

THREE KEY CONSTRUCTS FOR JUVENILE OFFENDERS

Niarhos and Routh (1992) highlighted some of the shortfalls of psychological testimony in juvenile courts. In part, they questioned whether psychological assessments of delinquent youth addressed the specific issues relevant to the court. Provorse and Sarata (1989), in their study of juvenile court judges, also noted that the courts expressed dissatisfaction with reports that were "couched in jargon," "ignored dispositional realities," and did not address the pertinent issues. Despite some progress, recent studies echo some of these same concerns regarding the clarity and transparency of psychological reports written for the courts (Hecker & Steinberg, 2002). Specifically, Hecker and Steinberg (2002) examined the quality of 172 predisposition psychological evaluation reports from a juvenile court in the Philadelphia area. They looked at the association between report quality and judges' acceptance of the mental health professionals' recommendations. According to Hecker and Steinberg, the reports were not addressing germane issues. The authors recommended that both practicing psychologists and judges become extra aware of the relevant domains of assessment for juvenile evaluations and of what constitutes quality reporting in each domain. Their findings suggest that greater precision regarding the assessment of psycholegal constructs should continue to be sought if reports and testimony are to address dispositional realities. It is quite likely that problems inherent in past reports stem from the improper integration of psychological theory into the legal concepts of risk, developmental maturity, and amenability to treatment.

The History Behind the Assessment of the Three Primary Constructs

Communication on the topic of disposition and transfer evaluations has increased over the past decade (Chu & Ogloff, 2012). Conference presentations at major psychology–law conferences like the American Psychology–Law Society now include significantly more submissions and resultant paper presentations, posters, and symposia on juvenile evaluations. Scholarly articles and chapters have also increased in number, resulting in marked advances in theoretical and scientific work on the topic of juvenile assessment and treatment. For instance, since the Melton, Petrila, Poythress, and Slobogin (1987, 1997) book provided chapters on the relevant topics of juvenile delinquency, juvenile disposition, and transfer evaluations, a proliferation of research has been evidenced on these topics. Melton et al.'s (1987, 1997) text has been helpful in that it provided specific information on how forensic psychologists might address the amenability-to-treatment question. Unfortunately, Melton and colleagues offered little information on risk and developmental maturity, which may be due in part to when that particular chapter was written, with only slight modifications made in the revised version.

In his book, Grisso (1998/2013) covered a variety of child and adolescent forensic evaluations, with two chapters centered on juvenile delinquency and rehabilitation evaluations. He identified a common set of psycholegal questions across different types of evaluations. Grisso's recommendations focused on having psychologists assess background characteristics of the youth and family (see also Hoge, Andrews, & Leschied, 1995, 1996). Borum and Verhaagen (2006) similarly provided information on the assessment of risk and protective factors that can be informative in the evaluation process. One issue with risk and protective factors is that, as mentioned in Chapter 3, the two sets of variables occasionally overlap, and mental health professionals will need to keep in mind that in some models the risk factor may run the chance of being counted twice against a young person. For instance, "poor school achievement" (a risk factor) is similar to "strong commitment to school" (a protective factor), and therefore these items are likely opposite sides of the same risk–protective factor coin. Thus, stating that a young person has a number of risk factors—let's say eight—and absolutely no protective factors sounds like the situation is much worse than it actually is because of the redundancy inherent in the model. Another example of this overlap is the long list of antisocial behaviors on the risk side and the protective variable of prosocial involvement on the protective side. One other issue is that risk- and protective-factor models may lack comprehensiveness for juvenile evaluations; that is, such models have no way of assessing developmental maturity, which seems like a major shortfall for juvenile assessment tools, where developmental maturity is key to the juvenile justice system philosophy (*Kent v. United States*, 1966; *Miller v. State of Alabama*, 2012). Moreover, amenability is not assessed in many of these conceptual models, or at least not directly assessed. Amenability and readiness are clearly key to the assessment of juvenile offenders and important in treatment outcome studies.

Clarifying Juvenile Constructs for Use in Forensic Practice

Over the past two decades, the constructs pertinent to disposition and transfer evaluation have been further clarified. As a consequence, the essential variables for forensic clinicians to examine have become increasingly salient. So pertinent are the concepts now that they are represented in many of the statutes for transfer and they are also represented in criminological and psychotherapy terminologies. For example, these constructs roughly reflect the risk–need–responsivity (RNR) model (Andrews, Bonta, & Hoge, 1990; Bonta & Andrews, 2007); that is, R (risk) in the RNR model maps onto the *Kent v. United States* (1966) criteria for risk or dangerousness, and NR (need and responsivity) of the RNR model maps onto the *Kent* concept of amenability to treatment. The second R (Responsivity), although most highly tied to amenability to treatment, also likely has indirect links to developmental maturity. Specifically, the more mature youth are, the more quickly they will respond to psychological therapy. Although I do not use the RNR terminology in this book, the philosophy behind the terminology has been helpful. This model has helped the field of criminology and correctional psychology to recognize individuals' needs more than their risk characteristics and to allocate greater resources toward young people who require higher dosages of intervention. This concept is not completely foreign to what is currently done in general clinical mental health practice. Specifically, clinicians identify the client's problem, determine the needs of the client, deliver the appropriate dosage of psychological therapy, see how the client responds to the intervention, and adjust therapy correspondingly to her or his progress. Within detention and correctional facilities, the model has served to shift attention back to the importance of correction. In the following sections, I discuss scholarly articles that have been useful in helping clinicians understand transfer evaluations.

Shedding Research Light on the Assessment
of Key Juvenile Constructs

Several articles on transfer can help clinicians better understand the focal juvenile constructs (Barnum, 1987). Ewing (1990) discussed ways in which psychologists could address dangerousness, sophistication–maturity, and amenability. Ewing noted that psychologists, because of their clinical training, might well be in the best position to address questions of developmental maturity. This viewpoint could very well be accurate given the material I just covered regarding the integration of psychological information (personality and stage models) into maturity assessments. Kruh and Brodsky (1997) also outlined ways in which youth might be assessed on the constructs of dangerousness, maturity, and amenability to treatment. At the time they wrote their article, Kruh and Brodsky believed that clinicians might be in a better position to address questions of developmental maturity, but they also provided suggestions for assessing dangerousness and amenability. Witt and Dyer (1997) discussed how clinicians could conduct scientifically grounded evaluations of juveniles when a waiver to adult court is being considered.

Grisso, Tomkins, and Casey (1988) refined the constructs of risk and amenability to treatment. Through a survey of court personnel the authors determined several key factors that were related to court decision making, such as self-reliance in maturity determinations. Building on their work, my colleagues and I provided additional empirical data on the core criteria that underpin the primary juvenile constructs of risk, developmental maturity, and amenability to treatment (e.g., Salekin, 2002a, 2002b; Salekin, Rogers, & Ustad, 2001; Salekin, Yff, Neumann, Leistico, & Zalot, 2002). I review this research below. Finally, Witt (2003) discussed how these constructs could be evaluated and interpreted. Fortunately, the scientific foundation for these juvenile constructs has begun to grow dramatically over the past decade.

Risk: Research-Based Assessment

Prototypical analyses provide information on the items that experts believe are most central, or core, to a concept. Thus, one aspect of risk assessment must involve examining the prototypes for dangerous behavior that have been derived from the ratings of juvenile court judges and clinical psychologists. Two prototypical analysis studies (Salekin, Rogers, & Ustad, 2001; Salekin, Yff, et al., 2002) revealed that the factors clinicians and juvenile court judges found to be pertinent included engagement in extreme unprovoked violence, severe antisocial personalities, lack of remorse/guilt and empathy, violent histories, and a leadership role in the crime. The tri-factor model identified in these prototypic and factor-analytic studies aligns with characteristics in the social science literature that suggest a higher likelihood, and stability, of future offending (e.g., Loeber & Stouthamer-Loeber, 1998; Moffitt, 2003). Moreover, the findings align with those of earlier prototypical studies, further validating the relevance and representativeness of the items (Grisso et al., 1988). In addition, the findings align with *DSM–5* terminology (CD, ODD, and LPE) and typology research (Loeber, 1991; Moffitt, 1993). This tri-factor model for dangerous behavior includes (a) planned and extensive criminality (which is similar to severe CD), (b) violent and aggressive tendencies, and (c) psychopathic-like (interpersonal callousness) features that likely entail a leadership role in crime. Because the research base for developmental pathways is well understood and the predictive validity for psychopathy is also fairly well established (Forth & Book, 2010; Leistico, Salekin, DeCoster, & Rogers, 2008), I focus on a couple of select topics related to risk assessment that require further consideration in the evaluation.

The first consideration has to do with the use of the term *psychopathy*. Although a good deal of research demonstrates that psychopathy (or "psychopathic characteristics") is a moderate predictor of violence and aggression in youth (Forth & Book, 2010; Forth & Burke, 1998; Frick & Scheffield Morris, 2004; Leistico et al., 2008; Lynam & Gudonis, 2005; Salekin, 2008), the term can certainly generate concern and remains controversial (Salekin & Lynam, 2010b; Seagrave & Grisso, 2002; although see Boccaccini, Murrie, Clark, & Cornell, 2008). Although one should always be careful about the terms he or she uses, the pertinent research suggests that personality characteristics such as those found in psychopathic-like individuals are an important consideration in predicting both general and violent recidivism in adult (Frick & Moffitt, 2010; Leistico et al., 2008; Salekin & Lynam, 2010a) and adolescent samples (Forth & Book, 2010; Gretton, McBride, Hare, O'Shaughnessy, & Kumka, 2001; Leistico et al., 2008; Salekin, 2008; Salekin, Rogers, & Machin, 2001; Salekin, Ziegler, Larrea, Anthony, & Bennett, 2003). Nonetheless, forensic clinicians should carefully consider the ways in which they use this term and should be specific regarding the correlates associated with the condition especially as they relate to, for example, intervention (e.g., Andershed, 2010; Fontaine, McCrory, Boivin, Moffitt, & Viding, 2011; Frick, Cornell, Barry, Bodin, & Dane, 2003; Kubak & Salekin, 2009; Lynam, Caspi, Moffitt, Loeber, & Stouthamer-Loeber, 2007; Salekin, Barker, Ang, & MacDougall, 2012; Salekin, Lester, & Sellers, 2012; Salekin, Tippey, & Allen, 2012; Salekin, Worley, & Grimes, 2010; see also Caldwell, Skeem, Salekin, & VanRybroek, 2006; Salekin, 2002a, 2002c, 2010; Salekin, Rogers, & Machin, 2001; Vitacco & Salekin, 2013; Vitacco, Salekin, & Rogers, 2010).

One other comment regarding the research on the prediction of dangerous behavior is required. Over the last two decades, antisocial pathways have been conceptualized in ways that may facilitate increasingly accurate appraisals of risk (e.g., DeLisi, Neppl, Lohman, Vaughn, & Shook, 2013; Loeber & Stouthamer-Loeber, 1998; Moffitt, 1993, 2003, 2007; Vaughn & DeLisi, 2008; Vaughn, Howard, & DeLisi, 2008). This research is most closely linked with the typology science I mentioned in Chapter 3. Developmental pathways may assist in the assessment of risk by distinguishing among different types of offenders. Recall that Moffitt (1993) proposed two distinct pathways to antisocial behavior: (a) adolescent-limited and (b) life-course-persistent delinquents (see Chapter 3). This model is particularly important because it addresses the issue of why many adolescents engage in antisocial behavior and then later desist. Presumably these youth live relatively normal lives afterward. Moffitt suggested that life-course-persistent offenders begin committing crimes early in childhood, continue well into adulthood, and manifest characteristics that seem categorically antisocial. In contrast, adolescent-limited offenders tend to commit their first offense in mid-adolescence and desist from illegal behavior as they enter adulthood.

This taxonomy has been widely accepted, as evidenced by its continued acceptance in the DSM–5. Despite general support for Moffitt's (1993) life-course-persistent model, research should continue to track success and failure rates for this and other typology models (e.g., Loeber, 1991). For example, although such taxonomies generally apply to youth with conduct problem, not all young people who are categorized as adolescent limited desist from criminal behavior. Also, we now know that not all early starters are antisocial throughout their life span. It is important to keep in mind that taxonomies account for patterns of behavior in young people (group-level analyses) but of course do not explain every young person's behavior. Providing the most recent data on these pathways and how youth fit into respective pathways is most helpful. Even more important is providing the percentage of youth who persist on a pathway, because this information will be incredibly helpful to the courts. Loeber (1990, 1991) generated such data with the Pittsburgh Longitudinal Study and has continued to provide these important pieces of data to his pathway model. In addition, Moffitt and Odgers and their colleagues have shed light on this issue with their model using longitudinal data from the Dunedin sample (see Odgers et al., 2009; Odgers, Caspi, et al., 2008; Odgers, Moffitt, et al., 2008).

Developmental Maturity: Research-Based Assessment

Two prototypical analyses studies have produced a clear tri-factor model for developmental maturity that include (a) autonomy, (b) cognitive control, and (c) emotion regulation skills (Salekin, Rogers, & Ustad, 2001; Salekin, Yff, et al., 2002). These factors have both content and construct validity

(M. Jordan, 2008; Leistico & Salekin, 2003; Salekin, 2004). This tri-factor model is also supported by other key research conducted on the concept of maturity of judgment (Greenberger, Campbell, Sorensen, & O'Connor, 1971; Greenberger, Josselson, Knerr, & Knerr, 1975; Greenberger & Sorensen, 1974; Greenberger, Steinberg, Vaux, & McAuliffe, 1980; L. Steinberg et al., 2008; L. Steinberg & Cauffman, 1996). Steinberg and colleagues have referred to the three concepts of (a) responsibility, (b) temperance, and (c) perspective (L. Steinberg et al., 2008). These facets can be mapped onto the tri-factor model of maturity, with autonomy in the model being similar to responsibility in the Steinberg model. Cognitive capacities in the tri-factor model would be similar to temperance in the Steinberg model. Finally, emotion regulation skills in the tri-factor model would be similar to the perspective component in the Steinberg model (see Table 4.2).

That these two models align so closely shows the great deal of convergence between the important constructs that underpin developmental maturity. Moreover, L. Steinberg et al.'s (2008) model originated from theory (top-down), whereas the tri-factor model originated from empirical research (bottom-up), giving the overall model even further credibility. Because the concepts offer greater clarity to clinicians and court personnel, they are likely to better inform juvenile disposition and transfer evaluations, thereby addressing some of the concerns raised by Niarhos and Routh (1992), Provorse and Sarata (1989), and Hecker and Steinberg (2002). Although both sets of terms would be useful for the courts, the terms *autonomy, cognitive*

TABLE 4.2
Developmental Maturity: Converging Bottom-Up and Top-Down Models

Tri-factor (empirical bottom-up development)	L. Steinberg et al. (2008; rational top-down development)
Autonomy	Responsibility
Healthy autonomy, internal locus of control, clear self-concept and use of self-reflection	Healthy autonomy, self-reliance, clarity of identity
Cognitive capacities	Perspective
Ability to weigh consequences of behavior, cost–benefit analysis, ability to anticipate consequences	Ability to recognize the complexity of the situation and to frame a specific decision within a larger context
Emotion regulation skills	Temperance
Able to delay gratification, moral development, self-regulation of emotion, conflict resolution skills, interpersonal skills	Ability to limit impulsivity; avoid extremes in decision making; and evaluate situations thoroughly before acting, including seeking advice of others when appropriate

capacities, and *emotion regulation* might be most easily recognized and understood across a range of professionals.

As mentioned earlier in this chapter, with respect to the physiology of maturity we now know that the myelination and pruning process has an impact on developmental maturity (Barbot & Hunter, 2012; Leuner & Gould, 2010b); that is, a considerable amount of research shows that youth continue to develop myelin sheaths for brain neurons and that there is an increase in the myelinated neurons in the brain from childhood until roughly age 26 (Giedd, 2004; Paus, 2005). Research also has shown that there is a pruning process whereby neurons are pruned back over the developmental years. This process also facilitates decision making and forethought (Giedd, 2004; Gogtay et al., 2004; Paus, 2005). In fact, the pruning process is thought to play a major role in the development, shaping, and sculpting of circuits (Gogtay et al., 2004). Although age and maturation are related, there is clearly variation in youth developmental maturity, and it is not the case that being an adolescent can be consistently equated with exercising poor judgment in real-world environments. This is because adolescents take many different life paths. Some adolescents regulate their emotions and make good decisions more frequently than not, whereas others make less sound, and sometimes impulsive and erratic decisions (Jahn et al., 2010).

Developmental maturity can also be impaired by many of the deficits that are often seen in juvenile offender populations, including family dysfunction, learning deficits, mental illness, substance use, and poverty (Barker, Oliver, Viding, Salekin, & Maughan, 2011; Barker & Salekin, 2012; Kazdin, 2000). This makes the inclusion of other relevant factors important in the consideration of developmental maturity and likely adds greater nuance to the discussion of biology and maturity. Of the many new neural connections that occur daily, development of maturity may well have to do with the types of connections that are made, specifically, the brain structures that are healthily developed.

New Hints on Developmental Maturity

The research and theory regarding developmental maturity suggest that when evaluating juvenile offenders, mental health professionals should consider issues such as moral reasoning and the development of conscience. Again, these are factors that could well be enhanced through the development of traits such as consideration, warmth, and kindness. The extent to which young people develop in a social versus an antisocial manner may have to do with the emotional valence of some of their neural connections that consequently affect their decision making (Damasio, 1994) or the manner in which they handle negative emotion (e.g., Davidson, Lewis, et al., 2002; Davidson, Putnam, & Larson, 2000; Hanson et al., 2010). Thus, in terms of understanding the young person's level of developmental maturity, it can be helpful to assess whether there is a mismatch between level of moral development and behavior.

One other comment about the research base of maturity is needed here. Maturity is a complex construct. On the one hand, research shows that higher levels of maturity can produce better treatment results. Youth with high-level cognitive skills, moral knowledge, emotion regulation, and clearer identity (including at least some aspect of prosocial identity) are likely to benefit from psychotherapy (Garfield, 1994; Salekin, Rogers, & Ustad, 2001; Salekin, Yff, et al., 2002). On the other hand, greater maturity might reflect more sophisticated criminal conduct that may be more challenging to treat. More research on this topic is needed; however, there exists a good incentive to try and shape developmental maturity. Assessment of amenability to treatment (e.g., motivation to change and responsibility) may help elucidate whether a young person high in maturity has the requisite motivation and openness to change. There is now some research to back this notion that motivation to change is a powerful attitudinal variable (Iselin, DeCoster, & Salekin, 2009; Kohlberg, 1981; Luthar, 1991; Miller & Rollnick, 2012; Salekin, Lee, Schrum-Dillard, & Kubak, 2010) and one that can help better understand the broader construct of amenability to treatment.

Amenability to Treatment: Research-Based Assessment

Clinical wisdom suggests that young people are more malleable than adults and are therefore more amenable to treatment, although this idea has not been extensively tested (Cauffman & Steinberg, 2000; Salekin, 2002c; Salekin & Grimes, 2008; L. Steinberg & Cauffman, 1999, 2000; Zimring, 1998). Nonetheless, there is quite a bit of indirect evidence to suggest that youth do have greater malleability. For instance, research on personality has shown a steplike increase in the stability of personality across age. This indicates that more change can be expected in young people than in adults (Roberts & DelVecchio, 2000). Also, in terms of plasticity, the brain is thought to be more malleable in younger years (Leuner & Gould, 2010b). Evidence for the plasticity of the brain and the development of specialty tracts is reflected in the research on musicians, who show stronger connections in certain brain regions (Chanda & Levitin, 2013; Herholz & Zatorre, 2012; Moreno & Bidelman, 2014; Wu, Zhang, Ding, Li, & Zhou, 2013). For instance, brain imaging studies have shown that an area in the somatosensory cortex that receives input from the fingers of the left hand is enlarged in string musicians, who constantly use the left hand to play the strings of their instruments (Elbert, Pantev, Weinbruch, Rockstroh, & Taub, 1995). Similarly, individuals given 3 months to learn to juggle showed structural changes in brain regions known to handle the processing of visual and motor tasks that are necessary to coordinate the act (Draganski et al., 2006, 2008; Pessiglione et al., 2007).

Aside from these important findings, we know from medical research that the earlier a disorder is detected, the better the prognosis. Thus, detecting conditions before they develop, or detecting them early, allows for the highest probability of survival. This notion has also been, in part, the basis for treating rather than punishing young people who come into contact with the juvenile justice system, in particular, those who have externalizing disorders such as ODD, CD, or other antisocial behavior problems. These ideals, of course, harken back to the early philanthropists of the late 19th century who held the ideals of protecting children when they make social errors early in life.

An important step in the amenability-to-treatment construct is to understand juvenile characteristics that are predictive of both positive and negative treatment outcomes. Earlier studies on this topic have suggested that factors such as cognition, self-evaluation, expectation, attention, engagement, values, and an understanding and appraisal of the world are important psychological variables in the treatment of juveniles (e.g., S. Adams, 1970; Carlson, Barr, & Young, 1994; Izzo & Ross, 1990). Amenable youth have also been described as being intelligent, verbal, anxious, insightful, aware of their difficulties, and motivated toward change (Salekin & Grimes, 2008; Salekin, Lee, Schrum-Dillard, & Kubak, 2010; Salekin, Worley, & Grimes, 2010).

Research has also been conducted on the treatment readiness construct, which has overlap with the concept of amenability (e.g., Ward, Day, Howells, & Birgden, 2004). Treatment readiness, like amenability, further reinforces the important factors related to concepts such as awareness of difficulties and openness to change. Prototypical analytic research has also shed light on this topic as well by delineating a tri-factor model for treatment amenability that aligns with research on the readiness for treatment concept (Salekin, Yff, et al., 2002). I discuss this model in greater detail below.

Clinical psychologists and juvenile court judges have provided core characteristics for the amenability to treatment (Salekin, Rogers, & Ustad, 2001; Salekin, Yff, et al., 2002). Important elements have included motivation to engage in treatment, awareness of difficulties, expectations that treatment would be beneficial, remorse/guilt, empathy, knowledge of right from wrong, anxiety about the circumstance, and a stable and supportive family environment. It turns out that these characteristics also yield three factors. This tri-factor model is underpinned by (a) psychopathology, (b) responsibility and motivation to change, and (c) consideration and tolerance of others.

A number of these characteristics have been studied in relation to treatment outcome and been found to be positive signs for treatment responsiveness (e.g., Carlson et al., 1994; Frank, 1959; Garfield, 1994; Salekin et al., 2001, 2002). Although not part of the tri-factor model, other prognostic variables that should be evaluated include family/support system considerations and protective factors that differ from risk factors, such as a prosocial role model or interests and hobbies.

For a small group of juveniles, treatment may be extremely difficult, and prognosis may be generally poor because of the type and severity of psychological disturbance (G. T. Harris & Rice, 2006). Having said this, I should also point out that it would be inappropriate to draw conclusions stating that severe antisocial personality or some other problem equates to such poor treatment prognosis that the disorder appears unalterable. Important in this regard is a meta-analysis on psychopathy and treatment that has shown that psychopathy, in particular in children and adolescents, may be more amenable to treatment than previously believed (Salekin, 2002c; Salekin, Worley, & Grimes, 2010; see also Caldwell et al., 2006). Research has shown that youth can benefit from treatment designed to reduce interpersonally callous traits (Hawes & Dadds, 2005; Salekin, Lester, & Sellers, 2012; Salekin, Tippey, & Allen, 2012). Consideration of whether and how deeply ingrained a young person is in a violent criminological lifestyle, coupled with consideration of whether the young person has stable psychopathic-like characteristics, may be more relevant in determining the degree of treatment needed to ameliorate the problem.

Because there are restrictions on the time to treat youth, the assessment of amenability hinges on how old a particular youth is and the time he or she has remaining in the system. Ewing (1990) suggested that two other factors to be considered are whether (a) the dispositions available to the juvenile court are likely to rehabilitate the juvenile before that court's jurisdiction ends and (b) the services available to the juvenile in the criminal justice system are appropriate to the young person's needs (Mulvey & Iselin, 2008). Also, as Ewing pointed out, some states have provisions for state-funded, out-of-state treatment of serious juvenile offenders, but only if the offender is assessed as being amenable to treatment and the agency or facility providing treatment is able to accept the young person pursuant to court order. Kruh and Brodsky (1997) and Mulvey and Iselin (2008) have suggested that child forensic clinicians should be less concerned with this issue than with whether treatment amenability is present. According to these authors, a finding of amenability places some pressure on the courts to provide adequate treatment to youth in the system.

Science has shown that adolescents are remarkably resilient and subject to positive change through both development (maturity) and treatment

(Weiten, 2013; Woolard, Fondacaro, & Slobogin, 2001). Research suggests that because of the potentially severe consequences associated with juvenile evaluations, resiliency factors must be given substantial weight (Salekin, Lee, Schrum-Dillard, & Kubak, 2010). Moreover, many of the treatment amenability factors are subject to change if the importance of change can be impressed upon the young person. Research indicates that some of this might be accomplished through motivational techniques and attempts to modify a young person's expectation of a positive outcome from the time of booking to the time of his or her release back into the community (Miller & Rollnick, 2012; Salekin, Lee, et al., 2010).

CONCLUDING COMMENTS

In this chapter, I have covered the science that supports the assessment of truthfulness/veracity, personality, risk, developmental maturity, and amenability to treatment. I suggested that deception, in general, should be viewed as a form of attempted adaptation. In addition, I delineated the connection among personality, stages of development, and the psycholegal constructs identified in Chapter 3. Personality was shown to be linked to risk, maturity, and treatment amenability. The same can be said for the use of stage models given that they also inform risk, developmental maturity, and amenability. The use of prototypical analyses to clarify constructs was also overviewed, showing clear tri-factor models. Selective research on brain development was reviewed and, as can be seen with individuals who learn to play string instruments (e.g., violin) or those who learn to juggle, the brain shows malleability and thus evidences changes in the pertinent regions that allow one to perform those tasks. This suggests that enhancing other skills like reading and writing, as well as effective self-talk and emotion regulation, will likely help with brain growth and general regulation skills. Such research suggests substantial hope for real change in youth involved in the juvenile justice system, who are often being asked to make substantial alterations in their lives. Much of this change, however, depends on accurate assessment, clear recommendations, and follow through on suggested interventions. The next chapter focuses on preparation for the evaluation.

5

PREPARATION FOR THE EVALUATION AND FORENSIC PRACTICE

The aim of this chapter is to help forensic clinicians prepare for the evaluation. Planning for the evaluation requires consideration of a number of ethical and targeted assessment issues. There are also considerations regarding the selection of appropriate psychological tools and the procedures for administering such tests. In this chapter, I discuss these practical issues, along with guidelines for best practice with child and adolescent offenders. However, with respect to the preparation, it is first necessary to briefly discuss the variability regarding the types of young people clinicians will see in the justice system as well as the specific training needs of practitioners who conduct juvenile evaluations.

Young people who come into contact with the law vary substantially, coming from different economic and social backgrounds and possessing different levels of knowledge about the legal system (Grisso, 1998/2013). All young people should be provided information regarding what the clinician

http://dx.doi.org/10.1037/14595-006
Forensic Evaluation and Treatment of Juveniles: Innovation and Best Practice, by R. T. Salekin

is planning to do during the evaluation and the significance of the evaluation. Forensic clinicians should be prepared to see each young person involved with the law as unique and not as a single type (e.g., a "delinquent"). Also, one may need to tailor one's approach—for example, basing the pace of questions on the young person's processing speed and comprehension and checking with them during the assessment process to see whether they have questions.

Mental health professionals differ in their level of training for child forensic work. Also, there is a considerable amount of continuing education that is requisite for optimal practice. Moreover, the literature with which forensic clinicians need to be conversant is growing exponentially, as is reflected by the increasing number of subdisciplines, specialized journals, associations, and societies. The broader field of psychology has grown since the American Psychological Association's (APA's) official journal, *American Psychologist*, was first published in 1946. At the time, *American Psychologist* was the only scientific outlet for psychological theory and research. Today, APA has a whole fleet of Tier 1 journals on a variety of psychological topics (e.g., *Journal of Abnormal Psychology*; *Psychological Review*; *Journal of Consulting and Clinical Psychology*; *Law and Human Behavior*; *Psychology, Public Policy, and Law*). In 1983 the Association for Psychological Science, which has its own panel of scientific journals (e.g., *Psychological Science*), was established. Other associations and private publishing companies also produce scientific journals. For instance, the Association for Child and Adolescent Mental Health is relevant to individuals who conduct forensic evaluations of juveniles and publishes a relevant affiliated journal titled the *Journal of Child Psychology and Psychiatry*. Similarly, the International Society for Research in Child and Adolescent Psychopathology produces a relevant journal titled the *Journal of Abnormal Child Psychology*. The Society for Research in Child Development has the affiliated journal *Child Development*. As one can see, the aforementioned associations and journals disseminate highly relevant ongoing research on many childhood disorders, including oppositional defiant disorder and conduct disorder, and callous–unemotional traits, that pertain to those conducting juvenile evaluations.

Currently, forensic clinicians are in a much better place in terms of the science available to inform their practice. However, with numerous affiliations and journal subscriptions, clinicians are also faced with many more nightly readings—stacks of journal articles—that require leaving the reading light on a little longer. This scientific growth in the field is healthy, but at the same time the volume of material can be overwhelming for new practicing clinicians working with young people involved with the law. To help narrow the field, in the following section I suggest major areas of psychology that are most relevant to forensic clinicians.

Forensic clinicians should be familiar with at least five dominant areas of research as they pertain to juvenile evaluation and treatment. These chief areas are (a) forensic psychology (Division 41 of APA, the American Psychology–Law Society); (b) life span developmental psychology (Division 7 of APA, Developmental Psychology); (c) clinical child and adolescent psychology and psychiatry (Division 53 of APA, the Society of Clinical Child and Adolescent Psychology, and the Association for Child and Adolescent Mental Health); (d) children, youth, and families (Division 37 of APA, the Society for Child and Family Policy and Practice, and the Society for Research in Child Development); and (e) correctional psychology (American Correctional Association). Currency with the research in these areas is the best strategy for maintaining sufficient knowledge. Fortunately, from what I have seen on the conference front, many individuals who work in child forensic psychology increasingly seek knowledge from the various disciplines to help inform their practice. This is an excellent and necessary step toward improving one's skills in order to offer the best practice in juvenile offender evaluations.

There are exciting opportunities for forensic clinicians to interact with legal professionals and to help shape, and ultimately improve, the juvenile justice system. This can be done through competent assessments and thoughtful intervention recommendations. Conducting such expert evaluations, however, requires a special set of skills. At present, training programs for mental health professionals in the United States are not geared toward the production of child forensic psychologists (or the training of allied mental health professionals who are also interested in forensic practice with children and adolescents). Present-day psychology programs have gaps in the training for individuals who are interested in child and adolescent forensic practice. This is because training typically occurs in one specific area, but what is actually needed is cross-training. For example, individuals may receive training in forensic psychology but not in clinical child psychology or developmental psychology. Alternatively, individuals may have training in clinical child psychology or developmental psychology, but not forensic psychology, and thus have little knowledge about the juvenile justice system, psycholegal constructs, and/or key legal cases (e.g., *Graham v. State of Florida*, 2010; *In re Gault*, 1967; *Kent v. United States*, 1966; *Miller v. State of Alabama*, 2012; *Roper v. Simmons*, 2005). As a consequence, under current training programs individual clinicians will have knowledge in some very important areas but not others (Grisso, 1998/2013). If one does not have the requisite knowledge in a particular area of psychology, he or she should address these gaps either through formal training at the graduate level or at the postgraduate level, through postdoctoral training, and/or continuing professional education.

The good news for individuals very early in the process who are contemplating a career in child forensic psychology is that the opportunities for practice in child and adolescent forensic psychology are increasing. The University of Alabama has the first-ever child and adolescent forensic emphasis, which combines aspects of the psychology law program and the child and adolescent clinical program to offer specialized training in this area. To obtain a degree with the child forensic emphasis, students attend a clinical child psychology seminar, a psychology law seminar, and a course in child and adolescent forensic assessment and treatment, and they complete a practicum in child and adolescent forensic psychology as well as other core requirements that are specific to their respective clinical programs (psychology law, clinical child). Drexel University also has opportunities for specialty training in forensic work with juveniles.

Training also is available in the Philadelphia juvenile court, which is modeled after the Miami, Florida, court system and thus allows for a strong connection between psychology topics and law topics as they pertain to the juvenile justice system. The University of Massachusetts offers an internship with a forensic focus for individuals seeking training within the juvenile and family court system (Fein, Appelbaum, Barnum, & Baxter, 1991). Brown University's Clinical Psychology Training also recently developed an internship specific to juvenile evaluation and treatment. The internship has primary rotations at a detention facility and a family court mental health clinic. These relatively new clinical internship programs recognize the importance of gaining supervised practical experiences with child and adolescent legal cases. Yale University has fewer formal opportunities for interns to learn about child forensic psychiatry and psychology but does offer fellowship opportunities for residents who are interested in training in child and adolescent forensic psychiatry.

Although training in clinical psychology requires 4 years of graduate school and a year of internship (as well as potential postdoctoral training), the training in child psychiatry is somewhat different. According to the American Academy of Psychiatry and the Law, training in forensic psychiatry entails education in medical school, a residency in psychiatry, and a forensic psychiatry fellowship. To be licensed, individuals must complete a designated number of years as mandated by the state in an American Medical Association- or American Orthopsychiatry Association-approved psychiatry program. The University of North Carolina at Chapel Hill School of Medicine has a forensic psychiatry residency that trains Fellows in criminal and civil settings involving both adults and children. Other opportunities are available at the New York University Langone Medical School, including a child and adolescent psychiatry program with a forensic component. A forensic psychiatry fellowship at Emory University has a number of ongoing research projects with juvenile offenders.

Whether clinicians have trained in psychology or psychiatry or some other mental health profession, the areas of developmental psychology and child and adolescent clinical psychology, as well as forensic psychology and psychiatry, pertain to all those who want to increase their precision as child forensic clinicians. Because knowledge in each of these areas is quite important to best practice for juvenile evaluations and treatment, a review of the extent to which the different training curricula cover key training areas is a necessary first step. Because of the current format of most programs, one will need to augment what has been learned with outside training and additional readings. Seeking consultations with experts will likely be the norm. Once adequately trained, one is ready to start preparing for the actual roles one might undertake.

EARLY STEPS IN PREPARING FOR THE EVALUATION

Clarifying the Referral Question

A good starting point for any evaluation is asking oneself, "What am I being asked to do?" and "Who is asking me to do this?" In typical child forensic evaluations the judge or an attorney makes contact with the forensic clinician. The focus and scope of the evaluation should be established during this initial conversation. Almost certainly, the three key constructs in juvenile evaluations of (a) the risk youth pose to the community, (b) their developmental maturity, and (c) their treatment amenability will arise. Although these variables are significant to the conceptualization of the case, they may not be the parameters set for all evaluations. In other words, the court may want information only on an adolescent's developmental maturity in some cases. Alternatively, the courts may want specific information on a young person's level of risk or treatment amenability. Conversely, the court may seek information only on whether a youth is competent to stand trial or whether a mental illness is present. These specifics can be used to guide the preparation phase of the evaluation. In the next few sections I provide an overview of the various expert roles forensic clinicians can take.

Mental Health Professionals' Expert Roles Within the Juvenile and Criminal Courts

Within the juvenile justice system, forensic mental health professionals may perform varying expert evaluator roles. Most often, they provide information that can inform the specific disposition of a young person. This role involves direct contact with a particular individual (Kalogerakis, 1992a, 1992b). At other times, however, a mental health professional may serve as a scientific expert without direct contact with the child. In this role, he or she educates the court about a particular topic but is not providing information or opinions with respect to a specific child or adolescent. This type of scientific testimony can be very influential and have significant ramifications for the young person. Thus, both types of testimony—forensic evaluations of individuals and providing testimony of a more general nature—are critical to the young individual and the court system. Fortunately, these two areas of practice typically overlap. Discussed next are the two major forensic clinician roles: (a) foundational science expert and (b) individualized forensic assessment.

Foundational Science Testimony

Top experts in the forensic field have stated that mental health professionals' roles involve scientific testimony on "the use of general conclusions from clinical and social science research in determining factual issues in a specific case" (Monahan & Walker, 1988, p. 470; see also Cunningham, 2010; and Otto, DeMier, & Boccaccini, 2014). For example, foundational science testimony could detail research findings regarding the developmental pathways for antisocial behavior. Here the expert might discuss major theoretical models and the science behind them. To elaborate on this example, after outlining the theory the expert would then provide the latest cumulative estimates regarding the total number of children and adolescents who meet the markers for a pathway and then provide information on how many of those young people actually pass all the way through the pathway as specified by the model. For example, an expert could use Moffitt's (1993, 2003) taxonomy to determine, cumulatively, how many life-course-persistent offenders with early onset, frequent, and severe antisocial behavior in childhood (before age 11) continue on to be persistent offenders later in adulthood. Similarly, the expert, in a written document or during testimony, could also discuss the number of offenders who follow the pattern articulated in the theoretical model for adolescent-limited antisocial behavior (a less severe pathway; see Chapter 3, this volume). With this group one could examine the percentage of youth who start their antisocial behavior in adolescence but then soon desist or provide information on the number of life-course-persistent offenders who desist but were expected to continue as well as provide information on the number of youth who start offending in adolescence and continue into adulthood, even though they were expected to desist.

Along this same line, an expert may provide information specific to a young girl's risk for continued delinquency. Specifically, he or she may provide information on how early physical development in girls, such as the early onset of menarche, can be a risk factor for delinquency. The expert may also explain the process and contextual factors for this risk factor and point to relevant scientific research on the issue (Caspi, Lynam, Moffitt, & Silva, 1993; Moffitt, Caspi, Belsky, & Silva, 1992). In short, forensic clinicians may offer information that science has shown that girls who demonstrate early physical maturity are at heightened risk for being chosen as girlfriends of older, delinquent boys who then have a negative influence on developing girls. The lifestyle of the older boys brings them into contact with the world of delinquency, including such behaviors as early underage drinking, smoking, and general misbehavior. Because early maturing girls, in all-girl schools, do not experience this rise in delinquency, there is evidence for the early menarche–older boy–delinquency connection (Caspi et al., 1993; Silverthorn & Frick, 1999). Of course, like all theoretical models, there are also error rates for this risk marker. Accuracy estimates (or hit rates) for this model show that not all early physically maturing girls evidence the aforementioned negative outcomes. However, early menarche does present as a risk factor, and as such might be referred to in foundational science research, including specific information on the model's accuracy. This type of expert information can be illuminating because the court is able to examine not just the explanatory taxonomy but also the statistical accuracy of the model. With this type of information, the court can use this evidence to make a more informed judgment.

Another area where scientific information may be requested pertains to developmental maturity. Questions on psychological maturity may extend beyond paper-and-pencil tests and interviews. Given the trend in the field to look to cognitive neuroscience, questions could extend to neuroscience findings. Testimony could include information on age-related brain differences and specifics regarding scientific studies on electroencephalography, functional magnetic resonance imaging, and/or diffusion tensor imaging research that may show age-related differences between adolescence and adulthood. One might testify on what is known about the myelination and pruning process and the implications this has for speed of neural transmission and other aspects of brain functioning. Forensic clinicians might delve further into neuroscience and describe what specific findings may mean in terms of decision making and, ultimately, developmental maturity.

Although this type of testimony can be very informative to the courts, one's foundational footing can get a little less solid on some of these cognitive neuroscience topics. This is because the requisite myelination and pruning needed for sufficient inhibition (to use the brain's brake system, to stop an impulse) is not clear (see Chapter 4, this volume). Moreover, the links between brain development and culpability have not yet been established (Aronson, 2010). Nonetheless, with adequate preparation clinicians likely can make some basic foundational comments regarding age-related differences in myelination and pruning as well as very general statements with respect to decision making. Testifying with certitude about brain development and culpability or about adolescents as a group being poor decision makers, for example, is likely going beyond the science (Aronson, 2010; Brodsky, 2013). Again, preparation and an understanding of the literature in this area will better inform forensic clinicians regarding the appropriate parameters of testimony. Other areas of foundational scientific preparation and testimony may center on the implications of particular factors such as attention-deficit/hyperactivity disorder, prenatal risks (e.g., poverty, substance use), and other variables that may affect a young individual's ability to learn from punishment and reward (Barker & Salekin, 2012).

Without expert guidance, juvenile court judges would be prone to a number of typical conceptual errors. For example, by failing to take into account error rates and detailed contextual factors that may limit an adolescent's risk, the court might overestimate an adolescent's poor (impulsive) decision making or his or her dangerousness when a young person fits criteria for a life-course-persistent pattern. Whether judges weigh such information heavily when making their decisions is not always known until the final judgment; however, forensic clinicians should do their best to convey the science related to the case.

A prominent forensic psychologist with whom I frequently consult told me of a case in which he had served as an expert witness providing only foundational science testimony. This expert was called on to provide information regarding whether a teenager, diagnosed with Asperger's disorder at the time, could reasonably be expected to fully understand that the content of communication with him over a police telephone line would be recorded and could be used against him in a court of law. The adolescent had provided considerable information about the case on the telephone. Even though this young person had been previously tested and shown to have a very high IQ (> 130), it was deemed that he would not have been able to grasp the significance of many of the communicated messages. Despite the provision of this foundational scientific testimony, the adolescent was transferred to adult court and later sentenced to significant prison time. Although the legal result was not what the expert had expected, the testimony that detailed the young person's Asperger's symptoms at the very least provided the courts with psychological information pertaining to his ability to understand his actions that could then have been considered in context with other relevant legal information.

Individualized Forensic Assessment

Assessing individual juveniles who have come into contact with the law requires mental health professionals to draw on what they have learned from science. This entails knowing about a variety of pertinent concepts and issues (see Chapter 3, this volume), knowing the research information supporting those concepts (see Chapter 4), and then applying that science to the evaluation to arrive at the best conclusions for the specific referral question. To get to this stage, one must be aware of a number of essential issues regarding preparation that are important in all forensic evaluations, including considerations such as due process, informed consent, and accuracy.

Legal and Ethical Guidelines: Due Process. Assessment of juvenile offenders and the information obtained from that assessment guides important
juvenile justice decisions, including pretrial detention, pre- and postcharge
diversion, referral to the mental health system, and disposition placements
and transfer. The importance of these decisions places a burden not only on
the system but also on forensic clinicians to ensure that relevant legal and
ethical guidelines are followed. Fortunately, as I discussed in Chapter 2, the
legal system, through the federal courts, has generated guidelines to ensure
that due process is followed in the handling of juvenile cases (e.g., *In re Gault*,
1967; *Kent v. United States*, 1966). In the 1960s, U.S. Supreme Court Justice
Abe Fortas provided guidelines for transfer and articulated the need for due
process. Some of these rights related to the *In re Gault* (1967) Supreme Court
decision included, of course, the ability to question an accusing witness, the
right to an attorney, and the right to avoid self-incrimination. The guidelines
delineated by the Supreme Court apply to the treatment of young people at
all phases of the juvenile justice process, from arrest through disposition. The
state juvenile justice systems generally provide statutory guidelines. Forensic mental health professionals who acquaint themselves with due process
and are sure that due process is abided by will be aiming for best practice in
this area.

For youth who are charged with delinquent acts, the juvenile justice system has a mandate to ensure that the legal process judges their responsibility
for the alleged delinquencies fairly and that the system does not abuse its discretion when deciding on penalties and rehabilitative measures when young
people are found delinquent (Grisso, 1998/2013). Forensic clinicians should
remain aware of the laws and regulations. Under certain circumstances,
this may mean that the information revealed in the assessment will not be
reported because it is not relevant to the forensic issue. The young person and
his or her family must be fully informed of any limits on confidentiality. Some
suggest that youth may require access to legal representation to ensure that all
ethical and due process rules are observed in the assessment. Although this
is an option, mental health experts hold mixed views of this because it can
hamper the process of obtaining assent and the flow of information during the
interview. Nonetheless, this is something that mental health professionals
may have to consider and accommodate.

Confidentiality and Honesty Forms. The young person and his or her
family also should be informed about the purpose and procedures of the assessment as well as all potential uses of the information collected. Best practice
entails the clinician's ensuring that the young person fully understands the
terms of the assessment and confidentiality, and it is important for systems to
have in place clear rules for the uses of the information collected in forensic
assessments (Grisso & Vincent, 2005a). In planning the evaluation, it might

be useful to generate a statement that can be read and signed by the child or adolescent and possibly by a parent. These forms should be administered before the forensic clinician engages the youth in any form of the assessment. Figure 5.1 is a notification and assent statement that can be used and that may serve as a template, or, example, for other honesty forms.

Confidentiality and Honesty Form for Parents and Third Parties. When parents accompany the young person to the assessment, forensic clinicians will also want to explain to them the limits of confidentiality and the importance of honesty. When reviewing the confidentiality and honesty form with youth, forensic clinicians should also advise parents and third parties of their

---

I'm Dr. Salekin. I am a clinical psychologist who works with children and adolescents. Sometimes, I work with children and adolescents who have come into contact with the law. I have been asked by the juvenile court judge (or, by your attorney/or prosecuting attorney) to provide him/her with an assessment of you that is specific to your case. My job here is to provide the court with a report and potential testimony regarding your psychological functioning and information that may pertain to your potential rehabilitation or placement. The information that I obtain from you and other people I will be talking with is not private (confidential), and I will use this information to write a report. This report will then be given to your attorney and the judge in juvenile court. Anything that I have learned from talking with you or anyone else may go into the report. Also, even if information we discuss is not in the report, I may be asked about this material, and I will likely have to offer this information to the courts. You may decide not to answer any or all of my questions. However, I would have to talk about this refusal in my communication to the judge either through my report and/or testimony. The judge would then have to decide how to move forward with your case. Do you have any questions about this? Are you willing to further talk with me and complete some assessment measures? [If answer is yes] Honesty is important in these evaluations. In order for me to conduct a thorough evaluation that is of high quality and accurate, it is important for you to respond to questions in a complete and honest manner. Although you may not be aware of this, dishonesty can show up in a variety of ways and it can negatively impact the evaluation. Because of this, you are encouraged to answer honestly. If you have any questions about the issues of confidentiality or honesty, please ask me at any time. If you have any legal questions about your participation, such as your rights, or you want to know more about the legal ramifications of participating, you would need to direct those questions to your attorney. Do you have any questions for me at this point? Your signature below indicates that you have read, or had this information read to you, and that you understand the information presented.

Name (print): _____

Signature: _____

Date: _____

Signature of Examiner:

_____

Figure 5.1. Sample Notification and Assent Statement.

professional identity (e.g., psychologist, psychiatrist), provide information on who assigned them the case (i.e., judge) or retained their services (i.e., attorney), as well as the purpose of the evaluation and how the findings could affect the pending juvenile disposition decision or transfer and the limits of confidentiality. This must be stated clearly enough to be understandable to the family, because many families have only limited knowledge of the juvenile justice system. For a family member of the young person, the honesty statement could take the form given in Figure 5.2.

I'm Dr. Salekin. I am a clinical psychologist who works with children and adolescents and sometimes with young people who have come into contact with the law. I have been appointed by the juvenile court judge (or your attorney/opposing attorney) to evaluate your son/daughter. To conduct such an evaluation I will also need to spend some time asking you questions and have you fill out questionnaires. I will also be asking your son/daughter questions and having them fill out questionnaires. My role here is to provide the court with a report of your son's/daughter's psychological functioning and to provide information that pertains to his/her placement in a rehabilitative setting as well. I will also have to provide some information on the degree of restriction that might be needed. The information I obtain from you, and other people that I will be speaking with, will be used to write a report to present to the judge. Once I provide this report to the judge, I may be questioned about the report as well as additional factors related to the report. Anything that I have learned from speaking with you and your son/daughter or anyone else, I can be asked to provide information about. And I will likely have to convey what I learn to the court. You may decline to answer any or all of my questions. If you decline to speak with me, I will need to relay this refusal verbally, in my written report, or testimony to the judge. The judge would then have to decide how to proceed with your son's/daughter's case without this information. Do you have any questions about this? Are you willing to further speak with me and complete some assessment measures? [If answer is yes] Honesty is important in these evaluations. In order for me to conduct a thorough evaluation that is of high quality, it is important for you to respond to questions in a thorough and honest manner. Although you may not be aware of this, dishonesty can show up in a variety of ways and it can negatively impact the evaluation. Because of this, you are encouraged to answer honestly. If you have any questions regarding the issues of confidentiality or honesty, please ask me at any time. If you have any legal questions about your participation such as your rights or you want to know more about the legal ramifications of participating, you would need to direct those questions to your son's/daughter's attorney. Do you have any questions for me at this time? Your signature below indicates that you have read, or had this information read to you, and that you understand the information.

Name (print): _____

Signature: _____

Date: _____

Signature of Examiner:

_____

Figure 5.2. Sample Confidentiality/Honesty Form.

Whereas young people are court-ordered to participate in the evaluations, it is important to keep in mind that the parents may not be. Thus, parents may decline to participate in the evaluation. When informing the young individual and the adults to be interviewed, clinicians should be careful that their role as a professional does not override the young person's and the parents' decision making. Specifically, being a professional from the mental health field (the "helping" field) combined with the hierarchical roles (the degree and title you worked so diligently to obtain; e.g., PhD/doctor) requires that one be careful that the adolescent and/or parents do not feel as though they have little choice regarding participation. Also, when introducing and administering the evaluation, it is helpful to keep the young person and the parents cognizant of its purpose. This can be done by repeating parts of the notification at different time points during the evaluation.

STANDARDS FOR JUVENILE EVALUATIONS

Although there are few legal guidelines for the conduct of juvenile assessments, standards and procedures for best practice in psychology exist and can be located by examining the relevant professional guidelines. Specifically, mental health professionals should look to broader professional organizations, such as APA, and to one's own specific organizations for help in preparing themselves for best practice assessments of juvenile offenders. APA and other relevant associations have specific guidelines delineating proper practice for general assessment and, even more specifically, for forensic practice.

The guidelines from various mental health professions tend to be relatively consistent in what are seen as important ethical principles. Thus, there are typically two levels of regulation that apply to the psychological and psychiatric professions. The first is through nonregulatory voluntary bodies. The most important of these are the national groups such as the American, British, and Canadian psychological and psychiatric associations (Cunningham, 2010). The major sources of assessment guidelines delineated by APA and more specialized organizations within the United States are listed in Table 5.1. Smaller groups include the various state associations and specialized groups such as the American Academy of Forensic Psychology, the American Academy of Psychiatry and the Law, and the National Association of School Psychologists. All have adopted codes of conduct, including standards regarding assessment. Members are expected to follow the ethical standards.

The second level of regulation occurs through governing bodies of professional mental health providers. Membership in these regulatory bodies is required of all psychologists and psychiatrists who conduct clinical activities. These are created by acts of the state legislatures and serve to regulate mental

TABLE 5.1

Guidelines and Standards for Mental Health Professionals

Guidelines and standards for mental health professionals	Source
Ethical Principles of Psychologists and Code of Conduct	American Psychological Association (2002)
Specialty Guidelines for Forensic Psychology	American Psychological Association (2013b)
Ethics Guidelines for the Practice of Forensic Psychiatry	American Academy of Psychiatry and the Law (2005)
Standards for Accrediting Forensic Psychologists	American Psychological Association (2007a)
Standards for Educational and Psychological Testing	American Educational Research Association, American Psychological Association, & National Council on Measurement in Education (2014)
Guidelines for Computer-Based Tests and Interpretations	American Psychological Association (1986)
Record Keeping Guidelines	American Psychological Association (2007b)

health professionals in their respective jurisdictions. Psychologists and other mental health professionals who conduct evaluations of young people in the legal system should be licensed psychologists or psychiatrists.

For best practice, one should also examine guidelines produced by groups that focus specifically on forensic assessment. For instance, the Committee on Ethical Guidelines for Forensic Psychologists' (1991) "Specialty Guidelines for Forensic Psychologists" has been updated by the American Psychological Association (APA, 2013b) as "Specialty Guidelines for Forensic Psychology." In addition, the American Academy of Psychiatry and the Law (2005) has a set of standards articulated in the "Ethical Guidelines for the Practice of Forensic Psychiatry." These guidelines apply to the practice of psychiatrists and their assessments in judicial settings and thus can further optimal practice. Mental health professionals can look to other sources of information regarding ethics and sources specific to forensic assessment (e.g., Bersoff, 1995, 2008; Eyde et al., 1993; Grisso, 1998/2013, 2003a, 2003b; Grisso & Schwartz, 2000; Grisso & Vincent, 2005a, 2005b; Melton, Petrila, Poythress, & Slobogin, 1987, 1997; Otto et al., 2014).

Other issues also are pertinent to the assessment of juvenile offenders. For instance, guidelines relating to the conducting of assessments with youth from culturally diverse backgrounds are increasingly relevant. APA's (1990) "Guidelines for Providers of Psychological Services to Ethnic, Linguistic, and Culturally Diverse Populations" may be helpful given the changes in the demographics of the population in the United States and many other countries. The *Diagnostic and Statistical Manual of Mental Disorders* (5th ed.,

DSM–5; American Psychiatric Association, 2013) provides guidelines for forming diagnoses of children from racial and ethnic minority groups. These guidelines relate to risk and prognostic factors and gender-related diagnostic issues. The DSM–5 no longer has a specific section for childhood disorders but instead views all disorders longitudinally. The *International Classification of Diseases* (World Health Organization, 2012) is also likely to follow this developmental and dimensional approach. In its opening pages, the DSM–5 also has a cautionary statement for forensic use of its guidelines that forensic clinicians should read and be familiar with (Kok et al., 2013).

A key issue with many of these guidelines is the fairness of testing and the choice of appropriate assessment techniques, procedures, and tests to describe young individuals. Unfortunately, on occasion clinicians are less concerned with a test's psychometric properties than its ease of administration. The problem with this approach is that some measures do not have adequate validity. Moreover, simply because tests are commercially available, forensic clinicians may assume that they are well vetted, but occasionally they are not, and often tests promise more than they can deliver. A central tenet of best practice is to be knowledgeable about the psychometric properties of the tests one chooses for the evaluation and to understand what specific psychological information the test provides.

The standards of educational and psychological testing (American Educational Research Association, APA, & National Council on Measurement in Education, 1999) constitute additional important sources of information. The standards provide thorough guidelines with respect to the construction, application, and interpretation of all formal psychological assessments and present information on the reliability and validity of the measures used. Key terms and definitions these constructs are provided in Exhibit 5.1, with comments concerning the evaluation of juveniles. Although some of the terms in the exhibit will be familiar to many readers, they are worth briefly reviewing here. *Change sensitive validity*, although a somewhat new form of validity, is especially important to consider in treatment outcome evaluations.

Understanding the psychometric properties of tests is a key factor in improving one's ability to prepare for the evaluation. Serious errors can occur when using scales that do not have appropriate psychometrics (e.g., content validity). Many clinicians are aware of these potential hazards, but because some psychological test manuals present measures as quite sound, and they look very technical—with a dizzying array of correlations, beta weights, scree plots, and confirmatory factor analytic parameters and fit indices—one can be lured into believing that they are sufficiently sound for all purposes and hence miss subtleties or even glaring flaws and omissions regarding the tests' potential limitations.

The content of the test is critical, yet the content of certain scales may not actually pertain, or pertain well, to the construct purportedly being

EXHIBIT 5.1
Psychometric Terms and Brief Definitions

Reliability	The homogeneity of a scale, agreement between raters, and temporal stability are all forms of reliability. In essence, reliability is the level of agreement (across items, raters, or time). High reliability is generally considered important because one wants agreement when it comes to testing. There is one exception: High temporal stability can be important if one is trying to establish the stability of a construct (e.g., IQ), but it is less important if one wants to measure change.
Content validity	The extent to which the content of the test is relevant to and representative of the construct being assessed. This is an important issue with respect to juvenile evaluations because many tests and scales claim to tap a specific construct, yet the underlying items that constitute the scale may appear to misrepresent or underrepresent the concept.
Construct validity	The theoretical meaning of the construct and the extent to which the instrument taps the intended construct. Cronbach and Meehl (1955) used the term *nomological net* to refer to a construct that has a number of associations that capture, or are related to, a construct. This type of validity provides the meaning to the construct (e.g., what it means to have generalized anxiety disorder or depression, or even a common cold).
Criterion-related validity	Concurrent and predictive validity represent two types of criterion-related validity. *Concurrent validity* is the extent to which a measure of a construct correlates with a different measure of the same construct. *Predictive validity* is the extent to which the measure (construct) is predictive of a certain outcome (offending). One can also measure *incremental predictive validity:* the extent to which a construct predicts above and beyond other constructs.
Change-sensitive validity	The extent to which measures or assessment strategies are capable of tapping change. For instance, measures with only static items are likely to reflect the same level of risk for youth each time the youth is assessed and thus are not change sensitive. Change-sensitive tests should be used if one is attempting to examine improvement after an intervention (e.g., reduction in level of risk).

indexed. This point was recently brought to the forefront in a series of articles published in *American Psychologist* regarding "arbitrary metrics." According to these articles, some tests may not tap the targeted construct. Kazdin (2006), in jest, used the example of a measure that tested for the concept "hard-driving janitor." His argument was that one could have a test labeled *Hard-Driving Janitor*, but unless the measure actually captures the characteristics of the prototypical hard-driving janitor, the measure could be misleading. This is because those being assessed by the measure may be inappropriately classified (or not classified) as a hard-driving janitor. Though humorous, this example also serves as an excellent illustration of potential areas of concern for some of the field's psychological tools. If a test does not tap what it states it does, or does not tap the concept well, it brings up this important issue of arbitrary metrics.

Two quick examples may make this point even more salient to the assessment of adolescent offenders. First, when using an adolescent multiscale inventory such as the Minnesota Multiphasic Personality Inventory—Adolescent (MMPI–A; Butcher et al., 1992), mental health professionals may use a high scale score to describe a young individual, but the label for the scale may not represent the item content. This is a classic example of arbitrary metrics. With respect to the MMPI–A, this is perhaps most notable when a young person scores high on the MMPI–A Psychopathic Deviate scale, which was originally designed to tap psychopathic personality. Because the content underlying the scale does not reflect modern conceptualizations of psychopathy, the name of the scale does not accurately represent what is actually being assessed via the scale items. Clinicians should review the content of the scale to know specifically what the individual endorsed in order to accurately describe the child or adolescent's character. If the young person is having family problems or family discord, this alone could cause a spike on the psychopathic deviate scale. A second example is the Millon Adolescent Clinical Inventory (Millon, 1993), which includes scales labeled *Forceful* and *Sadistic*, names that could be misleading if elevations occurred. These terms could be less than precise regarding a young person's character but, because of subscale labeling, be the sole terms used to describe the individual.

It is important to plan to provide a description of what your findings actually signify. It is necessary to ensure that the instruments and procedures used in the evaluation have demonstrated reliability and validity for the individual assessed and for the purposes for which the test was designed. Furthermore, if scores are being interpreted with reference to normative samples, the samples on which the test was validated should be examined to determine whether they are relevant for the individual being assessed. Moreover, when clinicians attempt to examine change, they should use change-sensitive measures. If clinicians conducting progress outcome evaluations use scales that are not sensitive to progress in psychological therapy, they could mistakenly conclude that a young person has been unable to make significant gains in treatment. Using a static risk measure based on past behaviors to rate change after some intervention is inappropriate because it will produce the same risk score each time it is administered. M. Jordan (2008), as well as Salekin, Tippey, and Allen (2012), demonstrated that the scales of the Risk–Sophistication–Treatment Inventory (RST-I; Salekin, 2004) are change sensitive. These studies showed that scores on the RST-I rating scale that were expected to either drop (i.e., risk) or rise (i.e., amenability) after an intervention actually did so, demonstrating that the measure is capable of indexing expected changes. The Antisocial Process Screening Device (Frick & Hare, 2001) and the Hare Psychopathy Checklist: Youth Version (Forth, Kosson, & Hare, 2003) have also been found to be change sensitive (Caldwell et al., 2006; Salekin, Tippey, & Allen, 2012). It is clear that forensic clinicians preparing for the evaluation should select their measures carefully and plan to use change-sensitive measures. Before returning to assessment specifics a few words on examining one's expertise are necessary.

EXAMINING ONE'S EXPERTISE AND DISCLOSURES

Clinicians who conduct forensic evaluations not only need the proper length and type of training and education, but they should also periodically review their training needs. It is imperative that they restrict their areas of practice to ones in which they are qualified and that they stay current in regard to pertinent legal statutes and the relevant scientific literature. It also is important to take steps to ensure one's ability to remain objective when carrying out forensic evaluations and to plan for the anticipated time commitment a potential case will entail.

Expertise

In the first few sections of this chapter, I discussed the training needs of forensic clinicians. Once trained, it is important to periodically examine one's own level of competence and expertise and provide relevant information to clients. Developing children who come into contact with the law require a high level of dedication to scientific rigor and a significant degree of professional expertise. This dedication can be shown by determining what capabilities one has for forensic juvenile evaluations and intervention and limiting one's practice to areas that one is qualified to undertake. For example, if a forensic clinician has never participated in a transfer evaluation, he or she may first wish to seek consultation, and even regular supervision, from an expert who has experience in this area. Specifically, one may want to be mentored by an experienced senior colleague on several cases before independently conducting evaluations. Finally, if a specialty assessment (e.g., involving neurology, brain functioning) is required, this aspect of the assessment should be performed by a qualified expert. This individual could then become part of a team of experts who address issues pertinent to the particular juvenile evaluation (Cunningham, 2010; Turner, DeMers, Fox, & Reed, 2001).

Board certification or other indicators can be used to determine a clinician's expertise in certain areas. Expertise regarding the psycholegal issues in juvenile evaluations can be enhanced by continuing education, seeking consultation, and ongoing self-examination. One might ask oneself, "How well prepared am I for such an evaluation?" Workshops on juvenile evaluations sponsored by the American Academy of Forensic Psychology are valuable, and I recommend them. Experts may also benefit by attending juvenile justice conferences, such as those sponsored by the Office of Juvenile Justice and Delinquency Prevention, the National Association of Juvenile Court Judges, and the American Psychology–Law Society, as well as regional organizations.

Portability of One's Expertise to Other States

Forensic clinicians who work with children and adolescents may be contacted by attorneys from other states, or even other countries, to provide their expertise. Hence, mental health professionals may need to obtain licensure in a specific state or province in order to conduct the evaluation. Fortunately, there is an ongoing effort to standardize this process as well as to allow for the portability of one's license and thus one's skills to work in other states. If one is not licensed in a particular state, then, as Cunningham (2010) noted, it will be necessary to contact that state's licensing board and learn what needs to be done to practice there. Clinicians should keep all documentation of their efforts to accomplish the evaluation. For instance, it can be helpful to retain e-mails and other communications as one works through the requirements to practice in the particular state or province.

Ensuring Objectivity

Forensic mental health professionals evaluating juveniles facing legal action are, just like any other professional group, subject to attitudes, prejudices, and biases that could hamper their judgment. (Some of this information was covered in Chapter 2 in my discussion of the political climate surrounding the juvenile justice system.) If one's attitudes are inconsistent with the objectivity required of a juvenile forensic expert, then practice in this area would be unethical (Nagy, 2011).

Consider, for example, a mental health professional working within the juvenile justice system who holds a strong view for either the crime control model (which focuses on reducing crime through punitive measures, e.g., imprisonment) or the rehabilitative model (which focuses on treating an individual with limited or no restrictions). Strong views for either side may affect the fidelity of evaluations. For instance, if a mental health professional who supports the crime control model has a "sniping" attitude toward young people who have engaged in criminal behavior, this may affect the evaluation and recommendations, including the use of pejorative language. To elaborate on this point, mental health professionals may hold an attitude that juvenile delinquents are mostly untreatable because delinquency is inherited. However, these views would not be supported by the latest science regarding gene–environment interactions (Farrington, Ullrich, & Salekin, 2010). In the planning phase of an evaluation, a clinician's clinical training ideally will result in the consideration of potential bias before he or she accepts juvenile cases from the juvenile court judge, defense, or the state. As experts, forensic clinicians will benefit if they consider their own personal reactions, and the implications of those reactions, in advance of any specific case inquiry. Similarly, asking attorneys about their strategy in certain cases can be helpful in determining whether a particular case is a type one wants to accept. For instance, if an attorney's entire focus is on presenting functional magnetic resonance imaging research to paint a picture that adolescents' brains are highly impulsive and substantially limited regarding decision making, and that thus adolescents are not responsible for any of their behavior, some clinicians may want to consider turning down the case. Testimony that is influenced by a clinician's personal views will lack comprehensive theoretical and scientific grounding.

Time Commitment to the Evaluation

Preparing for any psychological evaluation involves substantial time, and—surprisingly, given what's at stake—the pay in this area is not always commensurate with the time devoted to the evaluation. Some mental health professionals have expressed dissatisfaction with the rate of payment in relation to number of hours required to complete the evaluation. Limited payment for juvenile evaluations, however, cannot serve as a reason for limited effort: Time-limited evaluations based on calculations of one's hourly rate could result in the clinician missing critical information. For example, if an evaluator quickly assesses a young person and his or her family and determines that the adolescent has conduct disorder, but she does not take the time to comprehensively evaluate the young person and misses symptoms of major depressive disorder accompanied with suicidal ideation, the youth may miss out on a needed hospitalization. Later, if the youth survives this incompetent practice, the judge is still left thinking that the adolescent has only conduct disorder, and not depression. This leaves the judge misinformed, and his or her decisions will rest on the inaccurate assumption that "this must be all there is," thus putting the youth at further risk. The point is that if a report is only skeletal in what it brings to the judge's attention, it is not helpful—and may even be harmful.

Second, juvenile evaluations can vary in their time demands depending on what is being requested. The broader the parameters, the more time will be required to competently perform the evaluation. Providing foundational scientific expertise may take less time than evaluations of youth that require extensive interviewing of the adolescent, his or her family, and other third party sources. In addition, the extent to which the expert already has familiarity with the relevant scientific literature can greatly reduce the time the evaluation will take. However, if extensive preparation, such as literature searches and reviews, is needed, this too can increase the length of time required to complete the task. Timeline increases can also be expected if consultations with other specialists are needed or if the forensic clinician needs to coordinate with other evaluators (e.g., neurologist, neuropsychologist). The cost of hiring an expert to conduct work in this area will obviously be greater than that which one would expect for a scientific witness alone who testifies solely on the science (e.g., an expert who testifies about adolescent-limited and life-course-persistent offending). In addition, one's time availability should be discussed prior to accepting various roles as an expert, and time should be allotted to write the report. Forensic evaluations can take up to 30 hours, depending on the complexity of the case.

PLANNING FOR THE EVALUATION

Because some of the information regarding what tests to use in the evaluation is also covered in Chapter 6, in this section I touch on several key evaluation issues. The most complete individualized assessment includes a review of records, interviews of third parties, and a direct interview and assessment of the young person. Thus, clinicians should plan to use each one of these assessment methodologies. In the sections that follow I review several issues that pertain to planning, including efficiency, use of structure, frame of reference, multi-time-point evaluations, and test and scale names. I begin with the topic of how forensic clinicians should plan to be efficient, which helps with the timeliness of report delivery.

Plan to be Efficient

A clinician is more likely to obtain a better understanding of a child's life and current circumstances when he or she has spent an extended time with the boy or girl. One should not necessarily be impressed when a fellow clinician speaks of how quickly he or she can complete juvenile evaluations. On the other hand, psychological evaluations do not need to be back-to-back marathon experiences, either. Plan to be thoughtful and efficient in gathering information for the evaluation. This can be accomplished by immediately requesting records (e.g., medical, psychological, legal); setting up all collateral source interviews for a single day, with back-to-back 1-hour interviews where possible; completing the bulk of interviewing with the young person over a 2- or 3-day period; and scheduling and protecting time for the actual writing of the report. Direct contact is, of course, essential. Using psychology technicians to do all the interviewing and testing, without the clinician him- or herself ever seeing the youngster, would be inappropriate.

To Be Structured Versus Nonstructured

There are different approaches to the conduct of forensic assessments, and one question that may arise is, "How much structure should the assessment involve?" Unstructured clinical assessments involve using minimally structured methods to collect information (or at least a less transparent structure) and a dependence on judgments made by the assessor. More or less structure may be represented in the information-collection process given that professionals vary in their preference for the use of such organization. One extreme preference is represented by (a) a completely idiosyncratic unstructured approach or one that is completely guided by the youth, and the other preference includes (b) the use of highly structured interviews, and possibly checklists, to guide information collection, ratings, and clinical judgment. What level of structure should be used in juvenile evaluations? Probably both, with traditional interviews that allow young people to talk with some freedom and less interruption regarding their perspective on family, life, and their current predicament, followed up and supplemented with structured methods (e.g., structured clinical interviews, structured psycholegal rating scales, psychological testing).

It is not uncommon to encounter clinicians who argue that structured procedures are not required. This may be true, especially if a given forensic clinician has superb clinical skills and can crunch numbers on the fly, but these types of abilities are rare. Out there somewhere, I am sure, is a forensic clinician who has a personalized "structured interview" memorized and at the ready for clinical use and who can instantly tabulate the responses to specific questions, thereby keeping track of which disorders are elevated and which symptoms show the greatest severity. In this regard, the interview and ratings are, in a real sense, structured and likely not such a risk to use (Litwack, 2002). However, although many experts would agree this in theory can be accomplished, clinicians relying on memory alone as a methodology can leave too much room for error, especially when attempting to make a detailed clinical diagnosis. Moreover, when clinicians are involved in court procedures, the use of structured interviews allows them to bring in data on reliability and validity that can be helpful to the case. The point here is that clinicians, for a variety of reasons, might benefit from standardized testing procedures that document the answers to a set of prespecified questions in a booklet and allow them to make ratings on an accompanying scoring sheet with a specific metric (e.g., 0 = *no, not present;* 1 = *subclinically present symptom;* 2 = *clinical symptom present*).

Frame of Reference: Be Prepared to Interpret

Developmental histories help build the background information necessary to provide a young person's life history, but when gathering this information clinicians should be prepared for answers that require a second look. For instance, in some cases the information added by the child on issues such as the impact of each risk factor can add only minimally to the understanding of his or her developmental history. Superb self-awareness and insight on the part of some adolescents from the broader world perspective may be too high of an expectation in some cases. A young person may not view certain family and other environmental shortcomings as adverse. For instance, poor parental monitoring, harsh and inconsistent parenting, corporal punishment, and economic deprivation may be considered "normal" by some youth, and they may even view some of these detrimental parenting practices as effective. Kids often believe that the parenting they receive is beneficial and they may also view their neighborhoods as enriched when they are deprived. However, in terms of risk factors, neither of these beliefs would be accurate. Thus, whether children and/or parents view a specific practice (e.g., harsh parenting) as a risk factor is not always relevant to whether the practice is in fact a risk factor that should be identified in reports.

Multi-Time-Point Evaluations

Although personality testing is key to describing the contours of a young person's character, such testing alone runs the risk of minimizing the young person's history, capturing his or her "personality" in one still time frame. Moreover, when it comes to transfer evaluations, which can occur some time from when the offense actually occurred, forensic clinicians should be prepared to consider asking questions about the youth at the time of the alleged offense (perhaps months earlier) as well as at the present time. Interestingly, developmental maturity scores constructed for near the time of the offense might be more beneficial to the youth, whereas current risk and amenability scores might be more beneficial from the current time (rather than near the time of offense). Fortunately, decisions regarding what to do with this information is left to the judge, but forensic clinicians should be prepared to conduct multi-time-point evaluations for this and other purposes, such as in progress–outcome evaluations and blended-sentence evaluations.

Test and Scale Names

Test and scale names and labels may also speak to the planning of the battery of instruments to be administered during a forensic evaluation. If the scale names of the subscales on a particular inventory are primarily negative, then it may be worth considering an inventory with greater balance between the positive and negative aspects of human functioning. But if measures with primarily negative labels are used, then it is important to accurately describe what the scales signify and to augment these scales with at least one strengths-based measure to provide balance. The next step is to examine the psycholegal constructs.

Specific Juvenile Psycholegal Mental Health Concepts

When assessing specific functional legal capacities, structured professional judgment tools are likely to improve the accuracy of pertinent judgments. The RST-I is one example of such a measure in that it taps all three constructs identified as important in the *Kent v. United States* (1966) decision and is very helpful in disposition and transfer evaluations. Other measures, such as the Youth Level of Service/Case Management Inventory (YLS/CMI; Hoge, 2005) and the Structured Assessment of Violence Risk for Youth (SAVRY; Borum, Bartel, & Forth, 2005) also exist on risk and protective factors (or treatment variables). They typically offer an examination of one to two of the three concepts outlined in *Kent* (i.e., potential risk for dangerous behavior, sophistication–maturity, and amenability to treatment) and could be augmented to measure all three. Because of the gravity of the issues at hand, I recommend that clinicians use interview-based measures and rating scales. Of the existent measures, the RST-I, YLS/CMI, and SAVRY may have the best potential for juvenile evaluations. However, forensic clinicians should be aware that the YLS/CMI involves a very short interview and very few items per domain area. Thus, this may need to be bolstered with additional interviewing. Neither the YLS/CMI nor the SAVRY addresses developmental maturity. Because of this, forensic evaluator should augment these areas by also using other developmental maturity scales that have validity for juvenile justice youth. These measures are covered in greater detail in Chapter 6.

CLARIFYING THE EVALUATION LOGISTICS

In preparing to conduct forensic evaluations, clinicians should think ahead to clarify some logistical issues, such as where the assessment will be conducted, facility access, and considering whether the youth being evaluated poses any threat to her- or himself, or to others.

Assessment Context

Where the assessment will be conducted is a primary issue to be considered in the planning of one's evaluation. When the assessment is conducted for the purpose of contributing to decisions regarding legal issues such as waivers or transfers, the assessment will likely be conducted by a psychologist or psychiatrist within a juvenile justice, adult correctional system, or mental health facility. When addressing placement or disposition planning purposes, it will likely be conducted by a mental health professional or juvenile justice personnel within a juvenile justice facility. Disposition evaluations that involve treatment in the community might be conducted in clinicians' or attorneys' offices, or the young person may be assessed at an assessment center like the one first initiated by Healy and Fernald (see Chapter 1, this volume; Schetky & Benedek, 1980, 1992, 2002).

Facilities Access

Most detention centers and juvenile court settings require some special considerations and procedures before access is allowed regarding face-to-face interviewing and assessment of the young person. These vary according to the jurisdiction, but usually access to the facilities is established by the juvenile court judge or the retaining attorney, who provide clinicians with some form of approval. This approval can come in the form of a telephone call or a letter. There are two steps that may be taken to help enable access to facilities. First, it is best if forensic clinicians call the detention facility or jail in advance to make sure facility personnel know they are coming and clearance has been granted. Second, if possible, it is a good idea to have written authorization when arriving at a detention center, jail, or residential facility. Sometimes other individuals, such as guardian ad litem or probation officer, arrange for the evaluations.

Planning for the Immediate Threat of Risk

On occasion in the forensic assessment of youth, a clinician may conclude that the young person poses an immediate threat of harm to others or him- or herself. Under these circumstances, the professional is responsible for notifying appropriate authorities immediately. However, caution must be exercised in concluding that an immediate threat exists. Calling this to the attention of authorities is likely to have ramifications for the young person, and harm can arise if this proves to be a false alarm. Nonetheless, if a problem of this sort is identified, clinicians should contact the attorney and let him or her know of their concerns. If the young person is not detained, then *Tarasoff* warnings (*Tarasoff v. Regents of the University of California*, 1976) may come into play. Per the *Tarasoff* case, this may entail warning an individual who is the target of the threat.

OTHER ETHICS ISSUES

External Pressures

As the juvenile justice system has become more adversarial, it is possible that forensic clinicians may be retained by a defense attorney or by a prosecuting attorney. Depending on the magnitude of the case, each team may include attorneys, investigators/law enforcement personnel, paralegals, a guardian ad litem, victim advocates, and potentially trial consultants. Although being formally retained is more typical with adult cases, it can occur at the juvenile level, in particular with high-profile transfer cases. Team members have an adversarial agenda in seeking either to have the juvenile remain in juvenile court or to be transferred and held accountable for potential offenses. It is important to keep in mind that forensic clinicians must support objective expert findings and opinions, informed by the best science available.

Preparation for Testifying

Forensic clinicians, when testifying, vary in what they typically decide to take to court with them. Along with the report, having one's notes available can help to ensure accuracy while in the court or on the witness stand. But if the report is written in sufficient detail, then it should capture the aspects of the findings that support the conclusions. Some experts I know have described testifying without anything available for consultation, including the report. Although some experts with computerlike memories may be able to do this, I recommend that clinicians bring the psychological report to court, even if it is not relied on. The psychologist who is testifying should be prepared to answer questions in sufficient detail on both direct and cross-examination. If that means taking notes, manuals, and the psychological report to court, then the psychologist should do so.

Recording the Assessment

Given the traditional focus of the juvenile justice system and the emphasis on privacy (sealed records), clinical notes may be the best method for recording the evaluation. Recording juvenile evaluations could be problematic if information about the recording is leaked. Because of this, vigilance regarding the security of recordings—in particular, never allowing a third party to video- or audiotape the evaluation—is recommended. Malpractice complaints have been raised in the past concerning psychologists in high-profile cases where third parties have been responsible for recording the evaluation. In one example, a close colleague of mine informed me of an interview that ended up on the television news program *Dateline NBC*. Thus, for more sensitive information it might be best practice to simply take clinical notes during the interviews. Notes should be kept rather than destroyed, because this case file information could be useful in the future. Evaluative contacts that the expert has in a juvenile case with the young person and his or her family, as well as all third party sources, should also be sufficiently recorded to support scrutiny of the basis of the psychologist's findings and opinions. Clinical notes and any audio or video recordings, if used, should be maintained in their original state (APA, 2007b).

Retention of Records

The evaluative information gathered by the expert may be critical to later determinations of disposition or pertinent to later psychological evaluations of the individual. The notes and report may be quite valuable for a number of reasons; for example, forensic clinicians' notes may be the most comprehensive and coherent historical information for the young person. The mental health professional may have a critically important role as a record keeper for juvenile cases in one's city or state, or even across the nation if the youth and family move. Also, clinicians who are asked to perform a second evaluation of a young person will have their previous report and notes. Alternatively, other psychologists may request reports, and it is helpful to be able to pass psychological information to a fellow expert. As long as the proper consents or court authorizations are obtained, providing the report could well help another mental health professional and the courts. This provides the necessary continuity in the individual's history and further improves the evaluation. One way to do this is to archive reports in paper format in file cabinets. Another option is to digitize psychological reports for electronic storage. The recommendation to maintain records is consistent with the Introduction section of APA's record keeping guidelines (APA, 2007b): "The process of keeping records involves consideration of legal requirements, ethical standards, and other external constraints, as well as the demands of the particular professional context" (p. 993).

Sealed Records

At a time when the courts were highly rehabilitative in their ideology, records for juvenile offenders were sealed; that is, if a young person broke the law, the only people who were privy to this information were the child, the child's family, the police, and the juvenile court personnel involved in the case. This precaution was thought to protect the young person, allowing him or her to correct his or her behavior without the commission of the crime being broadly communicated. However, in modern juvenile courts, whether the records are actually sealed depends on the jurisdiction as well as the nature of the offense. Protecting the identity of juveniles was standard practice until the mid-1980s. As a prominent forensic psychologist informed me, "No pictures or names were allowed in news articles, no release of information, and no discovery of juvenile records in criminal cases." Most of the states changed this in the mid-1980s, but in different ways (e.g., opening some juvenile hearings and not others, allowing serious offenses to be discoverable when a child is an adult). In the mid-1980s, Massachusetts, for example, legislated that juvenile hearings on murder and several other offenses were open to the public and press. Thus, according to this expert, it was entirely possible to testify in such cases and then to also see the case—and yourself testifying—on the evening news (Thomas Grisso, personal communication, August 25, 2012).

CONCLUDING COMMENTS

In preparing for the clinical evaluation of juveniles, clinicians face a number of ethical and practical considerations. Mainly, they need to prepare for due process and honesty of reporting whereby the young person understands what the assessment is for and comprehends that a psychological report and testimony will result. In addition, in this chapter I have discussed the requisite level of training needed and offered information on licensing for practice as a clinical psychologist or psychiatrist or another allied mental health professional working in this area. Information on the various roles a scientist can be involved in, including foundational and individual-based assessment, also was provided. I discussed ways to gain access to facilities and assess youth comprehensively and effectively and provided advice on how to develop an effective evaluation battery. Specifically, I recommended that cognitive testing, interviewing, and self-reports, as well as specific juvenile measures, be used and that measures be chosen that can inform the pertinent constructs. Finally, I discussed record keeping and the storage of juvenile evaluation and treatment files. As one can see, considerable planning goes into preparing for the evaluation and storing one's materials. Time management in such evaluations is of the essence, including carefully planning specific times to sit at the computer and type the psychological report. The next chapter focuses on data collection and includes detailed information on the types of tests to include in a comprehensive battery.

6

DATA COLLECTION FOR JUVENILE EVALUATIONS

The perspective of proper juvenile evaluation offered in this book is innovative and based on emerging theory and research. However, as new research emerges, the process should be advanced to incorporate this new information. Much of the hope in developing scholarly research on this topic is to stimulate further empirical inquiry to refine the evaluation process and to suggest even better ways in which to assess and treat young people in upcoming years. Quality mental health evaluations have the potential to produce positive change in the young person's life and to modify the juvenile justice system. Clinical evaluations can influence the law's definition as well as the application of laws to maximize the healthy development of young people while maintaining public safety.

In the preceding chapter, I discussed some practical considerations in the planning of a forensic evaluation and the selection of assessment instruments and procedures (e.g., structured vs. unstructured assessments). In this chapter, I address topics relevant to the data collection phase of the

http://dx.doi.org/10.1037/14595-007
Forensic Evaluation and Treatment of Juveniles: Innovation and Best Practice, by R. T. Salekin

psychological assessment, including how to collect data on youth that will later be used to complete the evaluation and write a report. The three major constructs of (a) risk, (b) developmental maturity, and (c) amenability to treatment are at the center of these evaluations, but many other factors, such as family practices, mental or emotional disorder, personality, and response styles, also figure in. The methods for collecting this information covered in this chapter include document review, cognitive testing, clinical and structured interviewing, administration of self-report measures, and the administration of measures that are specifically developed for juveniles. I also discuss cognitive deficit measurement and projective testing.

ESTABLISHING RAPPORT

On occasion, anxiety, stress, fear, or even anger are associated with the evaluation. If the child being evaluated is making a strong effort toward autonomy, or if he or she has a strong reaction toward individuals he or she views as authority figures, the evaluation may require a special set of rapport-building skills. Rapport with the young person and his or her family may also be hampered by notifying them that you have been appointed by a judge to provide an accurate assessment of the family history and present functioning, including information regarding risk, developmental maturity, and treatment amenability. Being honest about the evaluation and its process, as well as being respectful of the young person and his or her family, is a good starting point and facilitates rapport, interviewing, and testing with the proper warnings in place.

Adolescents may also be influenced in the assessment by their perceptions of psychiatrists and psychologists. Forensic clinicians should work toward demystifying their role with youth. Forensic clinicians should also work toward establishing rapport with youth but also be aware of their personal interviewing style and remain cognizant of any subtle messages they may be displaying during the interview. Acknowledgment or reinforcement of certain responses with a nod or a smile should be monitored. The occasional smile or head nod is perfectly acceptable; however, the key here is to avoid the reinforcement of only specific types of responses and to conduct the questioning in a manner that eliminates selective reinforcement. If the young person is very uncomfortable with the interview, then the clinician may want to consider altering his or her style; consulting with a colleague; and, in the worst-case scenarios, perhaps discontinuing the interview and transferring the case.

That said, many youth find the process of sitting in a room with an adult, being asked a mind-boggling number of questions, boring. This may lead them to fidget in their seat, ask when the interview will end, and even look uninterested and express fatigue (e.g., a heavy sigh). It is probably safe to say that the psychological assessment is not one of the top 10 most exciting activities for young people. Moreover, the young person is also in a predicament he or she would rather not be. If forensic clinicians were to discontinue their work at the first sign of a young person's discomfort, such as looking disinterested, or yawning, there would be a long list of incomplete juvenile evaluations. It is acceptable to encourage kids to give their best effort in a process that is long and perhaps, at times, tiring. Being a creative but considerate evaluator may be important to finishing the evaluation.

Through a polite, respectful, and encouraging style, clinicians and young people can successfully make it through the evaluation. Of course, this might mean using various strategies, such as going on to a different topic, taking a break, or getting the child something to eat or drink, all of which may improve the chances that the evaluation will be completed without a compromise in the young person's performance. Purchasing a young individual a soda or candy bar from a vending machine may help counter the extensive labor involved with the evaluation, and it is not such a high-level incentive that the young person being assessed will feel uncomfortable declining. It also can be helpful to be lively in conducting the evaluation. For instance, one might say something like, "Look, there is a lot of work here, but it's manageable, and together, we can get through it, and I will help guide you along the way." This does not mean that one should be unprofessional or not express the seriousness of the matter. It is perfectly acceptable for clinicians to have a bit of energy in their voice as they set up the next task; for example:

> OK, next we are going to do what is called a "self-report inventory." There are 344 questions about how you think feel and act that we would like to know about you. Some of the questions can be interesting as you think about and respond to them, trying to be as accurate as you can along the way.

Another example could be "In some ways, these questions will be similar to some of the things we discussed earlier, so you'll get another chance to answer questions that are specific to you and your family." All this said, if a youth is genuinely distressed, extremely angry, or adamantly refusing, it is important to discontinue the assessment.

Establishment of rapport with parents also is clearly important. Parents will be concerned about their son or daughter and may also be anxious about potential questions about their parenting practices or personal factors, such as education, or work performance, and financial responsibility, that may have contributed to their son or daughter's delinquency. Some youth involved with the legal system come from single-parent families, and sometimes only one parent is available to participate in the evaluation. Wherever possible, efforts should be made to reach both parents and related caretakers in order to establish rapport with them and obtain information from all guardians and relevant extended family members.

THE REFERRAL QUESTION

Before any psychological evaluation, forensic clinicians working with young people need to know the referral question. If the question forensic psychologists are asked to address pertains to a particular legal standard, then the clinician should learn the specifics of that standard. Once forensic clinicians know the standard being evaluated, as well as the criteria that underlie the standard, they can then proceed to the next stage of the evaluation, which is to comprehensively gather information about the young person.

DOCUMENT REVIEW

On beginning the evaluation, it is important that the forensic expert allow adequate time to gather and assess the data required. The first step should be to review all the relevant documents, including police, school, medical, psychiatric, and social reports. A carefully constructed developmental history should be a composite of information gathered about the child's home, school, workplace (if applicable), legal proceedings, and neighborhood. Contacting the young person's lawyer and teachers as well as any other relevant court personnel also is necessary. If the young individual is not at present in school, then gathering his or her previous school records alone will have to suffice. Contacting coaches, music instructors, and other potential mentors regarding hobbies and other activities can also provide valuable material. A broad perspective in gathering the information is chief because context may be at least as relevant as personality and behavior.

COGNITIVE TESTING

As a forensic clinician, one should frequently assess cognitive abilities, which can be tapped by administering an IQ test and an achievement test. This is helpful in determining the young person's general level of cognitive functioning and determining whether he or she has an intellectual deficit or a learning disorder (LD). If an intellectual deficit or LD is suspected, then in-depth IQ and achievement tests should be administered (e.g., the Wechsler Intelligence Scale for Children—Fourth Edition [Wechsler, 2004], Woodcock–Johnson Tests of Cognitive Abilities [Woodcock, McGrew, & Mather, 2001]). If an intellectual deficit or LD is not a suspected, then one can use a brief IQ test (e.g., the Kaufman Brief Intelligence Test, Second Edition; Kaufman & Kaufman, 2002) and a brief achievement test (e.g., Wide Range Achievement Test 4; Wilkinson & Robertson, 2006) to obtain rough estimates of each. Some clinicians will choose to use the aforementioned brief screens and diagnose LDs. When doing so, they should be aware that they may be on less solid ground when it comes to testimony. One can also, after using a particular screen, administer alternate full IQ and achievement tests. Some clinicians may use full battery IQ and achievement tests on all evaluations, although this can be quite time consuming. When it comes to diagnosing LDs, clinicians should be aware that observing a young person's response to intervention is best practice to determine whether the youth truly has an LD or whether he or she simply has not been taught certain skills. Youth who can easily be taught information likely do not have an LD.

CLINICAL INTERVIEWS

Traditional clinical interviews provide key information on youth functioning. Such interviews provide the necessary information regarding the young person's developmental history, his or her life experiences, and how he or she thinks and feels about his or her life (including relations with others), as well as the type and severity of symptoms. Clinical interviews are also critical inasmuch as they allow for rapport building and provide a meaningful account of the events that led to the youth's current legal circumstances, if this information is desired. Clinical interviews also allow for the comparison of information across interviews (traditional and structured), self-reports, checklists, and other sources. Child interviews alone may produce very good information and permit clinicians to examine the quality of details provided and determine whether the youth's story has a logical flow (Raskin & Esplin, 1991; Steller & Koehnken, 1989; Vernham, Vrij, Mann, Leal, & Hillman, 2014; Vrij, Mann, Jundi, Hillman, & Hope, 2014; Yuille, 1988). Parent, teacher, and other collateral source interviews, as well as records (e.g., school records), also allow for further examination across reports and facilitates the synthesis of information.

Clinical interviews can be very helpful in that clinicians can query young people in detail about the emotions that accompany their life experiences. Depending on the young person and the situation in question, in my own work as a forensic evaluator I may ask adolescents to describe basic emotions.

For instance, I might ask a young person, "Please recall a happy time in your life that you can remember and tell me a little bit about that time." It is important to try to glean as much information as possible about the emotional response. Similarly, it may be helpful to ask about a sad time that may have resulted in a negative emotion and how the interviewee handled that specific negative emotion. I also frequently ask about times that might have evoked feelings of anger, guilt, and remorse, to learn how the young person dealt with each one of those emotions.

Through clinical interviewing one can get a sense of the young person's planning and prospection. For example, it can be helpful to ask about specific plans she or he may have made in the past, how those plans were executed, and how they worked out. Some youth talk about money they may have saved to pay for football or basketball camp. When asked about planning events, young people have the opportunity to describe successful completion of plans as well as failures. Factors that facilitated the completion of goals, as well as the roadblocks encountered, should be queried about. Questions about the latter can elicit considerable information on the young person's ability to solve problems and handle emotion (both positive and negative), and on his or her outlook on life. This information helps shed light on how that person's emotions either facilitate or hamper effective decision making. A careful examination of the extent to which young individuals are able to recover from negative outcomes can help shape treatment recommendations. All this information is valuable and can be garnered through a thoughtful clinical interview.

STRUCTURED CLINICAL INTERVIEWS

Structured interviews are likely best considered as the fourth step, in addition to the document review, cognitive/achievement testing, and the clinical interview, in the assessment process. Structured interviews are advantageous in that they provide a very reliable and valid method of obtaining detailed systematized clinical information. Structured interviews of *Diagnostic and Statistical Manual of Mental Disorders* (DSM)–based diagnoses (e.g., *DSM–5*; American Psychiatric Association, 2013) can facilitate the orderly gathering of diagnostic information and the methodological rating of symptoms. The vast majority of structured interviews are being updated for *DSM–5*. For the purposes of this chapter, I cover *DSM–IV* (American Psychiatric Association, 1994) interviews, given that many of the *DSM–5* disruptive behavior disorders have been only minimally revised from *DSM–IV* given that the revisions to the interviews themselves will not be monumental and newer versions will likely rely on the *DSM–IV* reliability and validity estimates to some extent.

DSM-based structured interviews include the Diagnostic Interview for Children (DISC–IV; Columbia DISC Development Group, 1999; National Institute of Mental Health, 1991), the Schedule of Affective and Schizophrenic Disorders for School-Age Children (Ambrosini, 1992b), and the Missouri Assessment of Genetics Interview for Children (Reich & Todd, 2002; Todd, Joyner, Heath, Neuman, & Reich, 2003). Many structured interviews have 3- or 4-point scales that are used to score individual symptoms. Three-point scales commonly range from 0 (= *no*, the young person does not have the symptom) to 1 (= *somewhat*, the young person has the symptom at a sub-clinical level), to 2 (= yes, the young individual fully has the symptom). Semistructured interview booklets can guide clinicians in probing symptoms that require further clarification. Structured interviews also allow for the examination of the coherence of reported symptoms and psychological disorders.

Another benefit of structured interviews is that they protect forensic clinicians from confirmation bias; that is, they prevent forensic clinicians from asking only questions that pertain to their own belief, or working hypothesis, regarding a young person's diagnosis. Structured interviews also allow forensic clinicians to mark the onset and offset of symptoms and disorders. This is critical because a young person who has anxiety or depression prior to conduct disorder symptoms may be different from a young person who has conduct disorder preceding anxiety or depression. Knowledge of which disorder the young person may or may not have is crucial. Despite their many advantages, not all structured interviews are equal, and, depending on the case (e.g., when drug abuse is suspected), a clinician may prefer a specific interview. Table 6.1 describes the structured interviews currently available for children and adolescents.

An important prerequisite to structured interviewing is to ascertain whether the child or adolescent understands the questions he or she is being asked. Children typically have a lower level of comprehension of words and phrases than older adolescents and adults. This is especially true if the words and phrases are geared toward elucidating nuances of human emotion. Several established practices can maximize cooperation and quality of the interview data. First, open-ended questions minimize the possibility that a forensic clinician will lead the child to state conclusions that are suggested by the wording of the questions themselves. Yet, overreliance on closed-ended questions, especially leading questions, should be avoided because they may encourage acquiescence. Second, structured interviews allow for a broad-based set of questions, and, consequently, the young person does not feel as though the forensic clinician is zeroing in on a specific disorder (e.g., severe conduct disorder) without considering other conditions (Rogers, 2001).

TABLE 6.1
Comparison of Child Interviews

Feature	KSADS–IV	DISC	CAS	DICA–III–R and IV	MAGIC	DBD
1. Ages 2. User friendliness	6–18 Excellent interview, but low in friendliness. The interview is long, with many questions. The Hamilton Rating Scale for Depression (Hamilton, 1967) is also included and may not be necessary given all the SI questions on depression. KSADS–PL: Reduced time to administer with a screen.	6–18 Very child oriented, but the SI is also long, with numerous questions. Computerized version strays from the rationale of a traditional SI in which the clinician conducts the interview. Paper-and-pencil versions are recommended for juvenile evaluations.	6–18 Easy to use, the measure is innocuous and designed to develop rapport. An excellent SI, but it needs to be updated for *DSM–5*.	6–18 The authors improved the ease of administration. The most current version, like the DISC, is computer run and thus arguably is better conceptualized as a self-report measure and no longer a traditional SI.	6–18 Appears to be a newer version of the DICA. This measure is user friendly and has excellent questions. It is a traditional SI with the clinician at the wheel.	6–18 Moderately friendly and easy to use. Clinicians require some training on the measure as some aspects are not self-evident. Training is expected for all interviews.
3. Parent vs. child oriented	The SI is administered to the parent first and then the child. A nice aspect is that questions about discrepancies are then asked after the interview with the parent and the child.	Given to both child and parent. No specific order is recommended.	The CAS–Parent is not required but it is preferred that both SIs be administered. For juvenile evaluations, it is best to give both SIs.	Has both child and adolescent versions. With the DICA, the parent version is recommended.	Parent and child and adolescent versions are available and should be administered.	Both child and parent versions are administered, and the interviews are followed by a clinician agreement meeting.

4. Symptoms vs. problem areas	• Research diagnostic criteria (*DSM*) • Not all versions are comprehensive.	• *DSM–IV* simplified • Comprehensive	• ADHD • ODD • CD • Anxiety • Mood • Psychosis and other problem areas	• *DSM–III–R;* self-report version based on the *DSM–IV* • Comprehensive	*DSM–IV* and problem areas	*DSM–IV* and disruptive behavior emphasis
5. Treatment and treatment–outcome	• KSADS–E current and past diagnosis • Treatment prediction rating	• Treatment prediction rating	• Excellent for treatment outcome information. Has a separate form for treatment outcome. • Problems in life before treatment and problems in life after treatment. • Also has a section for assessing where the young person needs improvement.	Gives both current and past diagnoses. There is nothing specific on treatment outcome or treatment prediction.	Treatment prediction rating	Treatment outcome rating

(continues)

TABLE 6.1
Comparison of Child Interviews (Continued)

Feature	KSADS–IV	DISC	CAS	DICA–III–R and IV	MAGIC	DBD
6. Prediction of problematic behaviors (e.g., suicide, aggression)	Very strong at measuring depression. Initially designed for measurement of depression and schizophrenia.	Very good at measuring problematic mood and behavior such as depression and aggression. This measure may show an edge over the others in this area.	Very good at measuring problematic behavior.	Very good at measuring problematic behavior.	Very good at measuring problematic behavior.	Good at measuring disruptive behavior.
7. Response styles	No	Measures response styles.	No	No	No	No
8. Family pathology			Measures family problems. SI begins on a positive note (e.g., "How do you get along with your mom?") and then asks questions that pertain to family pathology.			
9. Linkage w/ traditional child tests (e.g., CBCL)	Fair	Good	Good	Good	Good	Good

	Use with nonnative speakers of English					
10. Use with nonnative speakers of English	More than 20 translations, including Hebrew, Farsi, Persian, Korean, Greek, Spanish, Portuguese, Afrikaans, French, Turkish, Icelandic	Spanish, Dutch, German, Japanese, Icelandic, Chinese, French, (previous versions in Vietnamese and Hosa). Other non-English versions of the NIMH DISC–IV are in preparation by various investigators.	None	Arabic, Portuguese, Spanish	None	None
11. Psychosis	Comprehensive	Comprehensive	Some inferences could be made from observation section of interview; however, no direct questions	Good	Most comprehensive of the SIs	No
12. Substance use	Good coverage	Good coverage	Good coverage	Very good coverage	Excellent coverage	No

Note. KSADS–IV = Schedule for Affective and Schizophrenic Disorders, Childhood Version (4th ed.; Ambrosini & Dixon, 1996; Chambers et al., 1985; Kaufman et al., 1997); DISC = Diagnostic Interview Schedule for Children; CAS = Child Assessment Schedule (Hodges, Kline, Fitch, McKnew, & Cytryn, 1981; Hodges, Kline, Stern, Cytryn, & McKnew, 1982); DICA = Diagnostic Interview for Children and Adolescents (Herjanic & Reich, 1982); MAGIC = Missouri Assessment of Genetics Interview for Children (Reich & Todd, 2002); DBD = Disruptive Behavior Disorders Interview (Massetti, Pelham, Chacko, et al., 2003; Massetti, Pelham, & Gnagy, 2005); KSADS–PL = Schedule for Affective Disorders and Schizophrenia for School-Age Children—Present and Life Time Version (Ambrosini, 1992a; Kaufman et al., 1997); SI = structured interview; *DSM = Diagnostic and Statistical Manual of Mental Disorders*; ADHD = attention-deficit/hyperactivity disorder; ODD = oppositional defiant disorder; CD = conduct disorder; KSADS–E = Kiddie–SADS Epidemiological Version (Orvaschel, Puig-Antich, Chambers, Tabrizi, & Johnson, 1982); CBCL = Child Behavior Checklist; NIMH = National Institute of Mental Health. Additional structured interviews that may be of interest include the Anxiety Disorders Interview Schedule (e.g., Albano & Silverman, 1996); Children's Interview for Psychiatric Syndromes (Weller, Weller, Fristad, Rooney, & Schecter, 2000); Beck Youth Inventories (e.g., Beck, Beck, Jolly, & Steer, 2005), Child Symptom Inventory (e.g., Gadow & Sprafkin, 2002), and specialized interviews such as the Hare Psychopathy Checklist: Youth Version (Forth, Kosson, & Hare, 2003). Although it is not covered here, see also Silverman and Albano (1996).

SELF-REPORT MEASURES AND CHECKLISTS

Best practice in the assessment of juvenile offenders entails the consideration and administration of a self-report measure. Self-report measures can facilitate the evaluation in that they allow the young person to reflect on his or her characteristics and report on them in a private setting. Some self-report inventories also come with parent and teacher report forms that can be useful for direct comparisons across raters. The self-report measures differ noticeably in their content as well as their psychometric properties, so thoughtful consideration with respect to choosing a multiscale self-report inventory is vital. In this section, I provide a brief introduction to self-report indexes that may be helpful when deciding which measure to use. Forensic clinicians will need to gather supplemental information on each multiscale inventory. Self-report manuals should be perused before administration. Most multiscale inventories were developed and validated on adult populations before downward extensions were created for children. In some instances, measures may not have been extensively tested for their developmental sensitivity or their validity with juvenile offenders (Rosenfeld & Penrod, 2011). A careful reading of the manual and recent research can help determine whether such a measure is appropriate and scientifically supported for use with a specific young person in the justice system.

Several frequently used self-report measures for children and adolescents exist. These include the Minnesota Multiphasic Personality Inventory—Adolescent (Butcher et al., 1992), the Behavioral Assessment System for Children, Second Edition (Reynolds & Kamphaus, 2004), the Millon Adolescent Clinical Inventory (Millon, 1993), the Personality Assessment Inventory—Adolescent (Morey, 2007), the Adolescent Psychopathology Scale (W. M. Reynolds, 1998), and the Personality Inventory for Youth (Larchar & Gruber, 1995). Each of these self-report instruments has a set of clinical scales (e.g., depression, anxiety, atypical), some have personality scales (e.g., borderline personality), and others have adolescent-specific scales (e.g., expressed concerns). A few of the multiscale inventories contain strengths-based scales, and some include maturity-like scales (e.g., self-concept, adaptation, leadership). Each multiscale inventory also has a set of validity scales for determining the accuracy of the report.

Other self-report measures, such as the Achenbach System of Empirically Based Assessment (e.g., Achenbach, 1991b, 1991c, 1991d) or the Conners 3 (Conners, 2008), may be useful for forensic evaluations. Each of these measures focuses on different aspects of the externalizing and internalizing symptoms. For instance, the Child Behavior Checklist (Achenbach, 1991b) covers primarily externalizing disorders, and earlier versions had little correspondence with the *DSM–IV* or *DSM–5*. However, *DSM* scales were subsequently created for the

Child Behavior Checklist, and *DSM–IV* versions are available. The Conners 3 is one of the few tests updated at this point for *DSM–5*. With the proliferation of psychological tests, it is beyond the scope of this chapter to cover all broad-band self-report assessment measures. However, I note here that best practice with young individuals involved with the law requires that mental health professionals be aware of the psychometric properties of the measures they select and especially aware of the norming sample and the instrument's predictive validity to be sure the test is applicable to the young person being evaluated. See Table 6.2 for a list of self-report measures and their relative strengths.

Even if forensic clinicians are not frequent users of a specified measure, gaining knowledge about commonly used, and even uncommonly used, measures can be to one's advantage. This is because other mental health professionals who may testify in the same case might use an alternate test, and for this reason it is good to be knowledgeable about a variety of measures. Although it is impossible to know every test in the world of psychology, familiarity with the major instruments and some of the less commonly used measures can bolster one's competence and expertise.

INTERPERSONAL ADJECTIVE SCALE REVISED—BIG 5 VERSION AND OTHER GENERAL PERSONALITY MEASURES FOR ADOLESCENTS

Different approaches have been adopted to assess general personality dimensions in children and adolescents (Halverson et al., 2003; Shiner & Caspi, 2003; Slotboom, Havill, Pavlopoulos, & De Fruyt, 1998; Widiger, Lynam, Miller, & Oltmanns, 2012). Measures based on the five-factor model (Costa & McCrae, 1992a) initially developed for adults have typically been extended downward and used to describe differences in younger age groups (e.g., studies that have used the Revised NEO Personality Inventory [Costa & McCrae, 1992b] to assess adolescents' personality include De Clercq & De Fruyt, 2003; De Fruyt, Mervielde, Hoekstra, & Rolland, 2000; and McCrae et al., 2002). Other studies, to be more developmentally appropriate, adapted the phrasing of personality items for younger age groups (e.g., the Junior Eysenck Personality Inventory; S. B. G. Eysenck, 1963; S. B. G. Eysenck, Makaremi, & Barrett, 1994).

Because personality variables can be used to describe youth as well as facilitate the assessment of the forensic mental health concepts, they may be very helpful in case formulation. Several valid personality measures can be used to shore up the evaluation. The Interpersonal Adjective Scale Revised—Big 5 version (Trapnell & Wiggins, 1990; Wiggins, Trapnell, & Phillips, 1988; Wiggins & Trobst, 2002) is one such measure. It allows for the assessment

TABLE 6.2
Comparison of Self-Report Instruments

Feature	MMPI–A	BASC–2	MACI	APS	CBCL	Conners 3
Age range	To be used with adolescents ages 14–18. Can be used with 12- to 13-year-olds if they are bright/mature.	Geared toward children ranging between ages 4–18. The parent versions can go lower in age (PRS: 2–5, 6–11, 12–21), Teacher and parent: 2–21.	Designed to assess adolescents ages 13–19. There is now the M-PACI for younger children.	Designed for adolescents ages 12–19.	Has a number of different forms. Capable of assessing very young children and adolescents: YSR (11–18), TRF (1.5–5; 6–18) direct observation form.	Can be used to assess children ages 6–18 (PRS: 6–18). Self-report: ages 8–18.
1. User friendliness	Low in user friendliness because the measure is lengthy (478 items). The true–false format is friendly but the measure can take 120 minutes to administer.	Relatively easy to use. Has a reasonable number of items and a true–false format (C-152 TF; A-186 TF); there is also a 4-choice frequency index within the measure. The self-report can be completed in approximately 60 minutes.	Easy to use. Has only 160 items and a true-false format. Administration time is approximately 45–60 minutes.	Relatively easy to use. It consists of 346 items rated on a 3-point scale. Takes approximately 45–60 minutes to complete.	Easy to use. Time to complete is roughly 10–20 minutes.	Relatively easy to use. Has a long form (110 items) and a short form (45 items); rated on a 4-point scale. Administration time is approximately 10–20 minutes.

2. Parent vs. child oriented	Child self-report only	• Parents • Teachers • Self • Peers	Child self-report only	Child self-report only	• Parents • Teachers • Self	• Parents • Teachers • Self
3. Symptoms vs. problem areas	• Based on the MMPI–2 • Some say there is *DSM* correspondence.	• Description • Education • Some *DSM–IV* correspondence.	• Millon's system • Clinical • Residential • Correctional • Some *DSM* correspondence.	• Corresponds with *DSM–IV* clinical disorders, personality disorders, and psychosocial problems.	• Some *DSM–IV* scales, including ODD and CD, but some consider the measure to not be closely aligned with the *DSM* (Rogers, 2001); updated *DSM* scales for the measure may better tap *DSM* constructs.	Updated to *DSM–5* constructs. Scoring is based on updated scales. Five scales (Hyperactivity/Impulsivity, Executive Functioning, Learning Problems, Aggression, Peer Relations).
4. Scaling	• Linear T-scores • Overlapping items	Linear T-scores	• Base rate • Overlapping items	Linear T-scores	• Linear T-scores • Overlapping items	Linear T-scores

(continues)

TABLE 6.2
Comparison of Self-Report Instruments *(Continued)*

Feature	MMPI–A	BASC–2	MACI	APS	CBCL	Conners 3
5. Prediction of problematic behaviors (suicide, aggression)	Fair O-H scale Pd scale	Parent version picks up on aggression	Good suicide scale Aggression scales	Good suicide and aggression scales	Good—considerable data on the CBCL	Aggression
6. Response styles	• Yes • L • F • F1 (first half) • F2 (second half) • F-K • K • ?	• Yes • L index • V-random response pattern • Consistency	• Disclosure • Debasement • Desirability • Reliability	• Lie response • Consistency • Infrequency • Critical item endorsement	No	• Positive impression • Negative impression • Inconsistency
7. Family pathology	Yes–Pd scale	Yes	Yes—family discord scale	No	No	No
8. Linkage with traditional child Tests (e.g., CBCL)	Modestly well	Modestly well	Modestly well	Modestly well	Modestly well	Modestly well

9. Use with nonnative speakers of English	Bulgarian, Croatian, Dutch/Flemish, French, Hungarian, Italian, Korean, Spanish for Mexico and Central America, Spanish for Spain, South America, and Central America, Spanish for the United States	Spanish version	Spanish and Dutch versions	None	Translated into more than 80 languages, including Arabic, Bulgarian, Chinese, Dutch, Estonian, Farsi/Persian, French, German, Greek, Hebrew, Italian, Japanese, Korean, Lithuanian, Macedonian, Norwegian, Polish, Portuguese, Russian, Spanish, Turkish, Urdu, Vietnamese, and Zulu	Spanish and French versions
10. Psychosis	Scales 6 and 8	Atypicality scale	Not good	Good	Thought Problem scale	No
11. Substance abuse	Good	Poor	Good	Good	No	No
12. Personality	Fair	Fair	Good	Good	No	No

Note. MMPI–A = Minnesota Multiphasic Personality Inventory—Adolescent; MMPI–2 = Minnesota Multiphasic Personality Inventory—2 (Butcher, Dahlstrom, Graham, Tellegen, & Kaemmer, 1989); BASC–2 = Behavioral Assessment System for Children, Second Edition; MACI = Millon Adolescent Clinical Inventory; APS = Adolescent Psychopathology Scale (Reynolds, 1998); M-PACI = Millon Preadolescent Clinical Inventory (Millon, Tringone, Millon, & Grossman, 2005); CBCL = Child Behavior Checklist; PRS = parent rating scale; YSR = youth self-report; TRF = teacher rating form; C-152 TF = Child–152—true false; A-186 TF = Adolescent–186—true false; *DSM = Diagnostic and Statistical Manual of Mental Disorders*; ODD = oppositional defiant disorder; CD = conduct disorder; ADHD = attention-deficit/hyperactivity disorder; O-H = Overcontrolled Hostility Scale; Pd = Psychopathic Deviate scale; L = Lie; F = Infrequency; K = Correction; ? = unanswered items.

of personality from two overlapping theories, including the Interpersonal Circumplex and the five-factor model of personality (see Salekin, Leistico, Trobst, Schrum, & Lochman, 2005; Trapnell & Wiggins, 1990). Both conceptualizations allow the forensic clinician to view the young person's behavior problems through the lens of general personality. The Interpersonal Circumplex has octants and two broad domains (Dominance and Affiliation). The Interpersonal Adjective Scale Revised—Big 5 version also taps the separate scales for Openness, Conscientiousness, Extraversion, Agreeableness, and Neuroticism. Other personality scales may also be considered. Caspi and Shiner (2006) provided a detailed list of measures used for indexing personality in youth. Items that are typically contained in general personality indices are listed in Table 6.3. One potential consideration for these measures is to examine their opposite (i.e., Extraversion vs. Introversion). Information on both poles of personality domains to facilitate the adoption of measures for the purpose of assessing youth personality is provided in Table 6.3.

PSYCHOLOGICAL OR COGNITIVE DEFICITS

Forensic clinicians might consider several measures when they have concerns about a young person's cognitive impairment, including whether he or she is malingering, or faking symptoms. These include the Raven's Standard Progressive Matrices (Raven, 1996), the Test of Memory Malingering (Tombaugh, 1996), the Word Memory Test (Green, Allen, & Astner, 1996), and the Computerized Assessment of Response Bias test (Allen, Conder, Green, & Cox, 1997). If distorting information about a mental illness is a concern, then the Structured Inventory of Malingered Symptomatology (Smith, 1992; Smith & Burger, 1997) or the Structured Interview of Reported Symptoms (Rogers, Bagby, & Dickens, 1992) may be of assistance. However, all of these measures are designed for use with adults, with only limited data available on adolescent samples (Salekin, Kubak, & Lee, 2008). Forensic clinicians who decide that a cognitive examination is needed can search the available databases for the literature on cognitive deficits, including malingering, and determine what information is available on the desired test as it pertains to the child or adolescent. As more research is conducted on these and other related measures, they likely will become increasingly useful.

MEASURES RELATED TO PSYCHOLEGAL CONSTRUCTS

Over the past decade, juvenile assessment tools have been designed for the assessment of young offenders. For example, the Structured Assessment of Violence Risk for Youth (SAVRY; Borum, Bartel, & Forth, 2005), the

TABLE 6.3
Five-Factor Model of Personality Functioning and Opposing Poles

Factor	Pole	
Openness	Positive	Negative
Imaginative	Abstract, fantasy, a dreamer	Practical, concrete
Aesthetic	Aesthetic	Unaesthetic
Ideas	Odd, peculiar	Pragmatic, rigid
Values	Broad-minded, permissive	Traditional, inflexible
Feelings	Responsive, sensitive	Constricted, stoic
Actions	Unpredictable	Routine, habitual
Conscientiousness		
Competence	Efficient, perfectionistic	Lax, negligent
Order	Organized, methodical	Haphazard, disorganized
Dutifulness	Reliable, dependable	Casual, unreliable, untrustworthy
Achievement striving	Ambitious, goal oriented	Aimless, goalless
Self-discipline	Devoted, dogged	Negligent, hedonistic
Deliberation	Reflective, thorough	Careless, hasty
Extraversion		
Warmth	Affectionate, attached	Aloof, cold, indifferent
Gregarious	Sociable, outgoing	Withdrawn, isolated
Assertiveness	Forceful, dominant	Quiet, resigned, unassuming
Active	Vigorous, energetic	Passive, lethargic
Excitement seeking	Daring, reckless	Cautious, dull
Positive emotions	High spirited	Placid, anhedonic
Agreeableness		
Trust	Trusting, gullible	Skeptical, cynical
Straightforwardness	Honest, naïve	Cunning, manipulative
Altruism	Giving, sacrificing	Selfish, exploitative
Compliance	Cooperative, rule bound	Oppositional, combative
Modesty	Self-effacing, humble	Boastful, arrogant, confident
Tender-mindedness	Empathic, softhearted	Callous, ruthless
Neuroticism		
Anxiousness	Fearful, apprehensive	Relaxed, unconcerned, cool
Angry hostility	Bitter, angry	Even-tempered
Depressiveness	Pessimistic, glum	Optimistic
Self-consciousness	Timid, embarrassed	Self-assured, glib
Impulsivity	Tempted, urgency	Controlled, restrained
Vulnerability	Fragile, helpless	Brave, fearless, unflappable

Youth Level of Service/Case Management Inventory (YLS/CMI; Hoge, 2005), and the Risk–Sophistication–Treatment Inventory (RSTI; Salekin, 2004; see also Iselin & Salekin, 2014; Salekin, 2006; Salekin, Tippey, & Allen, 2012) all can be used to examine risk and provide other information relevant to the courts. The SAVRY or YLS/CMI might be used for risk-for-violence–related questions. Similarly, the YLS/CMI and RSTI can address treatment needs (Hoge, 2012). It is important to know that all measures allow for the assessment of risk and protective factors that are linked to concerns regarding aggression as well as treatment amenability. The RSTI includes the most extensive data-gathering process, which is important in terms of comprehensiveness, but the interview-based version is time consuming (Salekin, 2004).

Although the aforementioned measures provide structure to the evaluation process, they do not supplant the need for extensive knowledge of adolescent development. Nor do they supplant the need to keep up to date with the current literature on personality and pathology as well as the need to keep pace with the research on risk for dangerous behavior, developmental maturity, and treatment amenability. In deciding which factors to use to address the questions raised by legal standards, forensic examiners should look to the body of knowledge—scientific, theoretical, and clinical—in which they are expert. The tools discussed in the next section are based on the latest science on the juvenile constructs discussed thus far and will be very helpful with the structuring of forensic evaluations.

RISK, DEVELOPMENTAL MATURITY, AND AMENABILITY MEASURES

Structured Assessment of Violence Risk in Youth

The SAVRY appears to be modeled after the adult risk assessment measures such as the Historical Clinical Risk Management-20, Version 3 (Douglas, Hart, Webster, & Belfrage, 2013). The SAVRY focuses on violence risk and is based on the structured professional judgment model. Its 24 risk-related items are divided into three categories: historical, individual, and social/contextual. The measure also has six protective items. The risk items are rated based on a three-level coding structure (high, moderate, low), and the protective items have a simple two-level coding structure, with the protective factor being denoted as either present or absent. The manual provides coding guidelines for each level. Research conducted to date has shown positive correlations between SAVRY scores and other measures of violence in juvenile justice and high-risk community-dwelling populations (e.g., Borum et al., 2005; Catchpole & Gretton, 2003; Spice, Viljoen, Gretton, & Roesch, 2010). Like many juvenile tools, much less research has been conducted with adolescent girls (Borum et al., 2005). Areas covered by the SAVRY are listed in Exhibit 6.1.

The SAVRY, like the RSTI and the YLS/CMI, includes dynamic risk factors. Recent research has indicated that these changeable factors are significant in assessing risk because the inclusion of dynamic factors allows for the ongoing assessment of the effectiveness of treatment (Douglas & Skeem, 2005). Change-sensitive measures are very much needed in juvenile evaluations. In addition, the SAVRY addresses protective factors, such as strong

EXHIBIT 6.1
Areas Covered by the Structured Assessment of Violence Risk in Youth

Historical Risk Factors
- History of violence
- History of nonviolent offending
- Early initiation of violence
- Past supervision/intervention failures
- History of self-harm or suicide attempts
- Exposure to violence in the home
- Childhood history of maltreatment
- Parental/caregiver criminality
- Early caregiver disruption
- Poor school achievement

Social/Contextual Risk Factors
- Peer delinquency
- Peer rejection
- Stress and poor coping
- Poor parental management
- Lack of personal/social support
- Community disorganization

Individual/Clinical Risk Factors
- Negative attitudes
- Risk taking/impulsivity
- Substance use difficulties
- Anger management problems
- Psychopathic traits
- Attention-deficit/hyperactivity difficulties
- Poor compliance
- Low interest/commitment to school

Protective Factors
- Prosocial involvement
- Strong social support
- Strong attachments and bonds
- Positive attitude toward intervention and authority
- Strong commitment to school
- Resilient personality traits

social support or a strong bond with a positive authority figure, although some of these items appear to be the opposite of the identified risk factors, which suggests some redundancy in SAVRY model. According to the developers of the SAVRY, situations are possible in which risk factors are moderated by the presence of protective factors and, as such, the protective factors can make a difference in outcome. However, moderation requires the addition of a new variable (or new variables) to examine its moderating role on the relation between two separate variables. Another potential drawback to the measure is the lack of a specific interview. Forensic clinicians may have considerable variability in their interview content, and this likely will affect the rating of items. Finally, the measure is specific to violence and does not include developmental maturity of treatment amenability or treatment need scales. For risk, however, the measure has shown reliability and validity in previous research studies and for that reason has promising psychometric properties (Catchpole & Gretton, 2003; Dolan & Rennie, 2008; Spice et al., 2010; Vincent, Chapman, & Cook, 2011).

Youth Level of Service/Case Management Inventory

The YLS/CMI is based on the Level of Service Inventory—Revised (Andrews & Bonta, 1995) and is designed to assess risk and need factors in youth ages 12 to 18 (Hoge & Andrews, 2002; Hoge, Andrews, & Leschied, 1995). It is also designed to assist in case planning and management. Part I of the YLS/CMI provides for the assessment of risks and needs. Similar to the adult form, it was designed as a checklist to be used by professionals following the collection of clinical information. This section consists of 42 items that are divided into eight subscales: (a) Prior/Current Offenses/Dispositions, (b) Family Circumstances/Parenting, (c) Education/Employment, (d) Peer Relations, (e) Substance Abuse, (f) Leisure/Recreation, (g) Personality/Behavior, and (h) Attitudes/Orientation. The items were selected by the authors to reflect the full range of factors identified in the literature as related to youth crime (Cottle, Lee, & Heilbrun, 2001; Hoge, 2002; Lipsey & Derzon, 1998; Loeber & Hay, 1997). An opportunity to indicate areas of strength relevant to each young person is also provided. Other parts of the YLS/CMI allow for recording information regarding additional considerations relevant to the case, the specification of goals of service, and the means for achieving those goals. A professional override feature is also built into the instrument.

The YLS/CMI is used to classify youth in order to inform judicial disposition decisions, placement into programs, institutional assignments, and release from custody. It has been shown in some studies to be a valid predictor of recidivism for both male and female juvenile offenders (Marczyk, Heilbrun, Lander, & DeMatteo, 2003; Olver, Stockdale, & Wong, 2012;

Rennie & Dolan, 2010; Schmidt, Hoge, & Gomes, 2005). A revised version, the YLS/CMI 2.0 (Hoge & Andrews, 2010), was released in 2010 using an updated sample that is demographically representative of the current juvenile justice population in terms of age, gender, and ethnicity. A few changes were made to some sections of the instrument; however, much of it remains the same as the earlier version. Both versions of the YLS/CMI are currently available for use. The YLS/CMI also contains items that are not used as part of the risk/needs score calculations but are included as additional information for case management planning and to inform security placement decisions as well as any decisions to override the risk score classification. The updated 2.0 version of the instrument contains several revisions to this section, including new questions on gang involvement, bullying, and pregnancy. The YLS/CMI domains and items are listed in Exhibit 6.2.

The YLS/CMI may be readministered periodically to evaluate changes in the young individual's domain scores. The earlier version of the instrument may be scored by hand or by using computer software. Online scoring for the updated YLS/CMI 2.0 is reported to be under development at its publisher, Multi-Health Systems in Toronto, Ontario, Canada. Two types of reports are available, the prescreen report and the full assessment report. The prescreen report provides a score that can be used to determine whether additional assessment is needed. Any factors the rater considers to be exceptional are rated as strengths, which may then be integrated into a case management plan or may influence the professional override and the contact or supervision level. Although the YLS/CMI has many strengths, one concern is the relatively short set of questions designed to provide information on the pertinent constructs, and the computer-generated reports would need to be augmented with clinical judgment.

Risk–Sophistication–Treatment Inventory

The RSTI is a semistructured interview and rating scale designed to assist clinicians in the assessment of juvenile offenders ages 9 to 18 across gender (Salekin, 2004; Zahn, Hawkins, Chiancone, & Whitworth, 2008). The RSTI measures risk, developmental maturity, and treatment amenability using three scales, each composed of 15 items. Items are rated on 3-point scales (0 = *absence of the characteristic/ability*, 1 = *subclinical/moderate*, and 2 = *presence of the characteristic/ability*) that reflect the extent to which the individual demonstrates the specific characteristic or ability. Each scale contains three subscales, referred to as *clusters*. The Risk scale is composed of Violent and Aggressive Tendencies, Planned and Extensive Criminality, and Psychopathic Features. The clusters of the Developmental Maturity (Sophistication) scale include Autonomy, Cognitive Capacities, and Emotional Skills. The

EXHIBIT 6.2
Domains Covered by the Youth Level of Service/Case Management Inventory

Prior and Current Offenses/Adjudications
- Three or more prior convictions
- Two or more failures to comply
- Prior probation
- Three or more current convictions

Family Circumstances and Parenting
- Inadequate supervision
- Difficulty controlling behavior
- Inappropriate discipline
- Inconsistent parenting
- Poor relations, father–youth
- Poor relations, mother–youth

Education and Employment
- Disruptive classroom behavior
- Disruptive behavior on school property
- Low achievement
- Problems with peers
- Problems with teachers
- Truancy
- Unemployment/not seeking employment

Peer Relations
- Some delinquent acquaintances
- Some delinquent friends
- No/few positive acquaintances
- No/few positive friends

Substance Abuse
- Occasional drug use
- Chronic drug use
- Substance abuse interferes with life
- Substance abuse linked to offense(s)

Leisure/Recreation
- Limited organized activities
- Could make better use of time
- No personal interests

Personality and Behavior
- Inflated self-esteem
- Physically aggressive
- Tantrums
- Short attention span
- Poor frustration tolerance

Attitudes and Orientation
- Antisocial/procriminal attitudes
- Not seeking help
- Actively rejecting help
- Defies authority
- Callous, little concern for others

Developmental Maturity scale is neither prosocial nor antisocial; instead, it taps developmental maturity broadly while allowing clinicians to then rate on a separate scale the extent to which the related emotional/cognitive skills are used for criminological purposes (Criminal Thinking Style). Finally, the Treatment Amenability clusters are Psychopathology Degree and Type, Responsibility and Motivation to Change, and Consideration and Tolerance of Others. The items for each RSTI scale and cluster are listed in Table 6.4.

Strengths of the RSTI include its incorporation of dynamic items and its comprehensiveness in terms of tapping chief juvenile constructs. Because of its inclusion of maturity and amenability items it has considerable range in terms of coverage. The RSTI can be administered multiple times if desired and has the capability to index change that can occur in a young person across treatment. The RSTI interview booklet contains questions that are designed to obtain background, clinical, and historical information, as well as a sample of the juvenile's behavioral and psychological functioning. Items on the rating form reflect information central to the three scales. Scoring of items involves reviewing and synthesizing information from an interview and collateral sources such as school, police, detention, and previous treatment records, as well as consultations with parents or guardians. Proper administration and coding of the RSTI requires professional knowledge and skill.

TABLE 6.4
Scales and Clusters of the Risk–Sophistication–Treatment Inventory

Scale	Clusters
Risk for Dangerous Behavior	Violent and Aggressive Tendencies • Engage in unprovoked violent behavior • Aggression toward animals • Aggression toward other individuals • Easily angered and physically aggressive • Generally oppositional and cruel Planned and Extensive Criminality • Severe antisocial behavior • Premeditated crimes • Leadership role in crimes • High frequency of past criminal acts • Early age of onset • Delinquent peer group Psychopathic Features • Lacks remorse or guilt • Lacks empathy • Egocentricity • Manipulative

(continues)

TABLE 6.4
Scales and Clusters of the Risk–Sophistication–Treatment
Inventory   *(Continued)*

Scale	Clusters
Developmental Maturity (sophistication)	**Autonomy** • Autonomy • Internal locus of control • Development of self-concept • Self-reflection **Cognitive Capacities** • Aware of wrongfulness of crime • Understanding of behavioral norms • Able to identify alternative actions • Foresight (prospection) • Cost-benefit analysis in decision making • Ability to anticipate consequences **Emotional Maturity** • Able to delay gratification • Moral development • Self-regulation of emotion • Conflict resolution skills • Interpersonal skills
Treatment Amenability	**Psychopathology Degree and Type** • Degree of psychopathology • Treatability of psychopathology • Aware of difficulties/problems • Insight into cause of problems • Limited police/court/probation involvement **Responsibility and Motivation to Change** • Motivated to engage in treatment • Takes responsibility for actions • Open to change • Expects to change • Positive parental involvement **Considerate and Tolerant of Others** • Anxiety • Feels guilt/remorse • Considers and generally cares about others • Has positive attachments (e.g., parent, grandparent)

Training with an experienced rater can be helpful for the first few administrations and scorings. The RSTI has been shown to have good psychometric properties (e.g., M. Jordan, 2008; Leistico & Salekin, 2003; Salekin, 2004; Salekin, Lee, Schrum-Dillard, & Kubak, 2010; Salekin, Tippey, & Allen, 2012; Spice et al., 2010; Zalot, 2002a, 2002b). For instance, Spice et al. (2010) found that the RSTI performed well in differentiating youth who were waived to adult court from those who remained in juvenile courts in Canada. This has also been found in U.S. samples (Leistico & Salekin, 2003; Zalot, 2002a, 2002b). The RSTI and the SAVRY risk scales are highly correlated ($r = .79$; Spice et al., 2010).

Two shorter versions of the RSTI, an abbreviated clinical interview and a self-report scale are being empirically tested to determine their psychometric properties (Ang, Salekin, Sellbom, & Lee, 2014; Gillen, MacDougall, Forth, & Salekin, 2014; Salekin, 2014; Salekin, Tippey, & Allen, 2012). The abbreviated version has a shorter interview but retains chief questions central to rating the individual items. Thus far the psychometric properties appear promising in that the abbreviated interview and measure have shown internal consistency and convergent–discriminant validity (Gillen et al., 2014). The self-report version of the RSTI has shown both reliability and validity and appears to be a change-sensitive test in treatment studies (see Ang et al., 2014; Salekin, Lester, & Sellers, 2012; Salekin, Tippey, & Allen, 2012). Nonetheless, the RSTI also has shortcomings in that the original interview is lengthy and the Sophistication Maturity scale, although it has adequate reliability, is relatively lower on that construct than the Risk, Developmental Maturity, and Treatment Amenability scales.

There has been some discussion as to whether risk, developmental maturity, and treatment amenability are psychological concepts, psycholegal concepts, or legal concepts (Mulvey & Iselin, 2008; Page & Scalora, 2004; Penney & Moretti, 2005; Slobogin, 1999). Psychologists and allied mental health professionals typically view these concepts as psychological. However, they become psycholegal concepts insofar as they pertain to the court's decision-making process regarding disposition, commitment, or transfer. Another area within which the concepts become psycholegal is how judges decide to balance the concepts along with other information when they decide on disposition or waiver. For example, with respect to commitment or transfer, public safety may be seen as more important than amenability. Thus, categorical decisions regarding when a young person is going to be deemed higher risk is the legal aspect of the psychological construct and therefore makes the construct psycholegal. Another example is treatment amenability: The concept is psychological, but when the timeline is added in (i.e., whether the young person can be treated effectively in the time available within the juvenile justice system), it becomes psycholegal.

TEST BATTERIES FOR JUVENILE OFFENDERS: A BRIEF SUMMARY

Forensic assessments should incorporate a battery of measures that include standard intelligence testing, achievement testing, child and adolescent psychopathology measures, psycholegal construct measures, and strengths-based measures. The tools I have recommended in this chapter are useful because they help inform the evaluation and allow for systematic follow-up on treatment compliance, recidivism, and other outcome indicators (Salekin, Tippey, & Allen, 2012). No one measure should be used when comprehensive juvenile evaluations are requested. Another important point is that the risk, developmental maturity, and amenability information may need to be collected for two time points, as previously mentioned. This is especially true if the evaluation is requested after the youth has been in custody for some time. Although current estimates of risk and amenability are often used, the courts may want to know the young person's level of maturity at the time of the alleged offense. The only way to make this assessment is retrospectively via the clinical interview and rating scales and the gathering of information from the family from the specified time frame using the RSTI Developmental Maturity scale.

How Else Can Forensic Clinicians Bolster Assessments of the Psycholegal Constructs?

Up to this point in the chapter I have covered cognitive measures, broad-based psychopathology and personality instruments, and specific juvenile offender measures (i.e., SAVRY, YLS/CMI, RSTI) that are helpful in the evaluation process. Forensic clinicians may ask themselves, "How do other measures, like IQ tests and perhaps even projective tests, fit into the assessment battery, and can they be helpful in understanding risk, developmental maturity and amenability to treatment?" The answer to the latter part of the question is, yes, intelligence measures and projective measures can inform the psycholegal constructs if clinicians understand how to administer, score, and integrate the information. Moreover, although the above-mentioned juvenile measures (SAVRY, YLS/CMI, RSTI) are specific to juvenile psycholegal constructs, forensic clinicians should look for ways in which other measures can inform the juvenile offender evaluation and the psycholegal constructs. Further integration of psychological material can be accomplished by determining how test information might bolster measurement of constructs such as risk, developmental maturity, and treatment amenability. Covered in the next couple of sections are measures that might, for example, further help with the assessment of developmental maturity. These measures should not be used in isolation, of course, but instead to supplement specific juvenile measures because they may well add to the overall evaluation.

Further Information on Developmental Maturity

Because there are few measures designed for assessing maturity and, before 2004, there were no specific interview-based measures for this construct, researchers pointed to ways in which clinicians could gather data on this construct in youth (Salekin, 2002a, 2002b, 2004). Ewing (1990) recommended that juveniles evaluated for transfer be administered an intelligence test (e.g., the Wechsler Intelligence Scale for Children—Fourth Edition) and achievement test (e.g., the Wide Range Achievement Test 4). Ewing argued that such measures evaluate not only a young person's general intellect but also factors such as "perception, cognitive processing, attention, and judgment[,] all of which can be reflective of a young person's sophistication–maturity . . . [and the individual's] level of criminal responsibility" (p. 8). Similarly, he argued that the rationale for using achievement testing is based on the notion that many juvenile delinquents have co-occurring LDs that may negatively affect academic performance and contribute to their lack of age-appropriate maturity. Ewing recommended that a juvenile's level of emotional maturity also be examined through interviewing and psychological testing, which is consistent with best practice. With respect to psychological testing techniques, Ewing suggested that self-report measures (e.g., the Millon Adolescent Clinical Inventory; Millon, 1993) and projective techniques (e.g., the Thematic Apperception Test [TAT]; Murray, [1937] and the Rorschach inkblots [Rorschach, 1921/1951]) may be used to provide "indications of the juvenile's internal controls, ability to organize thoughts coherently, and reality testing" (p. 9). Ewing's point here is well taken in that youth who can organize and produce a coherent list of responses from ambiguous stimuli demonstrate an ability to structure very unstructured stimuli, which displays cognitive flexibility and thus a higher level of cognition and problem-solving ability. Despite some links to maturity, there is room for error with use of this assessment methodology because some of the scoring systems are overly complicated and can be somewhat negative in the interpretation of responses. Also, although one can certainly see Ewing's rationale for using the Rorschach, there are likely more efficient and perhaps more precise ways to tap developmental maturity. Nonetheless, this method could be used if clinicians had expertise in Rorschach interpretation, especially regarding cognitive and emotional skills.

It is possible that forensic clinicians could glean information on maturity from other projective techniques, such as the TAT or one of its variants, the Children's Apperception Test or other maturity tests (Adams, Bennion,

& Huh, 1989; Archer & Waterman, 1993; Bergh & Erling, 2005; Jones, Akers, & White, 1994). But one would need specialized knowledge on administering and interpreting the TAT. Westen et al. (1991; see also Conklin & Westen, 2001; Leigh, Westen, Barends, Mendel, & Byers, 1992) provided a method for scoring the TAT that outlines social cognition and object-relation variables that are likely linked to the concept of developmental maturity and consequently risk and amenability (R. Steinberg, 2008; Westen et al., 1991). These four rating categories and scales are (a) complexity of representations of people, (b) affect–tone or relationship paradigms, (c) capacity for emotional investment, and (d) understanding of social causality. These areas are rated on a level-based system from 1 to 5, with 5 representing greater maturity (see also Barends, Westen, Leigh, Silbert, & Byers, 1990). According to Westen and colleagues, these scales measure the extent to which a young person shows mature relations with others by understanding the complexity of relationships. In addition, the scales tap the extent to which individuals show an understanding of causality in relations as well as a capacity for emotional investment. The Westen system is likely useful for assessing developmental maturity in young people because it provides key information on internal representations, relationships, and social causality. However, forensic clinicians would need to be well trained on the TAT to effectively use the measure. Moreover, the scales would need to be augmented with other tests (e.g., the RSTI) because there also needs to be real-world indications that maturity is present.

Self-report measures may facilitate the assessment of developmental maturity. Clinicians can examine broad-band self-report indexes for relevant scales and use those scales to facilitate their determinations of developmental maturity. For instance, the Attention, Leadership, Adaptability, and Social Skills scales of the Behavioral Assessment System for Children, Second Edition, are relevant to developmental maturity (Reynolds & Kamphaus, 2004). Information from the general model of personality might also be used. As previously mentioned, measures of Conscientiousness and Agreeableness may add meaningfully to the clinical picture of developmental maturity. Finally, there are a number of self-report measures that might be used to inform the evaluation, including the Psychosocial Maturity Inventory (Greenberger, Josselson, Knerr, & Knerr, 1975), the Weinberger Adjustment Inventory (Weinberger & Schwartz, 1990), the Consideration of Future Consequences Scale (Strathman, Gleicher, Boninger, & Edwards, 1994), the Stanford Time Perspective Inventory (Zimbardo & Boyd, 1999), and the Criminal Decision Making Questionnaire (Fried & Reppucci, 2001; J. H. Goldberg, 2007). However, the measures tap different aspects of maturity, and most of them have primarily served as research tools (Hawes, Mulvey, Schubert, & Pardini, 2014). Nevertheless, once researchers begin to examine the measures in clinical settings, they might be found to be useful and further bolster developmental maturity assessments in clinical practice.

Further Information on Treatment Amenability

Currently, there are few tools for the assessment of treatment amenability. However, some assessment technology does exist on related concepts. Several amenability measures have been designed for adult populations, including the Treatment Motivation Questionnaire (Ryan, Plant, & O'Malley, 1995), the University of Rhode Island Change Assessment Scale (originally titled the Stages of Change Questionnaire; McConnaughy, Prochaska, & Velicer, 1983), the Treatment Readiness Questionnaire (Casey, Day, Howells, & Ward, 2007), and the Quality of Motivation Questionnaire (Martin, 1989). Most of these measures show support for their predictive merit (Treatment Motivation Questionnaire, University of Rhode Island Change Assessment Scale [Field, Adinoff, Harris, Ball, & Carroll, 2009], Treatment Readiness Questionnaire), but none have been adequately studied in juvenile offender samples (LeGrand & Martin, 2001), and some of these measures capture only aspects of treatment amenability (e.g., motivation). Nonetheless, these assessment tools could be used to supplement more comprehensive treatment amenability scales once they receive further validation. With regard to self-report measures, the Personality Assessment Inventory—Adolescent Version Treatment Rejection scale may be useful in comparison with RSTI results and other clinical information. In addition, the personality variables from the general personality measures can facilitate in the assessment of treatment amenability. Specifically, high scores on measures of Openness, Agreeableness, and Conscientiousness may suggest smoother interactions and quicker treatment gains in psychological therapy.

DATA COLLECTION REQUIRES DATA MANAGEMENT: HANDLING EXTENSIVE FILES

The nature of forensic work with young people is such that there are extensive interview notes, test protocols, materials, records, and research articles involved in the evaluation. This amount of information requires organization and logical awareness on the part of the mental health professional. As a first step, interviews, protocols, and records should be logged as they are completed and received. Forensic adolescent mental health professionals may then take varying approaches to organizing, filing, and digesting the information from test interviews, test protocols, and records. Some may find it useful to create summaries of the information on interviews, tests, and records with tables. Others may highlight and tag with Post-Its certain parts of the records they feel they may need close at hand. Whatever the mechanism, clinicians should keep in mind that the report and testimony based on these interviews notes, protocols, and records may occur downstream from when they are first obtained and reviewed. This calls for procedures that allow for the storage of the data in a single file or files that are in proximity to one another and ones that can be easily accessed. This can come in the form of electronic archiving of psychological reports, protocols, and notes, as hard copies stored in locked file cabinet drawers, or both. The point is that after the data are collected they will require safe storage.

CONCLUDING COMMENTS

In this chapter, I reviewed the important topic of data collection. I covered the importance of establishing rapport with young people and their families, which allows for the collection of accurate and comprehensive information. I then discussed the significance of intelligence and achievement testing, clinical interviews, structured interviews, self-reports, and measures of general personality before addressing specific juvenile measures such as the SAVRY, YLS/CMI, and RSTI. I pointed out that assessment of some concepts might be needed at two time points: (a) the time of the offense and (b) the present time when the assessment is being conducted. Finally, I provided an overview of the ways clinicians can augment assessments of developmental maturity and treatment amenability before offering a few additional words on the storage of the data gathered in the assessment of juvenile offenders. In the next chapter, I discuss the highly important topic of interpretation of forensic material gathered during the evaluation.

7

INTERPRETATION FOR JUVENILE EVALUATIONS

Interpretation in juvenile offender evaluations is based on multiple sources of information and science. This standard is the same whether the referral question is an exhaustive exploration of the young person's development and life history; a specialized assessment of a special issue, such as developmental maturity; or an evaluation of the risk a young person may pose to the community. In conducting an evaluation, a forensic clinician interprets the data on his or her desk, which have been gleaned from a multitude of sources, and arrives at a judgment of the young individual on the constructs delineated in Chapter 3 (i.e., risk for dangerous behavior, developmental maturity, and amenability to treatment). The clinician then types a high-quality report, prints it, and delivers it to the attorney and/or the judge. Information might also be conveyed through testimony, if requested by the judge or an attorney. In this chapter, I focus on best practices regarding the interpretation of a young person's assessment data.

http://dx.doi.org/10.1037/14595-008
Forensic Evaluation and Treatment of Juveniles: Innovation and Best Practice, by R. T. Salekin

Throughout this book, I have put forth a general model for the assessment of young people who come into contact with the law. Recall that this entails assessing the truthfulness/accuracy of reporting and personality/pathology as well as the young person's level of risk, developmental maturity, and treatment amenability/treatment needs. From this, as well as information on the young person's hopes and aspirations, and any information from strengths-based measures, the forensic clinician develops a set of detailed recommendations that includes a treatment plan. Regardless of whether forensic clinicians use the structure just described or some other structure, they should have a clear assessment model and theoretical framework in mind for describing the young person.

As I discussed in Chapter 6, the field of psychology provides a number of useful theories and typologies for delinquent youth on which clinicians can draw. These theories and typologies have been based on a considerable body of research (e.g., Achenbach, 1991a, 1991b; Jesness & Wedge, 1984, 1985; Loeber, 1991; Moffitt, 2003, 2007; Quay, 1987; Witt, 2003). Many of these theoretical models can be united and conceptualized together because they interlink with personality and pathology models as well as contemporary research on risk for dangerous behavior, developmental maturity, and amenability to treatment. Moreover, connecting these earlier typologies into a modern model can be helpful, given that the majority of these earlier theories (e.g., on "undersocialized aggressive" youth; Quay, 1966, 1987) are infrequently discussed in mental health fields and modern courts. This is because considerable research has been generated since they were originally introduced to the field and they are often now incorporated into broader conceptual models (e.g., conduct disorder [CD] in the *Diagnostic and Statistical Manual of Mental Disorders* [5th ed., *DSM–5*]; American Psychiatric Association, 2013). Providing integration for the courts to explain and connect the various typologies to newer classification systems is advantageous because this helps the courts understand psychological phenomena and psycholegal constructs in a contemporary model. Such integration provides the court with the pertinent court-related information that Niarhos and Routh (1992) and Hecker and Steinberg (2002) have suggested is needed in juvenile disposition evaluations.

Interpretation of the data entails describing the youth but may also involve delineating those situations in which a specific level of security is needed as well as what situations might prove to be a cause for concern. Specifically, when making management decisions, as well as determining when more specific mental health treatment is needed, it may be important to consider the types of situations that provoke antisocial actions in young people. In my own experience with juvenile offenders, the child's developmental history is, in many respects, the royal road toward obtaining some of the key information for interpretation of the data one has gathered about the child and his or her family.

DEVELOPMENTAL HISTORY

With respect to the youth's developmental history, clinicians using best practice in this area work much like an enthusiastic detective. The developmental history should be complete and include the records I mentioned in Chapters 4, 5, and 6 (e.g., interviews, formal cognitive assessment). To elaborate on this point, evaluators might consider using the family history to provide particular psychological material on the young person's prenatal risk, which can be judged on the basis of such influences as low socioeconomic status, maternal psychopathology, maternal substance use, single parenting, very young motherhood, and marital conflict. As research has shown, these factors may lead to a more fearless temperament in a toddler, which in turn may elicit a harsher parenting style; this is referred to as a *bidirectional effect*, whereby the child's temperament worsens parenting practices and the harsh parenting correspondingly worsens the child's temperament (Barker & Salekin, 2012; Burke, Pardini, & Loeber, 2008; Childs, Fite, Moore, Lochman, & Pardini, 2014; Jaffee, Caspi, Moffitt, Belsky, & Silva, 2001; Pardini, Fite, & Burke, 2008; Pardini, Lochman, & Powell, 2007; Patterson, 1976). Clearly, this is important information of which to be cognizant when gauging risk, making treatment recommendations, and identifying future interventions. Data on other important factors, such as how the young person was raised, the broader family functioning (e.g., relationship with siblings), school performance and involvement with peers, and contact with the legal system, are all very important to gather and interpret. These variables all have implications for interpretation and treatment recommendations. The ability to articulate the young person's life history as accurately as possible in a chronological and intelligible fashion is key to a high-quality interpretation. In the sections that follow, I discuss how clinicians can reconcile discrepancies in the data they have gathered so they can produce reports that are accurate.

TRADITIONAL INTERVIEWS: DEVELOPMENTAL LIFE HISTORY

A difficult aspect of the evaluation is the process of synthesizing the information and making sense of inconsistent data. One potential solution to this problem involves obtaining a thorough developmental history and gathering data from further sources of information. After the initial set of interviews and testing are completed, if the information is still unclear it is best practice to conduct a second and potentially third round of in-person or telephone interviews with individuals who have provided contrasting information. Interviewing might involve direct questions, such as asking individuals specifically about discrepancies. This process should be repeated until an accurate and increasingly coherent life story is obtained.

Multiple sources are needed to power this accurate interpretation. Interpretation based on the young person's account alone will lead to only partially precise life history information. Sometimes the information can be wholly imprecise. This inaccuracy negatively affects interpretation of the report.

STRUCTURED INTERVIEWS: PERSONALITY AND PATHOLOGY TESTING

Personality and pathology testing will require various levels of interpretation. For instance, one may observe elevations on structured interviews. These elevations may vary across disorders (e.g., CD, oppositional defiant disorder [ODD], attention-deficit/hyperactivity disorder [ADHD]) and sources (e.g., mother, father, youth report). Scoring programs for structured interviews provide a list of disorders that are most salient. This is usually determined by the frequency and severity of symptoms. Scoring programs also usually provide information about the onset and offset of symptoms that can facilitate interpretation. Life course detail, symptom severity, the family's history of mental illness, and the age at which a disorder may have started in family members also yield data that can help indicate whether a young person ever fully had a given diagnosis (e.g., CD or major depression). Each of these key pieces of clinical information can help clinicians dial in on the young person's psychological disorder, its onset, and its course of development, providing a nicely charted mental health history.

If computer-assisted charts are not provided for a given assessment instrument, mental health professionals may consider developing a table with pen-and-paper that delineates timelines for the onset and potential offset of symptoms and disorders as well as mark the severity of symptoms and disorders. In terms of arriving at a preliminary diagnosis, clinicians can use an *either–or strategy* or a *convergence strategy*. The either–or strategy requires that if either the parent or the youth reports symptoms that rise to the level of a diagnosis, the clinician may then consider the disorder to be present. Alternatively, with the convergence strategy, both the child and the adult would have to endorse the symptoms to some threshold level (e.g., five symptoms) to yield the conclusion that a particular condition is present. The symptoms need not be identical across raters because each reporter may see a different pattern of symptoms of the same disorder.

Once such a table has been developed, the clinician can start to examine the summarized information in context. Best practice in this area suggests that clinical judgment will be needed and that a diagnosis will be based on the onset, offset, and severity of symptoms. Unfortunately, there are no simple solutions to discrepancies across tests and reporters. For instance, a parent might rate the young person as having CD or ODD, but the young person does not endorse these same symptoms. Instead, he or she rates the symptoms of CD and ODD as absent or low in severity and may view his or her parents as oppositional. An in-depth level of investigation will be needed to make the final decision. Some symptoms, such as fighting at school, are difficult to dispute and can help forensic clinicians gain traction as to the accuracy of various reports regarding behavior problems. This is where record reviews can be incredibly helpful. For instance, if the young person states that he or she has not had behavioral problems in the past, but the records show a number of in-school and out-of-school suspensions or problems as well as previous contact with the law, then this information could factor into clinical ratings that may pertain to diagnoses of ODD or CD. However, forensic clinicians should make an effort to understand the motivation behind the problems at school (e.g., proactive aggression or self-defense in the context of being bullied).

SELF-REPORT MEASURES

Personality assessments based on self-report (e.g., the Behavioral Assessment System for Children, Second Edition [Reynolds & Kamphaus, 2004], the Millon Adolescent Clinical Inventory [MACI; Millon, 1993]) add another layer to the interpretation. If all test scores converge with the data gleaned from the types of interviews just discussed, the interpretation will be straightforward, but this sort of convergence is not always clearly evident. Often, there will be at least some discrepancies across self-report tests and interviews. A good place to start when examining multiscale self-report inventories is with an examination of the validity scales. This is because under- or overreporting can occur in some instances. If this is the case, forensic clinicians may consider the test results invalid or interpret them cautiously, placing less weight on their results. However, one has to be prudent because on occasion genuine pathology can lead to elevations on validity scales. The key is to examine test results in conjunction with interviews and other psychological information to make sense of the elevations and determine whether they are consistent with all other information gathered. Here again, one way to sort out discrepancies is to ask additional questions. For example, if a youth endorsed items of CD on the self-report but did not do so in the interviews, it might be that he or she felt more comfortable disclosing this information on the self-report but not during the face-to-face interview. Asking youth, or third parties, about discrepancies is solid practice for reducing incongruities so that one can more accurately understand the reasons for any differences, which will aid in interpretation and, thus, the final report. Similarly, youth may endorse depression items and even suicidal ideation items on self-reports when this information was not elucidated during either clinical or structured interviews. Forensic clinicians who notice such a discrepancy should ask about these endorsed critical items. Follow-up interviews regarding symptoms of depression also would be warranted. Reports from school and other third party sources as well as previous legal records might be used to further interpret inconsistencies.

GENERAL PERSONALITY ASSESSMENT

General personality assessment should be relatively straightforward and can be accomplished through an instrument such as the Interpersonal Adjective Scale Revised—Big 5 version (Trapnell & Wiggins, 1990; Wiggins, Trapnell, & Phillips, 1988; Wiggins & Trobst, 2002) or another broad-spectrum general personality measure (Caspi & Shiner, 2006; Shiner, 2006). General personality measures are relatively easy to interpret and can be administered to parents to obtain multisource personality information. Discrepancies can be handled in much the same way as previously mentioned. In terms of interpretation, personality indexes can be considered on their own or, more likely, integrated into the overall evaluation. Determining how scores map onto the *DSM–5* diagnoses should be straightforward. For example, ADHD and CD symptoms overlap with Extraversion, low Conscientiousness, and low Agreeableness. More specific *DSM–5* diagnoses can also be explained by the personality models, should the forensic clinician desire this. However, clinicians who make *DSM* diagnoses should obtain and interpret *DSM* structured interview information.

MECHANICS OF TEST EVALUATION AND COMPUTER-BASED INTERPRETATION

At this point in the chapter it would be beneficial to look even deeper into two specific issues regarding interpretation: (a) the mechanics behind test elevations and (b) computer-generated interpretation. With respect to the former, one might ask, "Why are certain scores considered elevated?" or "What goes into scale elevation calculations?" Other important questions are, "Can I trust the information I have obtained to be meaningful in terms of 'clinically significant' elevations?" and "How can I determine the accuracy of any predictions or conclusions drawn from test elevations?"

With respect to computer-generated interpretations, similar questions, such as, "How does the computer program generate its interpretation of my client?" might be asked. This seems like the one moment when a forensic clinician should be able to ease up, at least a little, after the considerable amount of work that went into the preparation for the evaluation, and data collection. Picture a forensic clinician sitting at a computer in his or her office, waiting for the interpretative summary statement to churn out of the printer and provide all the magic of a computer-generated interpretation and the clarification of the ins and outs of a given young person's character. Anyone who has used computer-based testing for the first time knows that this moment can feel very promising as one prepares to receive all the answers one has been awaiting, especially given that these answers will of course make life a little easier by providing a very nice shortcut to writing the report and providing information to the courts.

Unfortunately, computer-generated assessment results are, at least to date, never quite that simple in the world of interpretation of human behavior. Also, although forensic clinicians can and often do use computer-based scoring, as I emphasize in this chapter, knowing how the interpretative information is derived is crucial to accurately assessing the data and writing the report. In sum, knowing something about both (a) the basic mechanics of test scores and evaluations and (b) computer-generated interpretations is necessary so that one can interpret test data and clinical information with greater precision and competency. In the next section, I provide information to help clinicians understand test elevations and then move on to the related topic of computer-driven interpretation.

INTERPRETING TEST ELEVATIONS

Many psychological measures have a marker for each scale to designate the score as "elevated." In many cases the chosen elevation scale score is the same for each scale (e.g., scale T-score ≥ 65). It is the elevated scales that provide the forensic clinician with the descriptive information for the young person. Quantitative scores of these characteristics are expressed relative to a point on an underlying continuum. These quantitative test scores can fall into one of two categories, depending on how they were arrived at: (a) *criterion-referenced scores* or (b) *normative-referenced scores*. Criterion-referenced scores express results relative to behavioral or performance markers. For example, a young person exhibiting six out of 10 symptoms of CD would receive a score of 60%. Normative-referenced scoring is based on a comparison of a young person's score with aggregate scores from a sample of young individuals. Standardized individual intelligence tests illustrate the procedure well. Raw scores on a particular measure are interpreted with reference to a normative sample, such that, for example, a score on the Wechsler Intelligence Scale for Children—Fourth Edition (Wechsler, 2004) of 100 means that the young person's raw score matched that of the average of the comparison normative sample generally normed across the United States and Canada. A variety of procedures for calculating normative-referenced scores are available.

NORMAL CURVE OF INTELLIGENCE

Most standardized personality and rating/checklist behavioral measures utilize normative referenced scoring. For example, scores on the Risk–Sophistication–Treatment Inventory (RSTI; Salekin, 2004) and the Child Behavior Checklist (Achenbach, 1991b) can be expressed as T-scores calculated with reference to a normative sample, and these T-scores are available across gender. To illustrate, a T-score of 60 on one of the scales would indicate that the young person's score fell at 1 standard deviation above the mean relative to the standardization sample. The MACI uses prevalence rates of a disorder or condition as well as base rate scores, to determine how rare the condition is. Put another way, these scores inform clinicians of how elevated a score is in comparison to a standardization group. Although a bit more complicated, base rate scores are also informative benchmarks.

In many cases, descriptions are also qualitative in nature. For example, an individual can be described as gifted, having an autism spectrum disorder, explosive disorder, bipolar II disorder, ODD, or generalized anxiety disorder after exhibiting a high score on a relevant scale. As another example, an individual can be characterized in terms of the relative amount of intelligence displayed; degree of maturity; degree of ADHD, CD, and/or ODD; or probability of having difficulties in school. Descriptions or diagnoses yielded by clinical or structured interviews and self-reports are typically both quantitative and qualitative. Qualitative descriptions are often useful for summarizing and conveying information regarding young people at the time they take the test.

Diagnosing a young person with CD or ADHD provides information regarding his or her behavioral characteristics and can help guide treatment efforts. However, there are risks to this, especially if the formulas are too simple and/or if, as mentioned earlier, clinicians do not consider why a particular scale is elevated. For instance, if a test developer decides that one item (inattention while writing essays) is the primary marker (the *sine qua non*) for ADHD and categorizes youth on the basis of this single symptom, then use of that particular instrument likely would be hazardous because it would produce too many false positives. A great deal of caution is needed in interpreting test scores and understanding what constitutes an elevation. Another concern in interpretation relates to the use of computer-based scoring. I discuss this topic in greater detail next, given that computer-generated interpretations will likely increase in the future.

COMPUTER-BASED SCORING AND INTERPRETATION

Computer software has been used for some time in the calculation of raw scores to scale scores. There are now computer programs available for scoring structured interviews, self-report inventories, rating scales, checklists, projective measures, and so forth. For example, there are scoring programs for the Diagnostic Interview for Children (Columbia DISC Development Group, 1999; National Institute of Mental Health, 1991), Child Behavior Checklist, MACI, and Minnesota Multiphasic Personality Inventory— Adolescent Version (MMPI–A; Butcher et al., 1992). There are also scoring programs for the Conners 3 (Conners, 2008) and the Rorschach (Rorschach, 1921/1951). These scoring programs have the advantage of eliminating the cumbersome and potentially mind-numbing clerical work often involved in the tabulation of scale scores of psychological instruments. Computers can also eliminate human error and improve scoring accuracy. Despite many positive aspects of computer-entered and -scored data, there do exist some issues regarding their interpretation that require discussion.

A variety of computer programs now produce not only scores from the measure but also an interpretation of the scores. With some computer programs, this involves providing an assessment or diagnosis as well as treatment and programming recommendations, such as what should be done about the young person's problem. Perhaps one of the earliest efforts to develop a computer-based test interpretation was in connection with the original MMPI (Hathaway & McKinley, 1943) in the early 1960s. The MMPI computer scoring initiative led to similar efforts with other standardized measures of personality and pathology, such as the MACI, as well as computer scoring and interpretive efforts for tests of intelligence and achievement. Although few of the risk assessment measures specifically geared toward juveniles provide computer-based scoring and interpretation, some of the personality tests and behavioral checklist/rating measures I mentioned in Chapter 6 do offer such software.

The primary criticism regarding computer-based interpretations relates to the lack of validated information to accompany them (see the American Psychological Association's, 2010, "Ethical Principles of Psychologists and Code of Conduct"; Garb, 2000; Matarazzo, 1992). Although psychometric information may be available for the assessment tools themselves, this is typically not the case for the interpretations that are offered. This problem is complicated further by the fact that the interpretations are often made available to individuals who do not have the training and knowledge to utilize them effectively. Obviously, there are ethical issues associated with this practice as well (see American Educational Research Association, American Psychological Association, & National Council on Measurement in Education, 1999, in press; American Psychological Association, 1986). Therefore, best practice for the evaluation of young people involved with the legal system requires that interpretation involve a more hands-on, systematic evaluation of the data, using multiple sources of information. If forensic clinicians do use computer-based interpretations, then they should, as mentioned, understand the formula or algorithm used to arrive at the diagnosis or descriptive statement. They should also be able to explain the interpretation in court.

The aforementioned statements are not meant to undermine the use of computer technology. Computers have had a significant impact on the assessment process, and their influence will likely grow as improvements are made in regard to interpretation of the findings and interpretive statements. My colleagues and I recently outlined how the availability of smartphones and other daily rating devices (e.g., daily diaries) will, we hope, allow for further advances in the assessment and treatment fields (Salekin, Jarrett, & Adams, 2013). However, until the reliability and validity of such technology are well established, heavy use of computer-based programs for fast and simple solutions to typically very complex psychological problems is not responsible practice. Moreover, overreliance on computer-based interpretations will yield conclusions that are unlikely to stand alone, a problem that may arise if one is questioned by another expert on the rationale for one's conclusions. Nonetheless, computer-based tools have significant potential to eventually help with assessment and the treatment and monitoring of young people. Thus, when technological options are psychometrically ready, they might be introduced at the probation level and used in psychological evaluations, progress–outcome appraisals, and longer term tracking of progress in the community.

OVERALL INTERPRETATION OF PERSONALITY AND PATHOLOGY INFORMATION

After developing tables for each type of assessment (e.g., structured interview, self-report, general personality), if a clinician chooses to have done so, he or she might consider making one large, comprehensive interpretative chart or table. Physically writing out where elevations occur across measures and raters is one method of interpreting the wide array of information.

Alternatively, clinicians can develop charts or figures on a computer to illustrate where elevations are present, when disorders started and stopped, as well as when disorders co-occurred. By using a master table that includes all elevations, they can also insert, by rater, clinical notes for each interview, self-report measure, rating scale, and personality measure. They can include in this table computer-based scoring and interpretation information while knowing how each scale elevation was arrived at. Such a method can be used to further consolidate and prune diagnoses that are not supported. This allows the forensic clinician to develop a clearer picture of the young person's most salient characteristics.

Clinicians can then use the either–or strategy, a convergence strategy, or some weighting strategy to arrive at initial decisions. Perhaps highlighting elevations that seem most relevant (the highest level of convergence) can serve as a means by which to distill information. A number of clinicians put more stock in clinical (developmental history) and structured interviews, with self-report and rating scales being considered but only in the context of the broader clinical interview information. For example, if a young person scores high on the Psychopathic Deviate scale of the MMPI, but most of the items endorsed are "lack of acceptance of authority," and the child's oppositionality was evident from the interviews, it would not be correct to conclude that this youth has a psychopathic deviate personality or character; instead, it would be better to focus on the oppositional characteristics that were endorsed in the interviews and self-report measures.

Although I have suggested a number of strategies for sorting through data, with forensic cases it might be best to start with a consensus approach rather than an either–or strategy and therefore to look for convergence across measures and raters. If one reporter is more accurate than another, the clinician should consider this information. For instance, if information given by one reporter (e.g., mother) checks out against formal records and generally appears more coherent and consistent than information given by another reporter (e.g., father) who is inconsistent and whose report does not align with a record review, then one has reasonable grounds to consider putting more stock in the report that appears to be more truthful. However, with this method a consensus should be considered first. In other words, use of single-source information should be done only if one has a very good reason to believe that the single source is not only accurate but also more correct than other sources. If a clinician decides to use one report over another, he or she will need to explain how the reasons for this decision were well thought out and be able to articulate these in a psychological report and testimony. In general, one can make a well-reasoned argument for this focus, if certain aspects of reporting suffer from reliability and validity concerns. A step-by-step problem-solving approach to clinical decision making is outlined in Table 7.1.

TABLE 7.1
Step-by-Step Process for Reaching Decisions on Personality/Pathology

Step	Tasks
1	• Document all clinically significant findings and noteworthy personality elevations. • Develop a table to examine elevations discovered in traditional and structured interviews. • Develop a table to examine the elevations discovered on self-report, parent report, teacher report, and any personality and/or rating scales. • Create a combined integrative table.
2	• Look for convergent findings across method and across sources.
3	• Try to explain any discrepancies: ▪ Look for different demands in various settings. ▪ Look for differing knowledge of the young person's behavior (e.g., father has been fairly absent and does not know the child as well as the mother does).
4	• Develop a profile and hierarchy of strengths and weaknesses.
5	• Go beyond the profile and prioritize by delineating which problems are primary and which are secondary and note whether one problem (diagnosis) may have caused the other.

INTERPRETATION OF PERTINENT JUVENILE JUSTICE CONSTRUCTS

The next step in interpreting information on young offenders should be to evaluate the young person's level of risk, developmental maturity, and treatment amenability. Although much of the interpretation is similar to what was just mentioned in the preceding paragraphs, there are a number of special issues to consider in the interpretation of juvenile-specific constructs. In the past, most decisions regarding juvenile constructs were made by unstructured clinical judgment (see Chapter 5, this volume). This method has been criticized, although, as Litwack (2002) noted, it is possible that unstructured clinical judgments could well be accurate and informative, even structured in their own way. Nonetheless, clinical structured judgments based on results from assessment tools likely reduce error across clinicians. Even with structured risk measures, two points of caution are needed. First, with structured measures there is variation in the level of information gathered, which can influence scoring and interpretation. Second, interpretation based on these measures requires that the clinician know what high scale scores signify. A brief discussion of construct and criterion validity in the context of the psycholegal constructs is provided below. Finally, interpretation of results requires knowledge of the measure's accuracy; this is referred to as the *hit and miss rate*. This topic also is covered below, with an eye toward better informing interpretation.

STRUCTURED ASSESSMENT INSTRUMENTS AND JUDGMENT

It is useful to employ the kind of structured assessment tools described in Chapter 6 (e.g., the RSTI, Structured Assessment of Violence Risk for Youth [SAVRY; Borum, Bartel, & Forth, 2005], and Youth Level of Service/Case Management Inventory [Hoge, 2005]) for the assessment of psycholegal constructs in young people. The strength of structured evaluations is their assessment of relevant and representative items and the comprehensiveness of the interview used to glean information to rate the items. Structured evaluations require the examiner to collect information about a young person in a guided manner and then produce a summary statement of relevant concepts (e.g., high risk, high developmental maturity, high level of need for treatment with signs of low amenability). This structured method differs from unstructured approaches (e.g., unguided interviews) in that the scoring of items is based on a guided interview, thereby increasing objectivity. Because the items tapping the constructs have been empirically shown to predict some outcome, using the structured approach provides a direct link between the evaluation and the science. The better the science is, in terms of the psychometrics of the assessment tool, the better forensic clinicians can link the science to the specific assessment findings.

Once the forensic clinician has arrived at opinions relevant to risk, developmental maturity, and amenability to treatment, he or she should be able to explain how such opinions were reached and what the science states to support his or her opinions. This entails showing what information from the evaluation was relevant and what logic was used to move from the data to the clinical opinion (Grisso & Schwartz, 2000). The RSTI is one structured method for evaluating juvenile offenders because it takes into consideration theories of developmental pathways for antisocial behavior and prototypical analyses results to arrive at decisions regarding risk for offending as well as measuring developmental maturity and treatment amenability. These theoretical underpinnings to the RSTI also incorporate theories of juvenile offenders developed and tested by Loeber (1991), Moffitt (1993, 2003), and Quay (1964), as well as the empirical work of others (e.g., DiCataldo & Grisso, 1995). The same holds true for the RSTI's evaluation of developmental maturity (L. Steinberg & Cauffman, 1996, 2000) and amenability (Garfield, 1994; Leuner, Caponiti, & Gould, 2012; Leuner, Glasper, & Gould, 2010; Leuner & Gould, 2010a; Leuner, Gould, & Shors, 2006; Rains, 2002; Roberts, Walton, & Viechtbauer, 2006).

Whether using a highly structured test with defined items and a well-designed interview or an instrument with less structure, clinicians should keep in mind that they both require interpretive judgments. The question is, how much information is needed to make such judgments? For instance, assessment of a construct such as self-reliance calls for judgment on the part of the examiner, who may or may not have asked adequate questions to rate it. Presumably, an interview that addresses the pertinent questions would help mental health professionals arrive at, and formulate, appropriate ratings and consequent opinions. Some tests incorporate broad constructs such psychopathy, which, according to the best science, requires a separate interview to rate the symptoms, such as the Hare Psychopathy Checklist: Youth Version (PCL-YV; Forth, Kosson, & Hare, 2003). This would add more time to what might seem like a relatively short risk assessment measure, but the information from the PCL-YV would make the scoring of psychopathy-related items more accurate.

The point here is that the final translation of the information into a summary statement depends on the subjective judgment of the examiner. Therefore, even though the field of forensic evaluation uses words like *actuarial* or *professional structured judgment*, such terminology should be used cautiously with the courts because it may falsely lead court personnel to believe that these rating systems are without error, which is not the case. In sum, clinicians should know that there exists a certain level of subjective judgment in all testing and, as the research indicates, more standardized procedures are better than simple unstructured assessments, but they still require a level of clinical judgment.

THE VALIDITY OF MEASURES AND INTERPRETATION: CONTENT, CONSTRUCT, AND PREDICTIVE VALIDITY

Valid assessment has an important influence on the interpretation of the results (Floyd & Widaman, 1995; Foster & Cone, 1995; Haynes, Richard, & Kubany, 1995). Three forms of validity discussed earlier have particular relevance with respect to interpretation (Anastasi, 1998). The first, *content validity*, refers to the actual content of a scale or the face validity of the items that make up a scale (e.g., do the items appear like they tap the target construct?). If the content is inaccurate, then other forms of validity (construct and predictive) will be compromised. The second, *construct validity* (e.g., factorial and convergent–discriminant validity), refers to the theoretical meaning of a measure. It can also be defined in terms of the accuracy and significance of the measure. Cronbach and Meehl (1955) cogently proposed the use of theory and a nomological net for examining construct validity. According to Cronbach and Meehl, concepts should be surrounded (correlated with) by other meaningful concepts. For example, if a person has a cold, then he or she should also report feeling less than top-notch and may also report coughing, sneezing, a congested nose, and perhaps a sore throat.

All these correlates help one to understand that the person does in fact have a cold, as well as what it means to have a cold. The third type of validity, *predictive validity*, refers to the ability to forecast future behavior. The person with a cold may have a foggy head, and therefore one can predict that he or she likely will think less clearly at work, perform less well at sports, sleep later in the morning, and may even call in sick to work. In the sections that follow, I discuss each of these forms of validity in greater detail.

Content Validity

Content validity can be established rationally or through empirical methodology. Prototypical analysis, as I previously mentioned, is one empirical method for establishing the core characteristics of a construct. Experts are asked for the most central characteristics of a construct (e.g., "What's the most prototypical color of purple?" "What is the most prototypical microphone for a singer?"). This helps clarify the construct because there are many different shades of purple and even different types of microphones, but the core ratings help identify the most typical purple or most typical microphone, for example. Establishing the accuracy of risk, developmental maturity, and treatment amenability scores can present a problem if the items are irrelevant and nonrepresentative. Prototypical analytic research has converged to suggest a relatively coherent set of items for each of the juvenile constructs (Salekin, 2004; Salekin, Rogers, & Ustad, 2001; Salekin, Yff, et al., 2002). Without such specification, one is back to the problem of arbitrary metrics mentioned earlier in Chapter 5. Clearly, this would negatively influence interpretation.

Construct Validity

The construct validity of pertinent juvenile offender concepts should be of paramount concern in interpreting the assessments. If convergent validity is evidenced, it helps signify that the measure is tapping the intended construct. It is not sufficient to simply categorize the young person as high or moderate in developmental maturity or indicate that he or she has a high probability of treatment success without also knowing that the test being used has construct validity. With respect to psychological reports and testimony, it is helpful for forensic clinicians to be prepared to provide construct validity information to the courts by way of explaining how such information leads to conclusions regarding the young person's risk, developmental maturity, and/ or amenability.

Procedures for evaluating one aspect of construct validity involve comparing scores from a risk measure, for example, with scores from an alternate measure of the same construct (i.e., risk). For example Spice, Viljoen, Gretton, and Roesch (2010) compared the RSTI and the SAVRY and found their risk scores to be highly related. In addition, the RSTI has been significantly correlated significantly with measures of emotional intelligence (the Emotional Quotient Inventory: Youth Version; Bar-On & Parker, 2000), measures of the five-factor model of personality (the Interpersonal Adjective Scale Revised—Big 5 version), and treatment outcome variables (Leistico & Salekin, 2003; Salekin, 2004). This form of validity has been evaluated for most of the broad-based risk instruments discussed in Chapter 6.

Predictive Validity

Predictive validity (or *criterion related validity*, which is also a form of construct validity) is the third form of validity of particular relevance to the interpretation of risk, maturity, and treatment amenability. The issue, in this case, pertains to the ability of scores from the measures to actually predict future outcomes such as risk to the community, mature decision making, or future treatment success. Evaluations of predictive validity are usually based on correlations between the predictor and the criterion variables. For example, the criterion validity of a treatment amenability test might be expressed as a correlation coefficient; specifically, the correlation coefficient can be presented as follows: $r = .36$, $p < .05$. The correlation coefficient (Pearson r) value of .36 provides clinicians with information regarding the strength of the association between a test score and the criterion, and the probability (p) value of $< .05$ indicates that there are fewer than five chances in 100 of obtaining an association of that magnitude by chance.

It is also important to know the percentage of variance accounted for by the predictor variable on the outcome. In the example just provided, the percentage of variance would be 13% ($0.36^2 = 13$). Therefore, 13% of the variance in the criterion is accounted for by the predictor variable. Although this may not seem like a large amount of the variance, it is considered moderate to large in psychological research (Hemphill, 2003). The correlation offers one method for determining the magnitude of the effect. Other estimates of effect include Cohen's d, which can be helpful if one has information on young reoffenders versus young nonreoffenders, or nonviolent versus violent offenders, and are comparing two groups on a scale such as the PCL-YV. It might be that in comparing, for example, violent and nonviolent young offenders, an effect size of $d = 0.5$ is discovered on PCL-YV scores, which is a modest effect. This d score shows that the young violent offender group scored one half a standard deviation higher than the nonviolent offender group on the PCL-YV. Forensic clinicians can use this information when they examine a single score on the PCL-YV to determine whether a given young

TABLE 7.2
Prediction Accuracy Matrix for a Developmental Maturity Scale

Test score	Truly mature	
	Yes	No
Yes (high score—test specifies as mature)	a (100)	b (20)
No (low score—test specifies as immature)	c (30)	d (100)

person is closer to the violent or nonviolent offender group mean score on the PCL-YV.

Another method of examining the accuracy of a psychological instrument is to examine the measure's predictive ability using a 2 × 2 contingency table. This can provide clinicians and the courts with even more direct information about the predictive value of scores from an assessment tool (see Table 7.2). Two types of correct decisions, or *hits*, can be seen: (a) true positives (positive prediction and positive outcome) and (b) true negatives (negative prediction and negative outcome). Two types of incorrect predictions, or *misses*, can also be seen: (a) false positives (incorrect prediction of a positive outcome) and (b) false negatives (incorrect prediction of a negative outcome). These hits and misses are frequently discussed in the psychiatry and psychological literatures in terms of *sensitivity*, *specificity*, *positive predictive power* (PPP), and *negative predictive power* (NPP). In Table 7.2, the letters a, b, c, and d are used to help describe these indices and their calculation. Sensitivity, for example, can be calculated by the following formula: $a/a + c$. Specificity can be calculated by the formula $d/b + d$, PPP can be calculated with the formula $a/a + b$, and NPP can be calculated by the formula $d/b + d$.

As can be seen, there will be cases when a young person scores high on a psychological test but does not actually have the characteristic measured by the test. With any test there will be hits and misses, and the goal is to maximize the hits and minimize the misses. Psychologists conducting forensic evaluations will want to know the sensitivity and specificity, PPP and NPP of a measure, if this information is available. From Table 7.2 one can see that if an individual scores high on the developmental maturity scale (i.e., the test indicates the young person is developmentally mature), it is likely that the individual is in fact mature; that is, of the 120 individuals who scored high on the test, 100 were truly mature (display mature judgment in the real world). This could also be referred to as an *83% success rate*. Clinicians who want to know about NPP would examine all the individuals who scored low on the test to determine the percentage of correctly classified individuals. According to Table 7.2, the NPP is 77%. This means that 77% of the individuals who scored low on the test were actually developmentally immature.

Similarly, sensitivity and specificity can be calculated with the formulas noted above. These estimates provide slightly different pieces of classification information based on whether or not the young person is truly mature. Analyzing contingency tables in this way can provide forensic clinicians with key information regarding the predictive accuracy of a measure. However, interpretation of the information is complicated by the fact that the values yielded are very sensitive to base rates and the cutoff scores used with the predictor (referred to as *selection ratio*). Most manuals should specify hit and miss rates based on a specific cutoff score chosen, because this assists with the interpretation.

Finally, most predictive validity information will be limited to a particular time interval and to particular situations. For example, with regard to the risk construct, some validation studies are based on the collection of reoffending data for a 2- to 3-year period following termination of the disposition. Forensic clinicians will need to be aware of these parameters when arriving at their opinions. Also, when possible, forensic clinicians should attempt to be specific about the outcome they are attempting to predict. For example, forensic clinicians will want to know whether they are predicting aggression in the community, aggression in an institution, or some other outcome. As mentioned above, validity data on both of these risk outcomes exist, so mental health professionals who work with young people can, in this case, be specific. One of my former graduate students, Anne-Marie Iselin, conducted an extensive meta-analytic study of psychopathy checklists (including the PCL-YV). This study demonstrated the PCL-YV's ability to predict anti-social outcomes in the community and in institutions (see Leistico, Salekin, DeCoster, & Rogers, 2008). Another recent meta-analysis focused on youth has also been added to the literature base (Asscher et al., 2011). Such meta-analytic reviews are useful when one is attempting to drawing conclusions about risk because they rely on a sizable number of studies with a large number of participants and thus can help provide the types of quantitative data the courts find valuable.

PROVIDING CONTEXT FOR THE EVALUATION

It is critical that forensic clinicians put all information in context. Thus, if risk is linked to environment in which the young person lives (e.g., gang-infested neighborhoods), this should be noted in the psychological report. Also, in their reports clinicians should examine and characterize the extent of the young person's involvement with the law, the severity of past crimes, the nature of previous dispositions, responses to previous interventions, and the presence of personal and situational influences that might contribute to his or her risk for further offending. With respect to developmental maturity, the reports should center on the extent to which the young person is a mature participant, and the level of maturity he or she exhibited during the evaluation, including autonomy and cognitive and emotional maturity, and the context in which such maturity can develop. This is where examining psychological theory can be helpful. For instance, according to Marcia's (1966) theory, if adolescents are not provided sufficient chances to explore in life, they may not see the same options to commit to prosocial activities or to hold social values as youth who are provided such opportunities. In addition, although the courts might be interested in such information regarding maturity to help define the degree of culpability, psychologists may also want to describe how maturity might improve treatment outcome. With regard to amenability, a number of contextual factors, such as a lack of trust in adults, could be warranted because of the environment in which the young person has grown up. This would affect amenability scores and should be highlighted in psychological reports. Because a number of such factors are dynamic, or changeable through planned intervention, it is possible that many characteristics could in fact be intervention targets (e.g., improved adult behavior and improved trust in adults, improved emotion regulation and/or cognitive abilities).

WEIGHTING OF PSYCHOLEGAL CONSTRUCTS

Although in this chapter I have addressed the practice of interpreting the results of personality testing and examination of relevant juvenile constructs, I do not provide instruction to clinicians about the complex issue of weighing the juvenile psycholegal constructs (see Brannen et al., 2006). This task of interpretation is multifaceted, and the weighing of factors will be primarily left to judges in juvenile courts, at least with regard to disposition decision making and the ultimate decision. Nevertheless, forensic clinicians can provide more detail than simply a young person's standing on pertinent constructs (e.g., risk) in isolation (Brannen et al., 2006; Salekin & Grimes, 2008). If forensic clinicians can develop an appropriate road map for change, and if they view the young person as amenable to treatment (or as showing potential to improve amenability), then they can bring to light the treatment readiness of young individuals in their psychological reports and testimony.

PROFESSIONAL OVERRIDES

Examining a young person's potential risk, developmental maturity, and amenability to treatment on the basis of clinical and professional assessments depends ultimately on the examiner, who evaluates and weighs the available information and then arrives at a judgment about these factors. There may be occasions when mental health professionals override the estimates derived from a test, but this practice can be controversial. It can, however, be an option when all other information leads the clinician to believe that the young person he or she has assessed is actually lower or higher on the constructs than the test indicates. I should note that there is very limited research on the effectiveness of this method, and clinicians who choose this option should clarify this limitation to the courts. Also, clinicians who decide on an override should be prepared to explain the rationale behind their decision. An example of this might be when a youth commits a very violent act but has no other risk factors than the current offense. Because of the few risk factors, the youth would actually score low on many risk measures, even though he or she may be quite dangerous.

JUVENILE EVALUATIONS AND THE ULTIMATE OPINION

With regard to the interpretation of the data, clinicians are not responsible for arriving at an ultimate opinion. Similarly, interpretation of psychological data does not extend to weighing pertinent factors to determine whether public safety is more important than the development of the young person. This is because ultimate decisions are the domain of the juvenile court judge. Moreover, mental health professionals do not necessarily have access to all the evidence presented in a case. The best practice, given the state of clinical knowledge in this area, is to provide an opinion about the estimated likelihood that a young person with similar characteristics will be of risk to the community and to provide information on his or her level of developmental maturity and rehabilitation potential (e.g., how he or she may do in psychological therapy).

The judge balances the constructs in his or her decision making in conjunction with other information. The amenability-to-rehabilitation standard provides a good example of other considerations a judge may factor into a decision. Specifically, the standard, as defined in most states, does not simply ask whether the young person's conduct can be modified; instead, it asks whether the young person can be modified within the resources and time available to the juvenile court. Thus, the psychological concept of treatment amenability does not typically consider a time limit, but the juvenile justice system often requires this consideration (Grisso & Schwartz, 2000; Mulvey & Iselin, 2008). According to the legal system, the amenability question is not answered merely through an evaluation of the characteristics of a young person or a determination whether she or he is malleable; it also requires that one align those characteristics with the options available for rehabilitation in the community and consider whether treatment gains can be made within a specific time frame. The forensic clinician's role is to describe what the young person requires and to let others in the legal system know how to obtain the resources to address the young person's needs (e.g., probation officers, other mental health professionals). Once the judge has all the information, he or she must balance the interests of the juvenile against the risk to public safety. The interpretation of data, including veracity, personality/pathology, and juvenile-specific constructs, provides clinicians the opportunity to offer the courts psychological information that can then inform legal decision making.

CONCLUDING COMMENTS

In this chapter, I covered several pertinent issues, including the interpretation of developmental history information, clinical interviews, structured interviews, and self-report. In addition, I discussed scale elevations, computer-based interpretation, and specifics regarding the interpretation of psychological instruments designed for the assessment of juvenile offenders. I emphasized how clinicians must understand that judgments are made on the basis of the results these instruments yield and that examining the content, construct, and predictive validity of the measures one uses is essential in the interpretation of findings. Without such validity, one knows little about what the scale scores signify. I also highlighted how charts and tables might be used to help with the conceptualization and interpretation of elevations and other clinically significant points. Finally, I provided an overview of the topics of contextual assessment interpretations, the issue of ultimate opinion, and how those types of interpretations are left to juvenile court and criminal court judges. Nonetheless, psychological reports should be informative to the point that they facilitate legal decision making. In the next chapter, I address the important topic of report writing and testimony.

8

REPORT WRITING AND TESTIMONY

Best practice in juvenile forensic evaluations requires that clinicians be able to summarize their findings in a well-written psychological report as well as to testify about those findings. The written report may serve varying purposes depending on the requirement of the jurisdiction, the request of the judge or attorney, and the mental health professional's specific area(s) of practice. A report written in its best and most comprehensive format serves primarily to accurately tell a young person's life story to the courts, articulating his or her developmental history, personality, family context, and predicament. This information then needs to feed directly into specific communications regarding the young person's level of risk, developmental maturity, and amenability to treatment in relation to his or her current situation. The report should fairly and accurately reflect the evaluation procedures, reasoning, and the data-fueled conclusion of the clinician. In this chapter, I discuss general and specific guidelines that will help forensic clinicians write psychological reports related to juvenile evaluations. I also address the presentation of expert testimony.

http://dx.doi.org/10.1037/14595-009
Forensic Evaluation and Treatment of Juveniles: Innovation and Best Practice, by R. T. Salekin

Reports that focus more narrowly on evaluation of a specific construct, such as risk, amenability to treatment, or a specific treatment, may be appropriate under certain circumstances when the court requests this type of precision. In many cases, however, the assessment will focus on mental health, risk, developmental maturity, and treatment needs in concert. These concepts constitute the major aspects of the report.

REPORT PREPARATION

The structure and content of a report that is prepared to assist the courts will depend on the purpose of the report and the audience. A report designed to assist a judge or prosecution or defense attorney in making a postcharge detention decision will differ from one designed to assist a judge in determining an appropriate postadjudication disposition. Similarly, reports designed for transfer considerations will differ from general postadjudication nontransfer disposition evaluations. Although in this chapter I provide some recommendations for report writing, mental health professionals can also look to other scholarly works in this area that provide advice on report writing and testimony (Brodsky, 2013; Heilbrun, Rogers, & Otto, 2002; Karson & Nadkarni, 2013; Otto, DeMier, & Boccaccini, 2014).

Format of the Report

The length and format of juvenile evaluation reports vary depending on their purpose and the intended audience. For many purposes, early in the legal process, shorter reports that focus narrowly on the immediate risk and surface-level amenability issues will suffice. For these purposes, the terms *short* or *brief reports* are those that speak to a particular issue that needs to be quickly addressed. For example, brief reports are occasionally required and will be sufficient when focused on pretrial detention or a recommendation to move the youth to a hospital or mental health facility. Such reports may rely on more limited data collection efforts and include a clinical interview and possibly a brief self-report measure. Short reports based on checklists of static risk factors are sometimes also used, in disposition and placement decisions. In Alabama, juvenile court judges and court personnel recognize that short reports are based on limited information but, when rapid decisions are required, are able to facilitate speedy decisions with some information in hand.

Although short reports are clearly needed at times and are faster to prepare, they are also by their nature limited in what they can offer the courts. In addition, although such reports are economical they are unlikely to be helpful in most postadjudication disposition and transfer decisions. A short report can convey only a little information regarding the young person's history or psychological condition. With short reports little time is typically available to give considerable thought to what might be needed to help a young person recover from his or her current predicament and to function at a more healthy level in the community.

Brief reports most commonly focus on surface-level risk factors that are often static (e.g., the index crime), as well as on immediate clinically relevant information (e.g., agitation, threatening behavior, psychosis, suicidal ideation), but they do not consider a wider array of dynamic factors or delve into the complexity of the young person's background and character. Much of the information on life background and dynamic factors can be gleaned from in-depth interviews and questions designed to understand the individual's developmental maturity and treatment amenability.

Comprehensive psychological evaluations and reports will frequently be required in the case of decisions regarding disposition and transfer and for postadjudication referrals for mental health treatment. These may be in the form of a narrative-based letter or a more structured and sectioned report. Narrative letter–style reports are generally based on interview and file information and simply represent a written summary of the examiner's results and conclusions. The organization of the narrative report will be specific to the writer but generally outlines what was requested and what was done, briefly describes the young person's background and current situation, and lists conclusions that are accompanied by what needs to be done in terms of intervention. These reports are often based on the interviewer's clinical opinion and possibly one or two psychological tests, and thus they may not include the same level of structure as thorough psychological testing, which often entails a larger battery of tests. The structure, language, or terminology used, and the logical flow from data to conclusions, may vary among assessors, and therefore these brief reports can range from being fairly clear to quite opaque regarding the links from the data collection to the conclusion phase.

In this chapter, I describe a narrative letter–based approach because these types of reports are occasionally used in the very early phases of legal processing I mentioned in Chapter 1. However, using this approach would not be considered good practice for postadjudication disposition evaluations or transfer evaluations. In this book, much of the discussion has been devoted to developing an innovative model, ideas about what should be evaluated, how it should be done, how to interpret the findings, and how to consider the applicable research. In this chapter, I provide information on the best way to communicate this knowledge in a psychological report and testimony.

Organized and Sectioned Reports

Sectioned reports are organized under headings and subheadings to aid the reader. Some common features of these reports are shared in many psychological evaluations. This makes the reports more familiar to a wider range of professionals. Although the actual organization of the report can vary, most forensic mental health reports provided by psychologists and psychiatrists will follow a set format. Commonly, psychological reports contain the following 10 sections: (a) Identifying Information, (b) Reason for Referral, (c) Sources of Information, (d) Social/Developmental Background, (e) Psychiatric History, (f) Legal History, (g) Assessment Results, (h) Clinical Impressions, (i) Summary, and (j) Recommendations. This format and the use of structured instruments (see Chapter 6, this volume) will help guide the organization and terminology used in the report. This also provides some consistency across reports to aid communication among professionals. Clinicians may also choose to use specific headings for pertinent psycholegal constructs, such as "Risk," "Developmental Maturity," and "Amenability to Treatment." These specifics can be given in the Clinical Impressions section and followed up in the Summary and Recommendations sections.

Writing reports that are clear, concise, relevant, and accurate should be the primary aim in forensic practice with young people. It is important to identify and evaluate all the information used in the assessment and to discuss the rationale behind one's conclusions. However, this should be done in a succinct and focused manner. In the following sections, I offer further detail on the topics of content, test scores, and the use of labels, all of which need to be thoughtfully considered in report writing, with the ultimate aim of improving the clarity and fairness of the forensic juvenile report.

Content of the Report

The content of any report is driven by its purpose, which is to answer the referral question. If the question has to do with disposition within the juvenile justice system, then the report will likely require an assessment of personality, family support, risk, developmental maturity, and treatment amenability, within the various contexts. In addition, the report will require a Summary/Recommendations section that should contain information on potential treatment options. If the question is about transfer, then opinions of risk, maturity, and amenability become even more critical because they are identified criteria in state statutes. Mental health professionals should accompany any statements (e.g., the risk a young person poses to the community) with contextual information that helps explain and defend estimates to judges or attorneys. This is important from an ethical standpoint because professionals should not make judgments about individuals without providing contextual and research-based justifications.

Expanded reports will be needed when information regarding risk, developmental maturity, and treatment amenability and needs is required for case disposition planning and management decisions. In such cases, the report should provide sufficient information to identify relevant treatment needs related to the causes of the young person's problems. This type of report may be needed, for example, when a juvenile court judge or prosecutor is deciding whether the young individual would be eligible for a pretrial diversion program. If eligible, the report should be designed to outline the type of treatment that would be appropriate for rehabilitation. In Chapter 9, I provide an overview of specific information on treatment programs.

Most clinicians and legal scholars have encountered reports that lack structure and are lengthy; these qualities can make it difficult to sort through the material in order to arrive at what is most relevant. There are several ways to streamline reports so that they contain only applicable information. One method involves carefully considering the question of what should be in the report as well as what should not. There are two basic guidelines clinicians can use to reduce information and avoid including inappropriate information in the report. First, information that is not relevant for the purpose of the report should not be included. If, for example, the only purpose of the report is to estimate the young person's developmental maturity, then information about sports and hobbies may be relevant, but specific information about, for example, his or her choice of mountain bike equipment, downhill ski equipment, or brand of soccer ball may be irrelevant. Second, information that extends beyond the purpose of the report that may be prejudicial to the young person and violate the rules of due process should not be included (Melton et al., 1987, 1997). This situation might arise when an estimate of risk is requested and specific information on the index crime is specifically included in this request (e.g., by the defense attorney). Sometimes if it is presumed that the young person has committed the index crime, comments are expected regarding risk. For example, in a transfer case, the *Kent v. United States* (1966) criteria may require that one ask questions about the index crime as they pertain to risk, developmental maturity, and amenability to treatment. If this can be done effectively without asking about the index crime, it may be the preferred method.

Test Scores

Reporting test scores from assessment tools is generally helpful when the scores are easy to interpret and clearly relate to the purpose of the report. For example, scores from intelligence, achievement, personality, and rating and checklist measures can be described in a clear-cut manner that is then helpful to the court, as in the following hypothetical example:

> Peter obtained an IQ score of 100, and his achievement scores were in the average range (Reading, Writing, Arithmetic), placing him in the normal range of intellectual functioning, and his achievement scores are also in line with his IQ score. With respect to his behavior, Peter obtained a T-score of 70 (90th–93rd percentile) on the Social Problems and Rule Breaking subscales of the Child Behavior Checklist Teacher Report Form, placing him in the clinical range compared with a sample of youth in his own age group.

This type of information is generally valued and easily understood by a variety of individuals, including those who are not mental health professionals. However, other test scores are more technical and may not be readily understood by those unfamiliar with the interpretation of scores. For example, scores on the Millon Adolescent Clinical Inventory (Millon, 1993) that are derived from base rates may require further explanation. When explaining base rate scores, the forensic clinician may need to clarify that the scale scores are based on prevalence rates of the condition in adolescent clinical samples and specifically that elevations take into consideration prevalence (base) rates for each disorder (scale).

Scores on the Minnesota Multiphasic Personality Inventory—Adolescent Version (MMPI–A; Butcher et al., 1992) are sometimes expressed as code types, such as "4/9" or "6/8," with an evaluation on "A-Ang." Such descriptions are not particularly helpful and in fact can be confusing to people who do not know the code types and who may not be familiar with the acronyms or the short-form scale numbers or names. More recently, Restructured Format scales have been developed for the MMPI–A and are being tested with adolescent samples (Archer & Handel, 2014). These scales are also likely to be a bit too technical for individuals who are not mental health professionals, but fortunately they are contemporary and may offer an advance over the MMPI standard scale interpretations.

In general, for forensic clinicians who work with juveniles it is best practice to be as descriptive as possible and to use terms that a broad audience can understand. If some technical terminology is desired, an option is to include all technical information in an appendix to the report. Another option is to use the technical terms within the text and subsequently explain their meaning in a sentence or two following the presentation of the technical information. For example, base rate scores on the Millon Adolescent Clinical Inventory, or code types from the MMPI–A, could be presented in the text and then the meaning of the technical information subsequently described in the report itself. This strategy allows the reader to better understand the psychological material being presented in the psychological report and to follow along with the interpretative language.

Labeling the Problem

Reporting clinical diagnoses in psychological reports prepared by mental health professionals can be descriptive and helpful but also potentially harmful. In Chapter 3, I suggested that a personality and behaviorally descriptive framework be used. This method may allow the mental health professional to avoid terms that can be considered potentially damaging to the young person. A diagnosis of conduct disorder or oppositional defiant disorder (ODD) may be useful in some respects but misleading and even damaging in other respects. On the other hand, such terms may be important to consider given that they are contained in the formal system used in the United States (i.e., the *Diagnostic and Statistical Manual of Mental Disorders*, *Fifth Edition* [DSM–5]; American Psychiatric Association, 2013), and similar diagnoses are outlined in the World Health Organization's (2012) *International Classification of Diseases* (11th ed., *ICD–11*), signifying that the diagnoses will soon be even more applicable across the globe. In addition, they do have predictive validity especially as mental health professionals gain a more refined understanding of the various disorders, such as from recent research showing the three dimensions of ODD, including irritability, oppositionality, and spitefulness (see Chapter 4, this volume, as well as Burke & Loeber, 2010; Stringaris & Goodman, 2009a, 2009b; and Stringaris, Maughan, & Goodman, 2010).

Given that these diagnostic systems are used in many countries and offer a common way of communicating case information, it is best practice to integrate personality and behavioral information with them. Moreover, there may be diagnoses, such as major depression with psychotic features, autism, or bipolar disorder, that cannot be readily described by a general model of personality. Another issue that will require consideration is the use of the limited prosocial emotion specifier (see Chapter 3, this volume) and whether to use terminology such as *psychopathy* or *callous–unemotional traits* (Salekin & Debus, 2008; Seagrave & Grisso, 2002; Vitacco, Salekin, & Rogers, 2010). According to some research, use of these terms does not appear to affect judges' opinions regarding disposition (Murrie, Boccaccini, McCoy, & Cornell, 2007). Nonetheless, if such terms are used, they should also be accompanied by cautionary statements. For instance, forensic clinicians might note not only the stability of the condition but also the instability of the condition, as it applies to young people (Lynam et al., 2000; Lynam, Caspi, Moffitt, Loeber, & Stouthamer-Loeber, 2007). Alternate terms, such as *interpersonal callousness*, rather than *psychopathy*, may be indicated.

Another important point to consider here is that, in the mental health field, some conditions are viewed as more stable than others. This viewpoint can cause problems when court personnel believe that the condition is unalterable. This "permanence of a psychiatric condition" mind-set can be troublesome because it can lead to damaging disposition decisions. It is interesting that beliefs about stability are more ingrained for some disorders, such as attention-deficit/hyperactivity disorder (ADHD) and depression, than others, such as ODD. These beliefs regarding differential stability do not seem to be all that well supported by the research (Burke & Loeber, 2010; Hawes, Price, & Dadds, 2014; Salekin, 2010). Nonetheless, it is not altogether uncommon to hear even a mental health professional make statements like, "Well, his father has ADHD, so he/she must have ADHD." Forensic clinicians aiming for best practice should keep in mind that although there are familial and genetic links to clinical conditions, the links are never 100% accurate. Even monozygotic twins who share the same genetic makeup never show 100% concordance for a given condition. When studying co-occurrence in psychiatric conditions, the highest concordance rates are usually obtained are around 50%. This signifies that for some young people a particular condition may be passed on through a family member and expressed, and for other young people this expression may never be evidenced. In addition, for young people who develop the condition, the symptoms may well be stable, but for many other young people the symptoms may be unstable or may not arise at all. This variability requires consideration when making decisions about diagnosing (and thus labeling) a young person with one or more *DSM–5* or *ICD–11* conditions (e.g., taking into consideration that because a parent has a given condition, this is not grounds for diagnosing the young person with the condition and that because a young person meets criteria for a *DSM–5* and/or *ICD–11* condition at Point A does not mean he or she will necessarily meet criteria for the same *DSM–5* and/or *ICD–11* condition at Point B).

An explanation regarding the stability of a disorder and the factors that are apt to reduce its symptoms should be included in the psychological report. With respect to the assessment measures that yield risk categories or probabilities of reoffending, the issues are similar. Specifically, the term *high risk category* as a label can carry significant weight. Here, too, it is critical to discuss ways in which this condition of high risk can be reduced or eliminated.

Reviewing Past Treatment Records

When preparing for an evaluation, one should seek the juvenile's previous assessment and treatment records. This can be important given that past assessment and treatment records can give key information about continuity of diagnoses and effectiveness of previous treatment. Prior records can also facilitate accurate diagnoses. Specifically, if a forensic clinician's assessment independently confirms a previous diagnosis, this is very beneficial in that he or she now has two, or more, independent evaluations that confirm the diagnosis and show stability. This can provide greater confidence in the presentation of the diagnoses. However, the data from one's own independent evaluation must back such conclusions.

Alternatively, past psychological reports may show diagnoses that have changed from one disorder to the next across evaluations for a given young client. This may indicate the difficulty entailed in accurately reaching a diagnosis for young people and thus the potential for misdiagnoses. It also may underscore the dynamic nature of a young person's life and related characteristics and symptomatology. For example, a young person's record may contain a diagnosis of ADHD, yet the child who sits before a forensic clinician does not appear to have active ADHD symptoms; he or she, who is not medicated, appears attentive and calm and displays no excessive or extreme motor activity. After a thorough assessment, forensic clinicians should use their independent acumen to determine whether the disorder previously diagnosed should be carried forward. If the young person no longer exhibits symptoms of ADHD, then the forensic clinician should conclude that she or he no longer has ADHD while noting in the report that the young person was previously diagnosed with ADHD.

Other youth in referred cases may arrive with the label of severe conduct disorder accompanied with other descriptors, such as "limited capability for deep emotion" but, upon probing, the clinician discovers that the young person shows compassion for family members (e.g., a grandparent) and cares a great deal about the welfare of a former mentor (e.g., athletic coach) or perhaps a girlfriend or boyfriend. If there is corroborating support for this affect-related information, the clinician may have sufficient grounds for considering an alternate diagnosis. The point is that forensic clinicians should show a willingness to carry forward a diagnosis if their own data support such conclusions; similarly, they should be equally willing to provide an alternate explanation and/or diagnosis, especially when previous diagnoses are no longer held up, relevant, or applicable. In either case, abbreviated results from past reports should be included in ongoing psychological reports in order to continue the record forward and facilitate accurate diagnoses.

Clarity of the Report and Conversion of Data to Understandable Information

The report should be written in such a manner that it converts the psychological information to understandable information for attorneys and juvenile court judges. It should be easily read and understood. The judge should not have to turn to psychiatry texts, view lengthy videos on psychology and psychiatry, obtain diagnostic books, or seek out psychological test manuals to examine appendixes with T-scores to decipher the report. Some judges do in fact conduct their own research on psychological matters, but best practice entails providing sufficient information so that this is not a necessity. Checking one's report to ensure that it is clear and understandable to a wide audience is helpful in this regard and thus indicative of optimum practice.

One way to obtain this type of clarity and precision is to go through a draft of the psychological report several times with a pen, clarifying sentences and technical language or, alternatively, using a word processing function (e.g., Track Changes in Microsoft Word) to ensure that there are no confusing sentences in the report. Sometimes reading the report aloud can be helpful because, as the saying goes, the ears hear what the eyes cannot. Forensic clinicians will enhance communication if they provide clear transitions between their various thoughts. Also, providing examples can be illustrative. A professional psychological report should aim to leave no room for misinterpretation.

Use of Observations

Observations can be informative and should be outlined in the report. Structured interviews rely to some extent on observations. For example, the item "attention problems" appears in some structured interviews, rating scales, and some broad-based personality assessments. The assessor's response to this item will depend on information revealed in the interview or other sources, but it could also be informed by observations made during the course of the interview and other testing. With structured interviews, for example, a young person can state that he or she does not have attention problems, yet the mental health professional's experience with the young person during the interview reveals that attention problems do exist. For instance, the youth may not be able to sit still, needs to constantly fiddle with papers, and stares out of the interview room. This may or may not be indicative of ADHD, but it should be reported and considered with other relevant information, such as parent reports, school reports, and the like, to make determinations about attention. This information should be noted in the relevant section of the report.

To avoid producing symptoms, such as inattentiveness and even oppositionality, it is important to give adolescents breaks to refresh themselves and then restart interviews when they are re-energized. When practical, it is also wise to conduct these interviews over the course of several days (see Chapter 6 for more information about establishing rapport to reduce anxiety and inattentiveness). Observations of behavior can be useful when combined with all other information and with a variety of hypotheses, but only when youth are given fair and adequate time frames in which to complete the evaluation. Such observations can also be used to determine the adolescent displays thought (e.g., responses to internal stimuli) or mood (e.g., depressive affect, elevated mood) symptoms. For instance, pressured speech may be indicative of early onset bipolar disorder, a substance abuse problem, or some other related mental health issue, and this should be in included in the report.

Integrating and Reconciling Information

Putting the report together requires that forensic clinicians synthesize various pieces of information. This involves gathering data collected from different sources and examining both the converging and conflicting areas. I covered this important point in Chapter 7. It is the role of the forensic clinician writing the report to present the information in a coherent fashion. Clinicians should not leave it to the reader to sort through and make sense of discrepant information. This can be a common problem with poorly written reports. Psychologists in the early phases of their forensic careers may have to work on this. Coherent integration of information is primary to a good psychological report.

Mental health professionals should work vigorously to sort through informational discrepancies and make sense of divergent material so that they can identify broader convergent patterns in the final report. There may be some instances in which this is difficult to do, but synthesis can usually be accomplished with some effort. To illustrate this point further, a parent may report that a young person is well behaved, whereas a teacher reports that the child is highly disruptive and oppositional, and the results from personality testing do not indicate any difficulties in either of these domains. The contradictions in reporting can arise for a number of reasons. First, as noted, there can be true behavioral differences across settings. This means that the youth acts quite differently in dissimilar settings, for instance, calm and pleasant with parents but oppositional and argumentative with teachers. Second, one or more sources of information may be unreliable, such as a parent with some antisocial tendencies of his or her own, who may have just created a zigzag pattern down one of the test protocol forms. Alternately, parents may be rushed or may not put much stock in psychological testing, both of which can affect the accuracy of responding. In addition, reliability may be compromised because of the young age of the reporter or by a teacher who is biased in his or her reporting. Also, even though scales have the same name—say, for instance, "Oppositional Disorder"—the content that constitutes the scale could be quite different across different measures, resulting in divergent findings across sources. Finally, individual clinicians may vary in the content that they use to diagnose disorders (*ICD–11* vs. *DSM–5*) or the threshold at which they consider a disorder to be present. Table 8.1 contains definitions of the types of variance in reporting that can occur and that clinicians might note in reports to the courts to help explain any apparent inconsistencies.

A simple solution for inconsistent information does not always exist. However, it is the clinician's role to help make sense of the young person's developmental history. Recall that forensic clinicians can use their professional judgment to resolve the contradictions as well as seek further information. For instance, they could ask direct questions geared to solve the

TABLE 8.1

Variance in Reporting of Strengths and Difficulties/Problems

Type of variance	Definition
Setting variance	Variations in the client's presentation across settings
Information variance	Variations among clinicians (or self-report or teacher report measures) as to what questions are asked, which observations are made, and how that information is organized
Criterion variance	Variations among raters in applying standards for what is clinically relevant

discrepancy, such as, to a parent, "I noticed that when you were rating William on this test, you mostly filled out what we refer to as the 'oppositional symptoms,' whereas your wife filled out the irritable symptoms; does this make sense to you?" The parent may help the forensic clinician with this conflict:

> Yes, that makes perfect sense to me. My son is pretty much only oppositional with me; we cannot seem to get along, or agree on anything, but my wife and he get along quite well and when he is upset, he lets her know, and she sees the times when he is downright irritable.

Another issue related to synthesis has to do with integrating information from previous psychological reports. Illustrative here is that forensic clinicians may occasionally read previous psychological reports in which the writer of the report states, "It is unclear whether the young person was on a trial of medication for depression." This type of confusion can stem from inconsistent reporting between parents. For instance, one parent recalls a trial of medication, whereas the other does not. Leaving the report ambiguous in this regard and stating that "it is unclear whether the young person was medicated for depression" constitutes poor psychological reporting and practice, especially because medical records are generally fairly easy to obtain. It is the forensic clinician's duty to trace a young person's medical and psychological treatment histories in their entirety. Sufficient detail regarding prior treatments should be delineated. This includes the precise dates of those treatments, any medications that were administered, the dosage, and the beginning and ending dates of the intervention, as well as the outcome (positive, neutral, or negative). In addition, any reactions to medication and/or alterations in the treatment regimen should be noted in the past-treatment section of the report. If the previous treatment history is extensive, it can be beneficial to create a table to exhibit past treatment efforts that can be easily read at a glance. Information that is absent or not well delineated can lead to poorly informed new processing and treatment decisions. Requesting records and carefully charting past treatments represent the kind of investigation that is needed for effective psychological reports for the court.

OFFERING EXPERT TESTIMONY

Forensic clinicians are sometimes called to testify in a court or other judicial setting as an expert witness. Opposing professionals conducting juvenile assessments may also be required to testify. In addition, probation officers are often asked to offer guidance to judges in determining disposition. Probation officers also provide information on issues regarding the young person's mental health, likelihood of benefiting from treatment, and issues of public safety. As I mentioned in Chapter 1, in high-profile cases two experts may testify, which makes one's professionalism and knowledge about proper evaluation critical given that they will be scrutinized by the judge and by opposing professionals. The more knowledge one has on the topic of juvenile evaluations, the better prepared one will be for report writing and testimony. As forensic clinicians move along in their careers and make progress in the field, an important goal can be to continue to sharpen their clinical skills toward a level that could obtain national recognition.

Brain Development and Expert Testimony

Forensic clinicians should be cautious about research on adolescents and what that research means for the law. Arguments raised regarding the "impulsive brain of the adolescent" and links to law violations have sometimes been unclear or contradictory. For instance, one such argument purports that adolescents are less able to make sound judgments "in the heat of the moment." This may be true, although it is not all that well researched. These arguments were partially raised in cases such as *Roper v. Simmons* (2005), in which the individuals appear to have planned their actions in advance, were noted to be conversing about their lack of responsibility in the matter due to their juvenile status, and coordinated the act over the course of several days. Obviously, this is difficult to categorize as adolescent decision making in the heat of the moment. It appears instead to represent planning, premeditation, and at least a basic understanding of one's actions. A conservative and highly nuanced appreciation of brain science and adolescent decision making is recommended for clinicians who decide to testify on this topic.

Communication Skills

Communication skills and the ability to convey an understanding of one's work are what clinicians should aim for and are quintessential aspects of being an expert. There are some very helpful books on expert testimony that discuss how to testify in an effective manner. These books are detailed and cover topics such as how to look like an expert, dress like an expert, speak like an expert, and handle difficult questions like an expert (Barsky & Gould, 1996; Brodsky, 1995, 2013; Sattler, 1998; Sattler & Hoge, 2006). Moreover, they discuss courtroom procedures and etiquette. Familiarity with these aspects of providing testimony can be helpful to making an effective overall court presentation.

Clinicians should review the written report with whoever has retained them (usually the attorney) to better prepare for testimony. Experts who prepare complete, thoughtful, and unbiased reports will be less likely to be challenged and will be able to more easily withstand questioning by a juvenile court judge, adult criminal court judge, or counsel. Presenting information in a thorough and consistent manner will go a long way toward establishing credibility in the courtroom or when questioned privately by judges or attorneys. Being well prepared and polished but at the same time down to earth and nondefensive when presenting one's findings is an effective combination. Attending one or two hearings ahead of time, if permissible, with a senior colleague can be helpful to orient oneself to the courtroom and to forensic testimony.

After giving testimony, it can be helpful to gauge how confident a judge is regarding the information one has provided. Confidence and respect for one's work can also be based on how often one is sought by juvenile court judges to conduct subsequent evaluations, as well as how frequently one is referred by other clinicians and legal professionals to conduct additional evaluations. The frequency with which disposition decisions follow one's recommendations also can be a sign of how well one is doing. If a clinician's practice is becoming increasingly busy, then he or she likely is doing work that the courts appreciate. Alternatively, if the response to someone's initial work is less than enthusiastic (few calls or e-mails requesting that clinician's expertise), one may wish to seek feedback from those with whom he or she has worked to find out what he or she can do to improve. Critical feedback is essential in the field of forensic child and adolescent psychology, even for the very best clinicians in the field. A suggestion from a colleague that one needs to brush up on an aspect of the juvenile evaluation and/or improve the delivery of testimony to ensure that one is current, accurate, fair, and effectively heard could be very helpful and should be received with grace. A willingness to accept such feedback will help one flourish in the field.

Qualifications as an Expert

It is essential for clinicians who testify as mental health professionals to establish their credentials for offering expert testimony. Educational and professional experience is important in this respect. Formal licensing as a psychologist or psychiatrist is critical. Although possessing diplomate status with the

American Board of Forensic Psychology and the American Board of Clinical Child & Adolescent Psychology is optional, it may be desirable for some evaluators who want to further display their expertise. Licensing and board certification help guarantee that one has met the minimal professional standards and that one's performance is monitored. The next step as an expert is to build a reputation based on knowledge, fairness, and skill in writing reports and providing accurate and effective testimony. Fortunately, these are acquirable skills.

JUVENILE EVALUATIONS INFORM POLICY

Clinical evaluations of juvenile justice cases have a functional relationship with the law. Although clinicians look to the law for the types of information that courts require for making decisions, they bring their psychological expertise and interpretations of the law with them (Grisso & Schwartz, 2000; Schetky & Benedek, 1980, 1992, 2002). This subsequently influences the data forensic evaluators collect and how they examine and interpret that information. Therefore, courts influence the forensic process by providing legal guidance for clinicians. The ways in which clinicians structure their opinions in psychological reports for use by the legal decision maker can affect how the courts then frame their application of legal standards to questions of disposition and transfer. A product of this two-way interaction is the evolution of a better system. Fortunately, this bidirectional relation results in an ongoing refining of the meaning of the legal standards that guide judicial decisions regarding juvenile disposition and transfer practices (Grisso, 1998/2013).

Well-performed assessments for juvenile disposition and transfer cases serve a number of very positive purposes that are important for the young person, legal decision makers, and society. First, child and adolescent forensic evaluations can be effective in identifying youth who are likely to discontinue their delinquent behavior. Second, juvenile assessments can identify youth who are developing serious mental disorders and need psychological treatment. Third, well-performed evaluations contribute to the fairness of the juvenile or adult legal process. In sum, psychological assessments provide relevant information and structure to the system. This structure, along with the psychological material the assessments contain, allows the courts to think about the cases before them in relation to the legal standards.

CONCLUDING COMMENTS

In this chapter, I addressed the topic of report writing and testimony, providing information on the structure that reports can have, the use of test scores and labels, and reporting on psycholegal constructs. In addition,

I highlighted the importance of resolving discrepancies or making conceptual sense of inconsistencies and being sure to effectively and accurately delineate past treatment efforts, including both psychological and pharmacological interventions. I offered information on testimony, including how psychologists should inform lawyers about their testimony and details about how psychological reports can inform policy. Providing quality psychological reports and testimony is the first step toward delineating the best way for young people to transition to productive lifestyles. In the next chapter, I address the important topic of treatment of juvenile offenders.

9

TREATMENT OF YOUNG PEOPLE IN THE JUVENILE JUSTICE SYSTEM

A foundation of good juvenile forensic reporting includes being able to make sound recommendations for treatment. The penultimate aim of this chapter is to provide information on interventions that can be helpful to young people with oppositional defiant characteristics and conduct problems as well as other problems most commonly found in young people who are involved with the law. Specifically, in this chapter I provide information on the various blueprint treatment programs for youth in the juvenile justice system. Also reviewed are the key ingredients for improving young people's conduct. Decades of research have shown what principles, techniques, and modalities work in psychological therapy, and these broader principles are described in this chapter (American Psychological Association, 2013a; Lipsey, 2009; M. L. Smith & Glass, 1978). In addition, I offer information on the types of intervention recommendations that can be made for young people with mental health conditions that may require a multidisciplinary approach (e.g., mood disorders and psychotic disorders). I also describe how

http://dx.doi.org/10.1037/14595-010
Forensic Evaluation and Treatment of Juveniles: Innovation and Best Practice, by R. T. Salekin

specific recommendations for treatment can be outlined in the psychological report and discusses some new ways to conceptualize treatment delivery.

Many of the principles covered in this chapter, such as improving parenting skills and the use of positive reinforcement, have been incorporated into dozens of manualized treatment packages. Thus, the programs have similar ingredients for changing behavior, which perhaps highlights just how active these ingredients are. Forensic clinicians may choose to recommend such treatment packages to enhance the effectiveness of their planned intervention with young people involved in the legal system. Alternatively, in some situations, where the implementation of such programs is less feasible, clinicians may opt to recommend use of the psychological principles that are commonly administered in treatment programs (American Psychological Association, 2013a; Campbell, Norcross, Vasquez, & Kaslow, 2013; Leichsenring & Rabung, 2008; Shedler, 2010; Westen, Novotny, & Thompson-Brenner, 2004). Whatever is chosen, clinicians should provide a clear delineation of the rationale and empirical base for the recommended approach.

In this chapter, I provide an overview of five important treatment principles: (a) adequate treatment dosage, (b) strengths-based treatment focus (e.g., positive psychology), (c) mental health focus (an awareness of psychopathology and ability to immediately treat it), (d) use of immediate reinforcement in treatment and natural settings (e.g., immediate reinforcements that are available for youth when they exhibit a desired behavior), and (e) availability of prosocial activities in home and community environments (e.g., education, sports, artistic activities, and hobbies).

Other principles that have been raised primarily in the juvenile offender literature should be mentioned before I address the aforementioned broad principles in further detail. These include the notion of providing the most intense treatment to young people who are the most severe offenders as well as providing a high level of monitoring to the highest risk youth, targeting key criminological factors, planning interventions based on what has been shown to work, and using treatments that are sensitive to individual differences (and developmental stage). These factors may overlap with a variety of programs and principles and in many ways represent common therapeutic processes.

With respect to the notion of giving the most intense treatment to the most severe offenders, although this is a sound approach, I should note that, on occasion, providing intensive treatment to first-time offenders also can be beneficial (Greenwood, 2008; May, Osmond, & Billick, 2014). However, the level and nature of treatment depend on the case and the specific needs of the family. For instance, if parent training could help with redirecting a young person away from a risky pathway before he or she accumulates many problems (drug use, numerous law violations), implementing such parent training early would seem to be indicated. Thus, although the model of providing the most intense treatment to those who are the most severe offenders makes conceptual sense, so too does the notion of offering thoughtful treatment to first-time offenders to curtail further problems, when indicated.

BLUEPRINT PROGRAMS

Forensic clinicians can look to the Office of Juvenile Justice and Delinquency Prevention (http://www.ojjdp.gov) and other governmental bodies for model blueprint programs for violence prevention. These programs have been empirically tested and shown to have some effect on the prevention of violence; they include multisystemic therapy (Sawyer & Borduin, 2011), functional family therapy (Sexton & Turner, 2010), and aggression replacement training (Amendola & Oliver, 2010). In addition, there are bullying prevention programs and aggression prevention programs for elementary school–age children (Lochman, Wells, Qu, & Chen, 2013). A list of some of the representative programs are provided in Exhibit 9.1. The blueprint programs have not yet been shown to completely eliminate youth delinquency or recidivism, but they are nonetheless some of the better known programs and have demonstrated positive effects on unwanted behavior, such as recidivism (Borduin & Sawyer, 2011).

Searching for programs that offer one of the model treatment protocols mentioned above, or programs that encapsulate many of the treatment elements of blueprint programs, is best practice for securing effective treatment for young individuals in contact with the law. Unfortunately, not all cities or treatment venues have such blueprint programs, or even ones with the effective elements, and as a result the programs available may not work equally well. Where possible, the treatment programs mentioned above are likely most effectively implemented when they respond to the specific needs of the juvenile (e.g., parenting training, reduction in peer-related delinquency, reduction in substance abuse), and forensic clinicians should look for key elements that are designed to reduce delinquency, improve a young person's mental health, and alter life trajectories.

INEFFECTIVE PROGRAMS AND SYSTEMS

There also are ineffective programs and systems for juvenile offenders, of which forensic clinicians should be aware. There are three reasons why knowledge in this area is important. First, some ineffective programs are popular with judges and attorneys, and for this reason they may unknowingly turn to such programs when considering the rehabilitation of a young person. However, these

EXHIBIT 9.1
Model Blueprint Programs

Bullying Prevention Program
The Bullying Prevention Program is a school-based initiative designed to reduce victim/bully problems among primary and secondary school children. The program identifies and addresses incidents of bullying, ranging from teasing and taunting to intimidation and physical violence, and attempts to restructure the school environment to reduce opportunities and reward for bullying behavior (Black, Washington, Trent, Harner, & Pollock, 2010; Limber, 2011; Olweus & Limber, 2010a, 2010b; Schroeder et al., 2012).

Functional Family Therapy
Functional family therapy is a family treatment model designed to engage and motivate youth and families to change their communication, interaction, and problem-solving patterns. It has been applied successfully to a variety of problem youth (e.g., with problems ranging from conduct disorder to serious criminal offending, such as aggravated assault; Lucenko, Mancuso, & Felver, 2011; Phillippi, Below, & Cuffie, 2010; Rhoades, Campbell, & Bumbarger, 2011; Sexton & Turner, 2010).

Multisystemic Therapy
Multisystemic therapy targets a set of factors in a young person's ecology, including family, peers, school, neighborhood, and the support network, because this network is thought to contribute to the antisocial behavior. Multisystemic therapy is a short-term, intensive program developed by credentialed therapists that has been shown to be effective in decreasing antisocial behavior and violence in chronic juvenile offenders (Borduin, Schaeffer, & Heiblum, 2009; Butler, Baruch, Hickey, & Fonagy, 2011; Curtis, Ronan, Heiblum, & Crellin, 2009; Klietz, Borduin, & Schaeffer, 2010; Manders, Deković, Asscher, van der Laan, & Prins, 2013; Sawyer & Borduin, 2011).

Multidimensional Treatment Foster Care
Multidimensional treatment foster care has been shown to be an effective alternative to residential treatment for adolescents who have problems with chronic delinquency and antisocial behavior. Youth are placed in well-supervised foster families for 6 to 9 months and undergo weekly individualized therapy. Foster families receive weekly group supervision and daily telephone monitoring. Biological parents learn behavior management techniques to ensure that gains made in the foster care setting are maintained after a youth returns home.

Another, nonmodel program that may be of value:

Aggression Replacement Training
Aggression replacement training (ART) is a cognitive–behavioral intervention that focuses on training adolescents to cope with their aggression and potentially violent actions. It contains three components: (a) social skills training, (b) anger control training, and (c) moral reasoning. Aggression replacement training is not yet regarded as a model program but has been described by many scholars as a promising one (Amendola & Oliver, 2010; Currie, Wood, Williams, & Bates, 2012; Holmqvist, Hill, & Lang, 2009; Nugent & Ely, 2010).

Note. ART is not currently considered a blueprint program.

programs' popularity may be due to their ease of administration (large, peer-run treatment groups) and/or general appeal (e.g., Scared Straight, boot camps) rather than their effectiveness (Petrosino, Turpin-Petrosino, & Finckenauer, 2000). Despite their ease of use and appeal, forensic clinicians may need to help steer young people away from such programs because research has shown that a number of them can be counterproductive (James, Stams, Asscher, De Roo, & der Laan, 2013; Meade & Steiner, 2010; Petrosino, Turpin-Petrosino, & Buehler, 2002; Tyler, Darville, & Stalnaker, 2001). For instance, Dishion (2012) showed that group treatment, and especially peer-run groups, can be counterproductive and result in "delinquency training." Therefore, forensic clinicians should help the courts avoid programs that have been shown to be ineffective or counterproductive (James et al., 2013; May, Osmond, & Billick, 2014).

Second, even when young people initially receive solid psychological therapy following some contact with the law, there can be insufficient follow-up. This occurs when young people enter treatment programs and do quite well in the intervention program but then make little to no effort to maintain the treatment effects afterward. For instance, youth may need assistance in their transition from a residential facility to the community to safeguard the skills they learned and ensure that those skills are maintained. Moreover, parents may require some help understanding those changes in order to help the youth function in the home and in the community. In these cases, the parents may require some training that allows them to find new, constructive ways to interact with their child. This problem of a lack of effective follow-up may stem from limited resources. Nonetheless, if such follow-up is seen as essential for the young person's healthy adjustment, forensic clinicians should make appropriate recommendations for follow-up.

Third, and relatedly, problems with the effectiveness of probation may require consideration. I raised this issued in Chapter 1, but it requires reiteration here because of its importance to effective treatment. For instance, in the state of Alabama probation, officers have very heavy caseloads. This makes it difficult for them to have close contact with each young person involved with the law. Forensic clinicians may want to gather information on the probation system, to see whether certain aspects of the system are in need of augmentation to help with youth development. Fortunately, research has highlighted the aspects of probation that can be helpful with youth development. For instance, probation officers who are able to balance their authoritative and supportive roles not only to hold youth accountable but also to encourage them to assert control over their lives and to maintain optimism regarding prosocial involvement in the community can be incredibly helpful. Positive outcomes are more likely to occur when probation officers have sufficient time and appropriate supervision skills available to them to effectively interact with young people (e.g., Trotter & Evans, 2012; Umamaheswar, 2013).

Because of the aforementioned issues (e.g., the availability of blueprint model programs, the reality of the probation system in one's district, and the effectiveness of follow-up care), forensic clinicians will need to consider feasibility of effective treatments and follow-up care in their specific state. Where blueprint programs are not readily available, or are too expensive to implement, and follow-up care is minimal, forensic clinicians will need to consider new, economically sound models of intervention delivery. This may signify the need to develop a set of recommendations that include the chief ingredients for the successful treatment of young individuals involved with the law and a search for clinicians in the community who have expertise in treating disruptive disorders and other relevant conditions. In addition, because of follow-up concerns, clinicians may have to look for ways to extend a broad outreach to young people who live in communities where resources are scarce.

Kazdin and Rabbitt (2013) made the cogent point that with current methods in clinical psychology professionals are unlikely to resolve the mental health problems in the United States (see also Comer & Barlow, 2014; and Kazdin & Blase, 2011). The potential for solving the delinquency problem may be even more dismal without innovative and broader methods. One method is to have clinicians garner what they know from recent science and to make specific recommendations, including the use of well-known key ingredients, to young people and their families. In addition, clinicians could recommend in their reports the use of self-help guides to help spur the process of understanding such resources. This should help facilitate the overall therapeutic process where blueprint programs are not yet available.

WHAT WORKS: WHAT INGREDIENTS ARE IMPORTANT TO CONSIDER AND RECOMMEND IN A DISPOSITION REPORT?

Research on what is effective for juvenile offenders reveals a few common elements aside from the points mentioned in the previous paragraphs. Most successful programs appear to have similar ingredients, including:

- social learning approaches, whereby parents, peers, and/or staff model prosocial behavior that can be imitated;
- parent training and/or family therapy, in which resolving maladaptive patterns of relating and communicating with one another occur;
- modification of thought and emotion, whereby teaching thinking skills and emotion regulation skills result in better reasoning and regulation of emotion; and
- direct modification of behavior.

Such modifications improve problem solving and can enhance a young person's ability to generate nonaggressive solutions to interpersonal conflicts and improve functioning with family members and peers (Landenberger & Lipsey, 2005; Loeber & Farrington, 1998; Weisz & Hawley, 2002; Wilson, Lipsey, & Derzon, 2003).

A considerable amount of change can be accomplished by enhancing parenting skills. Parents have a significant amount of control over a young person's life; as a consequence, improved parental practices can help shape a young person's behavior in a functionally adaptive direction. Regardless of whether it is a child's difficult temperament that sets relations in a problematic direction, or parenting that leads to the difficult temperament, most forensic clinicians recognize that positive parenting is effective in bringing about change (Kazdin, 2010; Lahey, Moffitt, & Caspi, 2003; McMahon & Forehand, 2003; Patterson, 1975). If parents are inept at parenting a child with a difficult temperament, then improving parenting skills can be a recommended point of intervention. Any program that includes positive parenting practices is worth considering in interventions for youth involved with the legal system.

Parents can make manifold errors with youth, but there are a few common unhealthy parenting practices that generally affect youth in a negative way, and these errors may be more common in youth who are involved with the justice system. These ineffective parenting strategies have been highlighted in a number of research articles and monographs and in the popular media (e.g., Dishion & Kavanagh, 2003; Kazdin, 2010; McMahon & Forehand, 2003; Patterson, 1975, 1997). Pointing out ineffective parenting practices is critical in psychological reports because many parents believe their parenting strategies (e.g., corporal punishment) are helpful in the reduction of oppositional and conduct problem symptoms in young people, yet many approaches adopted by parents of youth with disruptive behavior disorders have the countereffect of increasing rather than reducing problematic behaviors.

Kazdin (2010) recently constructed a list of "the myths of effective parenting." Although these myths are well known to child clinicians, many parents steadfastly persist with these ineffective practices. For instance, Kazdin noted that many parents believe that punishment and threats of punishment are effective. In our practice at the Disruptive Behavior Clinic at the University of Alabama and in the juvenile facilities (detention and residential facilities in Alabama) where we conduct treatment, my colleagues and I encounter such parental beliefs regularly. It is likely that this incorrect view is common across the United States among parents of youth with disruptive disorders. Although some parents will argue adamantly about the benefits of punishment, a large number of studies indicate that punishment is not particularly effective for all youth and may be especially ineffective for some youth who have disruptive behavior disorders (Barker & Salekin, 2012). Instead, the opposite is true: It is better to use positive reinforcement rather than punishment.

Kazdin (2010) and other clinical psychologists also have noted that many parents believe that numerous reminders about behaving well will help reduce conduct problems. Many researchers have pointed out that it is better to reinforce young people for doing the right things from a very early age, and to continue to do this throughout the child's upbringing, than to punish unwanted behaviors (Kazdin, 2010; McMahon & Forehand, 2003; Patterson, 1975). Reinforcing desired behavior has been repeatedly shown to be incredibly effective in treatment programs (Weisz & Kazdin, 2010). Research has also shown that parents may also believe that explaining to youth why their conduct is counterproductive, and even illegal, is the key to reducing conduct problems. Although these explanations are important, especially for young people involved with the law, their effectiveness likely plateaus after one or two times. As Kazdin and other behavior modification experts have observed, repeatedly informing youth of the wrongfulness of their actions is unlikely to result in genuine behavior change (McMahon & Forehand, 2003; Patterson, 1975). Instead, as mentioned above, it is more beneficial to reinforce the desired behavior. Finally, some parents of youth who have oppositional or conduct problem behaviors believe that giving praise shows weakness and spoils the child, precipitating his or her bad behavior. Parents with this mind-set often argue that "tough" approaches, including punishment, are more effective.

It has been well documented that positive parenting that includes warmth and praise is an effective child-rearing practice, whereas punishment alone is not (Kazdin, 2010). This does not mean that forensic clinicians should endorse lackadaisical parenting in the Recommendations sections of their psychological reports. Instead, they should recommend that parents use verbal praise with their children, when appropriate, and set time aside for positive and warm interactions with them. Also, these positive nurturing practices need to be maintained (Sroufe, Carlson, Levy, & Egeland, 1999). Some parents who come to the Disruptive Behavior Clinic at the University of Alabama believe that if their child is acting properly and complying with the rules in one setting for a specified period of time, that that signifies that the child can do the desired behavior all the time, in all settings.

It is the continual shaping and mastering of a desired behavior that facilitates prosocial change. Several myths of effective parenting are listed in Exhibit 9.2. Some of these myths may be more frequently seen in juvenile casework. Finding ways to intervene by discussing them can be helpful. At the Disruptive Behavior Clinic, my colleagues and I share these myths with parents in a handout, and also discuss them. If we are concerned about

EXHIBIT 9.2
Parenting Practices That Can Help With Correcting Conduct Problems

Reward rather than punish

Many parents believe that punishment is an effective way to curb their child's delinquency. However, this is generally an ineffective method. Research has shown that it is better to find ways to reward a desired behavior (e.g., Patterson, 1975). This entails "catching" young people doing things right and rewarding the desired behavior immediately after it occurs (Kazdin, 2010; McMahon & Forehand, 2003).

Reward rather than remind

Many parents believe that if they remind their children frequently that certain behaviors are wrong, such reminders will fix the problem. Although instructing is helpful, after an initial instruction it is better to then focus on rewarding the desired behavior; otherwise, frequent reminders start to sound like nagging, and the child may stop paying attention to them (Kazdin, 2010).

Give frequent rewards: Rewards do not spoil children

Many parents believe that rewarding children will spoil them. This is not the case; instead, rewarding works very well if a reward immediately follows a desired behavior. Parents should not be too concerned if a young person gets a lot of rewards. If the desired behavior is attained, the child should be rewarded (e.g., Kazdin, 2010; McMahon & Forehand, 2003; Patterson, 1975).

Stay on the job: One-time parenting does not work

Many parents of delinquent youth believe that if they can get the child to perform a desired behavior once, then the child knows what to do and parents should not have to continue to elicit and reward that behavior. Research has shown that this is not the case (Weisz & Kazdin, 2010). Continual rewarding and shaping are needed to elicit the desired behavior and to ensure it becomes permanent (Patterson, 1975).

Keep your positive emotion high, especially warmth

Many parents spend little one-on-one time with their children. Children require individual time with their parents. Therefore, parents should spend as much time as they can (at least 2 hours per week) in meaningful activities with their child (Kazdin, 2010; Patterson, 1975). Such activities do not have to be expensive endeavors but could include hiking, playing a sport, going to a movie, dining at a favorite restaurant, and so forth. Giving a pat on the back and making eye contact that displays warmth and caring are important.

---

defensiveness or potentially offending a parent, we mention that parenting is an intricate practice and that we provide the handouts to many clients to offer opportunities to improve parenting strategies. We give the handout to all clients before asking any extensive questions about their parenting, to preclude potential defensiveness.

One other point is worth mentioning here in terms of making treatment recommendations; specifically, parents can learn to place a lot of blame on the child over the course of his or her run-ins with the law. Allocating blame is not always helpful. Training parents to reduce and even stop blaming their child should be a primary aim. Instead, treatment programs should focus on increasing positive behaviors and supporting those positive changes.

This does not mean that young people should not be held accountable for their behavior; there should be consequences for misbehavior. There should even be potential restoration plans; restoration may include making amends to persons who have suffered, providing community service, or some other form of reparation. Blaming, without proposing ways to resolve or correct the problem, is counterproductive. Similarly, adolescents who externalize blame may not be accepting responsibility for their own actions (e.g., they may inappropriately externalize blame onto parents). There likely are potential shortcomings on both sides (i.e., parenting and the young person's conduct) that will require work. If these issues are identified as problem areas during the evaluation, they may need to be outlined in the psychological report and highlighted in the Recommendations section.

Parent training, along with individual psychological therapy, can go a long way toward improvement in the vast majority of juvenile offender cases. Therefore, forensic clinicians should look for programs that embody the characteristics mentioned above (i.e., positive orientation, parent training, shaping, modeling). These methods for changing disruptive behavior in youth have been well supported by decades of research and documented in thousands of articles (e.g., Weisz & Kazdin, 2010). However, these methods work only if the treatment is effectively implemented and maintained. Clearly, the family needs to be engaged. Although these types of treatments will help with many of the young people who come into contact with the justice system, there are also more serious offenders and more severe mental conditions that will require tailored treatments (Jouriles, McDonald, Mueller, & Rosenfield, 2014; Piehler, Bloomquist, August, Gewirtz, Lee, & Lee, 2014). Thus, improving parent skills may go only so far; additional treatment modalities may be required.

Multisystemic therapy (MST) is obviously a very good choice for serious juvenile offenders. This program is effective because it handles the youth's entire ecology: parents, schools, teachers, peers, and neighborhoods. Specifically, MST is an intensive family- and community-based treatment program that focuses on addressing the environmental systems that affects chronic and violent juvenile offenders. Proponents of MST recognize that each system plays a critical role in a young person's world and that each system requires attention when effective change is needed to improve the quality of life of young people and their families. MST has been shown to be effective with difficult offenders who have long histories of arrest. Other considerations, such as foster care placement and homeless youth, require additional treatment considerations (see Jouriles et al., 2014).

Two special concerns with juvenile offenders are (a) the treatment of interpersonal callousness, or callous–unemotional traits (Salekin, Tippey, & Allen, 2012); and (b) treatment in secure residential facilities where parents are typically not available or much less likely to be available on a regular basis. Recently, my research team embarked on interventions with young persons with interpersonally callous traits in a residential facility with a theory-based treatment called *mental models*. The mental models treatment program has a positive psychology focus and provides education on brain development (e.g., the mechanisms of the brain that are responsible for planning, inhibition, and emotion) and helps youth plan meaningful life interactions during the intervention.

Across the delivery of the mental models treatment intervention, interpersonal callousness, positive emotion, risk, developmental maturity, and treatment were indexed and measured at pre-, mid- and postintervention. Youth who participated in the program reduced their level of risk, increased their developmental maturity, and increased their treatment amenability (e.g., motivation to change; Salekin, Tippey, & Allen, 2012). Psychopathy scores also declined across the intervention, and staff reported that the young individuals in the treatment program improved their conduct in the residential facility. We are in the process of analyzing additional data from this informative project at the Department of Youth Services residential facility in Alabama, but these initial findings are positive for youth in residential facilities. Michael Caldwell at the Mendota Juvenile Treatment Center in Madison, Wisconsin, has also attempted to tackle the difficult problem of treating youth in secure facilities with reported success. More efforts in this regard will shine further light on ways to effectively treat youth in residential facilities.

The mental models intervention has also been implemented in a program for first-time offenders at the Disruptive Behavior Clinic, where youth are referred for treatment who have come into contact with the law because of domestic violence in the community (e.g., hitting or pushing a parent or sibling, interfering with the operation of a motor vehicle with the intent of causing an accident). Young persons engaged in this program must complete 9 weeks of treatment. This program also focuses on teaching young persons (and parents) about brain development and teaching youth to set goals and to make plans for a better life by making specific proximal plans to improve these major life areas (e.g., relationships and academics). Unlike a residential treatment program, this intervention has a parent training component that helps parents learn how to use positive parenting skills. Parents are also taught about brain development, which helps them to better understand the level at which their child is capable of working. This also helps reduce the particular myths of effective-parenting (e.g., that punishment works). In our experience, this can change parents from viewing the child's behavior as manipulative and deceptive to, instead, viewing the child's behavior as adaptive (and developmentally appropriate). This helps alter the parents' view of their child from someone who needs to be punished to someone who needs to be helped, as Patterson (1975) cogently noted. Parents are taught to anticipate potential problems ahead of time and set up environments where they can place their new found parenting skills ahead of problem behaviors and reward appropriate behaviors before unwanted behaviors occur.

RESIDENTIAL TREATMENT AND ATMOSPHERE

The gains made in a residential setting have much to do with the atmosphere of the facility, and the atmosphere should be rehabilitative. Forensic clinicians who are provided access to such settings can attempt to improve the atmosphere of the environment, if needed, by offering to conduct workshops for staff. Relevant topics could include maturity, brain development, and the importance of shifting the ratio of positive to negative reinforcement much more heavily in the positive direction. Thus, some focus should also be on training staff while at the same time improving youth decision making and planning. Such an educational component helps create an environment that is considerably more conducive to positive changes and increases in both amenability to treatment and developmental maturity, characteristics that have been shown to decline when youth are placed in residential facilities that do not have a positive tone (Dmitrieva, Monahan, Cauffman, & Steinberg, 2012).

Forensic clinicians should look for climates that represent this positive atmosphere. Making recommendations such as the need for five-to-one ratios of positive reinforcement to punishment (e.g., time-outs) is one way to shift this balance. These specific recommendations can be delineated in psychological reports. Moreover, the particular ingredients underscored in this chapter could also help clinicians in private practice who agree to accept juvenile treatment cases, if the psychological reports clearly delineate these specific recommendations for intervening.

The additional principles for treating young people introduced at the beginning of this chapter require further discussion to facilitate the identification of effective treatment programs for young people in one's state. Specifically, the topics I cover in further detail in the following sections include treatment dosage, positive psychology emphasis, being aware of psychopathology, and changing the ratio of positive to negative reinforcement to facilitate prosocial behavior.

Treatment Dosage

With respect to dosage, or length, of treatment, forensic clinicians should recommend treatment lengths that are likely to be effective. This entails considering what the youth needs in terms of intervention, including treatment for conduct problems, substance use, and perhaps cotreatment with the parents. When youth have primarily conduct problems without a host of other problems, my colleagues and I have found that treatment can be relatively brief. For example, for first-time offenders, my colleagues and I provide nine sessions of treatment across a 9-week time span. This turns out to be effective for this group, striking a balance between adequate dosage and allowing youth time to try things out on their own in the community after they have developed new skills. We have found that by the end of the 9 weeks the parents are taking a different approach to parenting and the young person has learned to interact differently with his or her parents. In addition, many of the young people involved in the treatment tell us that they have a more positive outlook after they completed the treatment. Part of what may be working is that the kids and their parents are strengthening their relationship and learning to communicate with one another in a more effective way. Youth in residential facilities usually have sufficient time to allow for adequate dosage, but questions can be raised about effectiveness that pertain to the content of treatment programs and follow-up care. Thus, with regard to content, the forensic clinician may be concerned with what the program actually contains for youth. One should look for ways in which blueprint programs might be used, or try to ensure that the content contains a strengths-based and positive psychology emphasis. With regard to the second question, even if young people have received a good dosage of effective treatment, follow-up can be an issue when transitioning back into the community. If mental health professionals can make recommendations that allow for effective follow-up treatment once young people leave residential facilities, this would ease the transition and increase the chances of success in the community. Mentorship programs, if effective in one's state, can be a good option for follow-up.

Positive Psychology

Although positive psychology has had its fair share of skeptics (e.g., McNulty & Fincham, 2012), it has been shown to be a viable and valuable subfield of psychology and has yielded interventions that have been helpful in increasing positive affect (e.g., Bannink, 2014; Seligman, Rashid, & Parks, 2006; Walker & Lampropoulos, 2014). Forensic clinicians should look for programs that reflect this positive psychology focus; that is, the programs should increase positive affect in youth and also allow clinicians to remain positive with young people while they are working with them in psychological therapy. Examples of this emphasis include helping parents and/or staff notice young people doing things right rather than punishing them when they have done something wrong, as well as having youth focus on their strengths, evidence good moments during the day, and express gratitude for the good things that have happened to them because of someone else (e.g., mother, father, grandparent). Having a positive psychology emphasis that includes focusing on strengths and being constructive with young people models to youth that they can learn to be constructive with others. Positive psychology interventions are likely to affect brain development and promote healthy neural development between the frontal cortex and the amygdala and other regions of the brain, whereby youth will learn to inhibit impulsive decisions and use positive emotion in their decision making (see Damasio, 1994; Salekin, Tippey, & Allen, 2012; Vaughan, 1997).

Being Aware of Psychopathology

The psychological practices mentioned above will work for the bulk of cases; however, specialized treatment will be needed for young people who have conditions such as schizophrenia or depression. This will likely include a psychopharmacological intervention. These individuals need to be identified and diagnosed early and provided with the care that is needed. A number of additional team members will be required for such treatment efforts to be effective, including, possibly, psychiatrists to determine the appropriate psychopharmacological regimen. In their reports and testimony, forensic clinicians should include recommendations for evaluations to determine psychopharmacological interventions.

Changing the Ratio of Positive to Negative Reinforcement

Engineering environments that enable the desired behavior is primary in the treatment of youth involved in the justice system. Making recommendations for improving environmental conditions usually comes in the form of parenting advice and by placing greater expectations on the young person. This advice should be highlighted in one's forensic report. For example, use, and implementation, of a behavioral activation program is one way to engineer an environment in which prosocial behavior can be initiated and rewarded. Opportunities to work out at the gym, play a sport, go for a run, take a walk, or engage in a hobby provide the chance to increase health, increase positive affect, and build competencies in important life activities. When the desired behaviors are initiated, and performed, rewards should be available and immediate. Even verbal praise can be very effective in this regard. Because such ingredients are key to effective change, they should be standard recommendations for intervening with youth in the juvenile justice system. Mentoring programs can, where available, help implement some of the aforementioned behavioral activities and further augment treatment.

Thus, creating healthy environments improves one's chances of producing change and should be underscored in the recommendations section of forensic evaluators' reports.

CONCLUDING COMMENTS

In this chapter, I addressed the important issue of the treatment of juvenile offenders. Clinicians can look to the model programs discussed earlier in this chapter, where such programs are available, for reducing conduct problems and delinquency. When these programs are not readily available, clinicians should look to the chief ingredients that are most effective when intervening with young people who may have oppositional defiant and conduct problem disorders and recommend those key factors to improve youth behavior. These recommendations should be clearly outlined in the Recommendations section of forensic evaluators' reports. Many parent training techniques can be helpful in reducing oppositional and conduct problems. In addition, programs whose staff have been trained to understand youth development (e.g., brain development, developmental maturity) can be helpful in facilitating healthy youth development. Finally, it should be noted that evidence-based model programs, as well as newer innovative programs, have not yet solved the problem of delinquency. Because of this, forensic clinicians and researchers should continue to build on the many programs that exist for youth with disruptive behavior disorders. This is another area where a three-way interchange among forensic clinicians, juvenile justice administrators, and researchers could very well be fruitful by further refining and adding to the effective ingredients that improve and promote positive youth behavior (Schweizer, Grahn, Hampshire, Mobbs, & Dalgleish, 2013). Such efforts will help shape parenting and help youth better understand themselves and make more informed plans for the future that entail healthy social development, even in the most difficult environments.

10

CONCLUSION AND FUTURE DIRECTIONS

Numerous scholars have criticized the juvenile justice system for not meeting the rehabilitative goals it set out to accomplish (Fagan & Zimring, 2000; Schetky & Benedek, 1980; Zimring, 1998). For some young people, however, the juvenile justice system works quite well as a means for correcting delinquent behavior. This is evidenced by the many youth who come into contact with the law for the first time, whether through involvement with the police or juvenile courts, and never return to the legal system (Woolard, Odgers, Lanza-Kaduce, & Daglis, 2005). Although the reasons for this are not always clear, this initial contact with the law may provide the necessary admonition young people need to effectively adjust their behavior and subsequently behave lawfully. The favorable impact of the state system may occur through the discretion of a police officer or a juvenile court decision maker who decides to warn a youngster about the potential negative long-range consequences of his or her behavior rather than immediately turning to a reprimand. Decisions to warn rather than formally process youth allow many

http://dx.doi.org/10.1037/14595-011
Forensic Evaluation and Treatment of Juveniles: Innovation and Best Practice, by R. T. Salekin
Copyright © 2015 by the American Psychological Association. All rights reserved.

young individuals and their families to correct their behavior and return to healthy functioning in the community. Many of these young people return to their communities with little oversight from the government, without the potentially harmful impact of the legal system and with few costs to society. When the juvenile justice system works in this fashion, it is working effectively and is obviously the best possible outcome for all parties involved. As I have noted in this book, however, many young people do make their way further into the system. When this happens, the courts often recommend that the young person undergo a psychological evaluation and possibly receive intervention to correct his or her errant behavior.

In the chapters of this book, I detailed how such evaluations can be competently conducted by blending best practice with innovative methods of thinking about data collection and interpretation that allow for even greater amounts of scientific data to be gathered, such as the use of general models of personality, even projective testing, and the selection of measures with relevance to the psycholegal constructs. I also outlined the laws, legal processing, and various places where a clinician's psychological knowledge may come into play in the evaluation of young people in the legal system. Also discussed within the pages of this book were the statistics that are available to better understand juvenile offenders, the importance of being aware of the current political and social climate, and the major case laws and Supreme Court decisions that are relevant to juvenile offenders. I also provided detail regarding data on the main constructs to be assessed when evaluating juvenile offenders and the science behind the constructs. These constructs include the truthfulness of reporting, personality/psychopathology, risk, developmental maturity, and amenability to treatment. The difficult concept of developmental maturity was reviewed and considered in terms of neuroscience and recent case law. In addition, I covered information on how to prepare to train to conduct juvenile evaluations. Finally, I covered the important topics of report writing, testimony, and effective treatment, as well as how to develop a set of treatment recommendations when model programs are not available or are too expensive in a particular locale.

In these chapters, I discussed the complexity of the system using a subway analogy and the diversity of young people within it ranging from the fairly mild cases of youth with conduct problems, such as those embodied by the fictional characters Huckleberry Finn and Tom Sawyer as well as Calvin from the *Calvin and Hobbes* comic strip. Of course, more extreme cases exist, some of which, unfortunately, involve quite heinous crimes and have been covered on world news television and in national and international newspapers. Quite often these cases involve even more severe forms of psychopathology and significant caretaker problems, including considerable problems with attachment (Bowlby, 1958, 1977, 1978, 1984, 1988). Nonetheless, it is my hope that the foundation for assessment provided within this book will help prepare clinicians for the process of arriving at a clinical formulation and plan for even the most difficult cases.

In the future, much more can be done when one has adequate training as a forensic psychologist. One's forensic practice can be used to help increase the knowledge of the courts and to continue to learn from the courts and their various components (e.g., attorneys, judges, probation officers, detention facilities). The more that forensic clinicians can bring broad strands of research together, such as those on personality and temperament, the better they will be able to inform the courts. Therefore, in this book I have proposed a model that incorporates best practice and at the same time recommends innovation that can be used to broaden what the courts learn about the psychology of young people involved with the legal system and the effective treatment of juvenile offenders. In my opinion, grassroots efforts will be needed to help the courts better understand youth as well as to provide the many young people in the juvenile justice system with the treatment they very much need. Young people who come into contact with the law can benefit from treatment if it is readily available. Providing treatment in juvenile justice settings (detention and residential facilities) and in clinics has the benefit of immediate service to the courts and young people. The opportunity to work with youth by offering services where they are needed is a unique chance to change a young person's life when he or she may not have otherwise sought treatment.

The next steps will be to expand assessment and treatment practices across the United States and to expand these interventions into the community so that both assessment and intervention can help with the life transitions. Although arguments have been made that youth will never change because of the communities to which they return, this does not necessarily have to be the case. If assessments are focused and interventions are properly geared toward the young person's needs, then, with sufficient treatment dosage, significant strides in treatment can be made. Interventions that target environmental systems, such as multisystemic therapy (see Chapter 9), can have a significant effect on adolescent behavior and should be considered wherever possible.

The future of forensic assessment and intervention for young people holds much promise. There are several areas that will likely grow and continue to inform assessment and treatment. In the forthcoming years, psychological theories regarding young people involved with the law should be advanced, and these theories should be integrated with neuroscience (Rutter, 2000). Innovation in assessment and treatment technology also is needed. Advancements in these areas can further improve a young person's social development. Much benefit also can come from the provision of parent training and mentoring of youth. When parents are not available for treatment, youth can take what they learn in therapy, such as new ways to negotiate with family members, back into their homes, where they can initiate change with their parents.

Processing youth in the community or juvenile justice system rather than the adult system is likely to reflect best practice, especially if they can be treated before problems become too serious. Also, treatment in the community and within the juvenile justice system reflects a better representation of the *parens patriae* philosophy (see Chapter 1), which is in line with the original spirit of the juvenile court system. Given the wide array of problems in U.S. society, these bottom-up efforts are very much needed. Additional efforts that include the use of technology, going into the field where services are needed, and cross-training individuals for the delivery of service are key. In their evaluations and reports forensic clinicians should recommend treatments that encompass parent training and target primary psychological systems. In addition, broad lifestyle changes, to include exercise, nutrition, engaging in recreational activities, volunteering and contributing to others— all of which can improve a young person's physical and mental health—should be encouraged. Incremental success in the juvenile justice system is likely to begin with the effective training of mental health professionals who can then provide clear reports to the courts regarding youth characteristics and youth needs. Such competent evaluations will then lead to effective treatment and, correspondingly, the best opportunity for healthy youth development.

REFERENCES

Aalsma, M. C., & Lapsley, D. K. (2001). A typology of adolescent delinquency: Sex differences and implications for treatment. *Criminal Behaviour and Mental Health, 11,* 173–191. doi:10.1002/cbm.386

Abram, K. M., Choe, J. Y., Washburn, J. J., Romero, E. G., & Teplin, L. A. (2009). Functional impairment in youth three years after detention. *Journal of Adolescent Health, 44,* 528–535.

Abram, K. M., Washburn, J. J., Teplin, L. A., Emanuel, K. M., Romero, E. G., & McClelland, G. M. (2007). Posttraumatic stress disorder and psychiatric comorbidity among detained youths. *Psychiatric Services, 58,* 1311–1316.

Achenbach, T. M. (1985). *Assessment and taxonomy of child and adolescent psychopathology.* Thousand Oaks, CA: Sage.

Achenbach, T. M. (1991a). The derivation of taxonomic constructs: A necessary stage in the development of developmental psychopathology. In D. Cicchetti & S. L. Toth (Eds.), *Rochester Symposium on Developmental Psychopathology: Vol. 3. Models and integrations* (pp. 43–74). Rochester, NY: University of Rochester Press.

Achenbach, T. M. (1991b). *Manual for the Child Behavior Checklist/4-18 and 1991 Profile.* Burlington: University of Vermont, Department of Psychiatry.

Achenbach, T. M. (1991c). *Manual for the Teachers Report Form and 1991 Profile.* Burlington: University of Vermont, Department of Psychiatry.

Achenbach, T. M. (1991d). *Manual for the Youth Self-Report and 1991 Profile.* Burlington: University of Vermont, Department of Psychiatry.

Achenbach, T. M. (1995). Diagnosis, assessment, and comorbidity in psychosocial treatment research. *Journal of Abnormal Child Psychology, 23,* 45–65. doi:10.1007/BF01447044

Ackerman, B. P., Brown, E., & Izard, C. E. (2003). Continuity and change in levels of externalizing behavior in school of children from economically disadvantaged families. *Child Development, 74,* 694–709. doi:10.1111/1467-8624.00563

Adams, B., & Addie, S. (2010, June). *Delinquency cases waived to criminal court, 2007.* Washington, DC: U.S. Department of Justice, Office of Justice Programs, Office of Juvenile Justice and Delinquency Prevention.

Adams, G. R., Bennion, L., & Huh, K. (1989). *Objective measure of ego identity status: A reference manual.* Unpublished manuscript, University of Guelph, Toronto, Ontario, Canada.

Adams, S. (1970). The PICO project. In N. Johnson, L. Savitz, & M. E. Wolfgang (Eds.), *The sociology of punishment and correction* (2nd ed., pp. 548–561). New York, NY: Wiley.

Aharoni, E., Vincent, G. M., Harenski, C. L., Calhoun, V. D., Sinnott-Armstrong, W., Gazzaniga, M. S., & Kiehl, K. A. (2013). Neuroprediction of future arrest.

Proceedings of the National Academy of Sciences of the United States of America, *110,* 6223–6228. doi:10.1073/pnas.1219302110

Albano, A. M., & Silverman, W. K. (1996). *The Anxiety Disorders Interview Schedule for Children for DSM–IV: Clinician Manual (Child and Parent Versions).* San Antonio, TX: The Psychological Corporation.

Allen, L. M., Conder, R. L., Green, P., & Cox, D. R. (1997). *CARB'97 manual for the Computerized Assessment of Response Bias.* Durham, NC: CogniSyst.

Allport, G. W. (1937). *Personality: A psychological interpretation.* New York, NY: Henry Holt.

Ambrosini, P. J. (1992a). Schedule for Affective Disorders and Schizophrenia for School-Age Children—Present and Life Time Version (K-SADS–PL): Initial reliability and validity data. *Journal of the American Academy of Child & Adolescent Psychiatry, 36,* 980–988.

Ambrosini, P. J. (1992b). *Schedule for Affective Disorders and Schizophrenia for School Age Children (6–18 years): Kiddie-SADS* (present state version). Philadelphia: Medical College of Pennsylvania.

Ambrosini, P. J., & Dixon, M. (1996). *Schedule for Affective and Schizophrenic Disorders, Childhood Version* (4th ed.). Philadelphia: Medical College of Pennsylvania.

Amendola, M., & Oliver, R. (2010). Aggression replacement training stands the test of time. *Reclaiming Children and Youth, 19,* 47–50.

American Academy of Psychiatry and the Law. (2005). *Ethics guidelines for the practice of forensic psychiatry.* Retrieved from http://www.aapl.org/ethics.htm

American Educational Research Association, American Psychological Association, & National Council on Measurement in Education. (1999). *Standards for educational and psychological testing.* Washington, DC: Author.

American Educational Research Association, American Psychological Association, & National Council on Measurement in Education. (2014). *Standards for educational and psychological testing* (2014 ed.). Washington, DC: American Educational Research Association.

American Psychiatric Association. (1994). *Diagnostic and statistical manual of mental disorders* (4th ed.). Washington, DC: Author.

American Psychiatric Association. (2013). *Diagnostic and statistical manual of mental disorders* (5th ed.). Washington, DC: Author.

American Psychological Association. (1986). *Guidelines for computer-based tests and interpretations.* Washington, DC: Author.

American Psychological Association. (1990). *Guidelines for providers of psychological services to ethnic, linguistic, and culturally diverse populations.* Retrieved from http://www.apa.org/pi/oema/resources/policy/provider-guidelines.aspx

American Psychological Association. (2002). Empirical principles of psychologists and code of conduct. *American Psychologist, 57,* 1060–1073. doi:10.1037/0003-066X. 57.12.1060

American Psychological Association. (2007a). *Guidelines and principles for accreditation of programs in professional psychology.* Retrieved from http://www.apa.org/ed/accreditation/about/policies/guiding-principles.pdf

American Psychological Association. (2007b). Record keeping guidelines. *American Psychologist, 62,* 993–1004. doi:10.1037/0003-066X.62.9.993

American Psychological Association. (2010). *Ethical principles of psychologists and code of conduct (with 2010 amendments).* Washington, DC: Author. Retrieved from http://www.apa.org/ethics/code/principles.pdf

American Psychological Association. (2013a). Recognition of psychotherapy effectiveness. *Psychotherapy, 50,* 102–109. doi:10.1037/a0030276

American Psychological Association. (2013b). Specialty guidelines for forensic psychology. *American Psychologist, 68,* 7–19. doi:10.1037/a0029889

Anastasi, A. (1998). *Psychological testing* (7th ed.). Upper Saddle River, NJ: Prentice Hall.

Andershed, H. (2010). Stability and change of psychopathic traits: What do we know. In R. T. Salekin & D. R. Lynam (Eds.), *Handbook of child and adolescent psychopathy* (pp. 233–250). New York, NY: Guilford Press.

Andrews, D. A., & Bonta, J. (1995). *LSI–R: The Level of Service Inventory—Revised.* Toronto, Ontario, Canada: Multi-Health Systems, Inc.

Andrews, D. A., Bonta, J., & Hoge, R. D. (1990). Classification for effective rehabilitation: Rediscovering psychology. *Criminal Justice and Behavior, 17,* 19–52. doi:10.1177/0093854890017001004

Ang, X., Salekin, R. T., Sellbom, M., & Lee, Z. (2014, March). *Assessment of sophistication–maturity with the Risk–Sophistication–Treatment Inventory—Self Report.* Poster presented at the annual American Psychology–Law Society conference, New Orleans, LA.

Annin, P. (1996, January 22). Superpredators arrive: Should we cage the new breed of vicious kids? *Newsweek,* p. 57.

Archer, R. P., & Handel, R. W. (2014). The Minnesota Multiphasic Personality Inventory—Adolescent. In R. P. Archer & E. M. A. Wheeler (Eds.), *Forensic uses of clinical assessment instruments* (2nd ed., pp. 108–139). New York, NY: Routledge.

Archer, S. L., & Waterman, A. S. (1993). Identity status interview: Early and middle adolescent form. In D. R. Matteson, J. L. Orlofsky, A. S. Waterman, S. L. Archer, & J. E. Marcia (Eds.), *Ego identity: A handbook of psychosocial research* (pp. 177–204). New York, NY: Springer-Verlag. doi:10.1007/978-1-4613-8330-7_8

Arnett, J. J. (1999). Adolescent storm and stress, reconsidered. *American Psychologist, 54,* 317–326. doi:10.1037/0003-066X.54.5.317

Aronson, J. D. (2007). Brain imaging, culpability and the juvenile death penalty. *Psychology, Public Policy, and Law, 13,* 115–142. doi:10.1037/1076-8971.13.2.115

Aronson, J. D. (2010). The law's use of brain evidence. *Annual Review of Law and Social Science*, 6, 93–108. doi:10.1146/annurev-lawsocsci-102209-152948

Asendorpf, J. B. (1994). The malleability of behavior inhibition: A study of individual developmental functions. *Developmental Psychology*, 30, 912–919. doi:10.1037/0012-1649.30.6.912

Asendorpf, J. B., & van Aken, M. A. G. (2003a). Personality–relationship transaction in adolescence: Core versus surface personality characteristics. *Journal of Personality*, 71, 629–666. doi:10.1111/1467-6494.7104005

Asendorpf, J. B., & van Aken, M. A. G. (2003b). Validity of Big Five personality judgments in childhood: A 9-year longitudinal study. *European Journal of Personality*, 17, 1–17. doi:10.1002/per.460

Ashford, J. B., Sales, B. D., & Reid, W. H. (2007). *Treating adult and juvenile offenders with special needs*. Washington, DC: American Psychological Association.

Asscher, J. J., van Vugt, E. S., Stams, G. J. J. M., Deković, M., Eichelsheim, V. I., & Yousfi, S. (2011). The relationship between juvenile psychopathic traits, delinquency and (violent) recidivism: A meta-analysis. *Journal of Child Psychology and Psychiatry*, 52, 1134–1143.

Austin, J., Dedel Johnson, K., & Gregoriou, M. (2000). *Juveniles in adult prisons and jails: A national assessment*. Washington, DC: Bureau of Justice Assistance. Retrieved from https://www.ncjrs.gov/pdffiles1/bja/182503.pdf

Bandura, A. (1999). Social cognitive theory: An agentic perspective. *Asian Journal of Social Psychology*, 2, 21–41. doi:10.1111/1467-839X.00024

Bannink, F. P. (2014). Positive CBT: From reducing distress to building success. *Journal of Contemporary Psychotherapy*, 44, 1–8. doi:10.1007/s10879-013-9239-7

Barbot, B., & Hunter, S. (2012). *Handbook of juvenile forensic psychology and psychiatry*. New York, NY: Springer Science + Business Media.

Barends, A., Westen, D., Leigh, J., Silbert, D., & Byers, S. (1990). Assessing affect-tone of relationship paradigms from TAT and interview data. *Psychological Assessment*, 2, 329–332. doi:10.1037/1040-3590.2.3.329

Barker, E. D., Oliver, B., Viding, E., Salekin, R. T., & Maughan, B. (2011). The impact of prenatal maternal risk, fearless temperament and early parenting on adolescent callous–unemotional traits: A 14-year longitudinal investigation. *Journal of Child Psychology and Psychiatry*, 52, 878–888. doi:10.1111/j.1469-7610.2011.02397.x

Barker, E. D., & Salekin, R. T. (2012). Irritable oppositional defiance and callous unemotional traits: Is the association partially explained by peer victimization? *Journal of Child Psychology and Psychiatry*, 53, 1167–1175. doi:10.1111/j.1469-7610.2012.02579.x

Barker, E. D., Trentacosta, C. J., & Salekin, R. T. (2011). Are impulsive adolescents differentially influenced by the good and bad of neighborhood and family? *Journal of Abnormal Psychology*, 120, 981–986. doi:10.1037/a0022878

Barnum, R. (1987). Clinical evaluation of juvenile delinquents facing transfer to adult court. *Journal of the American Academy of Child & Adolescent Psychiatry*, 26, 922–925. doi:10.1097/00004583-198726060-00018

Bar-On, R., & Parker, J. D. A. (2000). *EQi:YV: Bar-On Emotional Quotient Inventory: Youth Version technical manual*. Toronto, Ontario, Canada: Multi-Health Systems.

Barsky, A. E., & Gould, J. W. (1996). *Clinicians in court: A guide to subpoenas, depositions, testifying, and everything else you need to know*. New York, NY: Guilford Press.

Bates, J. E., & McFadyen-Ketchum, S. (2000). Temperament and parent–child relations as interacting factors in children's behavioral adjustment. In V. J. Molfese & D. L. Molfese (Eds.), *Temperament and personality development across the life span* (pp. 141–176). Mahwah, NJ: Erlbaum.

Bates, J. E., Pettit, G. S., Dodge, K. A., & Ridge, B. (1998). Interaction of temperamental resistance to control and restrictive parenting in the development of externalizing behavior. *Developmental Psychology, 34*, 982–995. doi:10.1037/0012-1649.34.5.982

Beaver, K. M., Boutwell, B. B., & Barnes, J. C. (2014). Social support or biosocial support? A genetically informative analysis of social support and its relation to self-control. *Criminal Justice and Behavior, 41*, 453–470. doi:10.1177/0093854813504918

Bechtold, J., & Cauffman, E. (2014). Tried as an adult, housed as a juvenile: A tale of youth from two courts incarcerated together. *Journal of Law and Social Behavior, 38*, 126–138. doi:10.1037/lhb0000048

Beck, J. S., Beck, A. T., Jolly, J. B., & Steer, R. A. (2005). *Beck Youth Inventories— Second Edition manual*. San Antonio, TX: The Psychological Corporation.

Becker, S. P., Kerig, P. K., Lim, J. Y., & Ezechukwu, R. N. (2012). Predictors of recidivism among delinquent youth: Interrelations among ethnicity, gender, age, mental health problems, and posttraumatic stress. *Journal of Child & Adolescent Trauma, 5*, 145–160. doi:10.1080/19361521.2012.671798

Belsky, J., Bakermans-Kranenburg, M. J., & van IJzendoorn, M. H. (2007). For better and for worse: Differential susceptibility to environmental influences. *Current Directions in Psychological Science, 16*, 300–304. doi:10.1111/j.1467-8721.2007.00525.x

Belsky, J., Fearon, P., Bell, R. M., & Bell, B. (2007). Parenting, attention and externalizing problems: Testing mediation longitudinally, repeatedly and reciprocally. *Journal of Child Psychology and Psychiatry, 48*, 1233–1242.

Belsky, J., Hsieh, K., & Crnic, K. (1998). Mothering, fathering, and infant negativity as antecedents of boys' externalizing problems and inhibition at age 3: Differential susceptibility to rearing influence? *Development and Psychopathology, 10*, 301–319. doi:10.1017/S095457949800162X

Belsky, J., Jaffee, S. R., Caspi, A., Moffitt, T. E., & Silva, P. A. (2003). Intergenerational relationships in young adulthood and their life course, mental health, and personality correlates. *Journal of Family Psychology, 17*, 460–471.

Bergh, S., & Erling, A. (2005). Adolescent identity formation: A Swedish study of identity status using the EOM–EIS–II. *Adolescence, 40*, 377–396.

Bernstein, D. P., Cohen, P., Skodol, A., Bezirganian, S., & Brook, J. S. (1996). Childhood antecedents of adolescent personality disorders. *The American Journal of Psychiatry, 153*, 907–913.

Bernstein, D. P., Cohen, P., Velez, N., Schwab-Stone, M., Siever, L., & Shinsato, L. (1993). Prevalence and stability of the *DSM–III* personality disorders in a community-based survey of adolescents. *The American Journal of Psychiatry, 150,* 1237–1243.

Bersoff, D. N. (1995). *Ethical conflicts in psychology.* Washington, DC: American Psychological Association. doi:10.1037/10171-000

Bersoff, D. N. (2008). *Ethical conflicts in psychology* (4th ed.). Washington, DC: American Psychological Association.

Black, S., Washington, E., Trent, V., Harner, P., & Pollock, E. (2010). Translating the Olweus Bullying Prevention Program into real-world practice. *Health Promotion Practice, 11,* 733–740. doi:10.1177/1524839908321562

Boccaccini, M. T., Murrie, D. C., Clark, J. W., & Cornell, D. G. (2008). Describing, diagnosing, and naming psychopathy: How do youth psychopathy labels influence jurors? *Behavioral Sciences & the Law, 26,* 487–510. doi:10.1002/bsl.821

Bøe, T., Sivertsen, B., Heiervang, E., Goodman, R., Lundervold, A. J., & Hysing, M. (2014). Socioeconomic status and child mental health: The role of parental emotional well-being and parenting practices. *Journal of Abnormal Child Psychology, 42,* 705–715. doi:10.1007/s10802-013-9818-9

Bonnie, R. J., Johnson, R. L., Chemers, B. M., & Schuck, J. (2012). *Reforming juvenile justice: A developmental approach.* Washington, DC: National Academies Press.

Bonta, J., & Andrews, D. A. (2007). *Risk–need–responsivity model for offender assessment and treatment* (User Report No. 2007-06). Ottawa, Ontario, Canada: Public Safety Canada.

Bools, C., Foster, J., Brown, I., & Berg, I. (1990). The identification of psychiatric disorders in children who fail to attend school: A cluster analysis of a non-clinical population. *Psychological Medicine, 20,* 171–181. doi:10.1017/S0033291700013350

Boone, K. B., & Lu, P. H. (2003). Noncredible cognitive performance in the context of severe brain injury. *Clinical Neuropsychologist, 17,* 244–254.

Borduin, C., & Sawyer, A. (2011). Effects of multisystemic therapy throughout midlife: A 21.9-year follow-up to a randomized clinical trial with serious and violent juvenile offenders. *Journal of Counseling and Clinical Psychology, 79,* 643–652.

Borduin, C. M., Schaeffer, C. M., & Heiblum, N. (2009). A randomized clinical trial of multisystemic therapy with juvenile sexual offenders: Effects on youth social ecology and criminal activity. *Journal of Consulting and Clinical Psychology, 77,* 26–37. doi:10.1037/a0013035

Borum, R. (1996). Improving the clinical practice of violence risk assessment: Technology, guidelines, and training. *American Psychologist, 51,* 945–956. doi:10.1037/0003-066X.51.9.945

Borum, R., Bartel, P., & Forth, A. (2005). Structured Assessment of Violence Risk in Youth. In T. Grisso, G. Vincent, & D. Seagrave (Eds.), *Mental health screening and assessment in juvenile justice* (pp. 311–323). New York, NY: Guilford Press.

Borum, R., & Verhaagen, D. (2006). *Assessing and managing violence risk in juveniles*. New York, NY: Guilford Press.

Bowlby, J. (1958). The nature of the child's tie to his mother. *The International Journal of Psychoanalysis, 39*, 350–373.

Bowlby, J. (1977). The making and breaking of affectional bonds: I. Aetiology and psychopathology in the light of attachment theory. *British Journal of Psychiatry, 130*, 201–210.

Bowlby, J. (1978). Attachment theory and its therapeutic implications. *Adolescent Psychiatry, 6*, 5–33.

Bowlby, J. (1984). Violence in the family as a disorder of the attachment and caregiving systems. *American Journal of Psychoanalysis, 44*, 9–27.

Bowlby, J. (1988). *A secure base: Parent–child attachment and healthy human development*. New York, NY: Basic Books.

Brannen, D. N., Salekin, R. T., Zapf, P. A., Salekin, K. L., Kubak, F. A., & DeCoster, J. (2006). Transfer to adult court: A national study of how juvenile court judges weigh pertinent Kent criteria. *Psychology, Public Policy, and Law, 12*, 332–355. doi:10.1037/1076-8971.12.3.332

Brennan, E. M., Bradley, J. R., Allen, M. D., & Perry, D. F. (2008). The evidence base for mental health consultation in early childhood settings: Research synthesis addressing staff and program outcomes. *Early Education & Development, 6*, 982–1022.

Brent, D. A., Johnson, B., Perper, J., Connolly, J., Bridge, J., Bartle, S., & Rather, C. (1994). Personality disorder, personality traits, impulsive violence, and completed suicide in adolescents. *Journal of the American Academy of Child & Adolescent Psychiatry, 33*, 1080–1086. doi:10.1097/00004583-199410000-00003

Brent, D. A., Zelenak, J. P., Buckstein, O., & Brown, R. V. (1990). Reliability and validity of the structured interview of personality disorders in adolescents. *Journal of the American Academy of Child & Adolescent Psychiatry, 29*, 349–354. doi:10.1097/00004583-199005000-00003

Brodsky, S. L. (1995). Prison redux. *PsycCRITIQUES, 40*, 551–552. doi:10.1037/003722

Brodsky, S. L. (2013). *Testifying in court: Guidelines and maxims for the expert witness* (2nd ed.). Washington, DC: American Psychological Association.

Brownstein, H. H. (2000). *The social reality of violence and violent crime*. Boston, MA: Allyn & Bacon.

Burke, J. D., Hipwell, A. E., & Loeber, R. (2010). Dimensions of oppositional defiant disorder as predictors of depression and conduct disorder in preadolescent girls. *Journal of the American Academy of Child & Adolescent Psychiatry, 49*, 484–492.

Burke, J. D., & Loeber, R. (2010). Oppositional defiant disorder and the explanation of the comorbidity between behavioral disorders and depression. *Clinical Psychology: Science and Practice, 17*, 319–326. doi:10.1111/j.1468-2850.2010.01223.x

Burke, J. D., Pardini, D. A., & Loeber, R. (2008). Reciprocal relationships between parenting behavior and disruptive psychopathology from childhood through adolescence. *Journal of Abnormal Child Psychology, 36,* 679–692.

Buss, A. H., & Plomin, R. (1984). *Temperament: Early developing personality traits.* Hillsdale, NJ: Erlbaum.

Bussey, K. (1992). Lying and truthfulness: Children's definitions, standards, and evaluative reactions. *Child Development, 63,* 129–137. doi:10.2307/1130907

Butcher, J. N., Dahlstrom, W. G., Graham, J. R., Tellegen, A., & Kaemmer, B. (1989). *The Minnesota Multiphasic Personality Inventory—2 (MMPI–2): Manual for administration and scoring.* Minneapolis: University of Minnesota Press.

Butcher, J. N., Williams, C. L., Graham, J. R., Archer, R. P., Tellegen, A., Ben-Porath, Y. S., & Kaemmer, B. (1992). *Minnesota Multiphasic Personality Inventory—Adolescent: Manual for administration, scoring, and interpretation.* Minneapolis: University of Minnesota Press.

Butler, S., Baruch, G., Hickey, N., & Fonagy, P. (2011). A randomized controlled trial of multisystemic therapy and a statutory therapeutic intervention for young offenders. *Journal of the American Academy of Child & Adolescent Psychiatry, 50,* 1220–1235. doi:10.1016/j.jaac.2011.09.017

Caldwell, M., Skeem, J. L., Salekin, R. T., & VanRybroek, G. (2006). Treatment response of adolescent offenders with psychopathy features: A 2-year follow-up. *Criminal Justice & Behavior, 33,* 571–596. doi:10.1177/0093854806288176

Campbell, L. F., Norcross, J. C., Vasquez, M. J. T., & Kaslow, N. J. (2013). Recognition of psychotherapy effectiveness: The APA resolution. *Psychotherapy, 50,* 98–101. doi:10.1037/a0031817

Caprara, G. V., Alessandri, G., Di Giunta, L., Panerai, L., & Eisenberg, N. (2009). The contribution of agreeableness and self-efficacy beliefs to prosociality. *European Journal of Personality, 24,* 36–55. doi:10.1002/per.739

Carlson, B. E., Barr, W. B., & Young, K. J. (1994). Factors associated with treatment outcomes of male adolescents. *Residential Treatment for Children & Youth, 12,* 39–58. doi:10.1300/J007v12n01_03

Casey, S., Day, A., Howells, K., & Ward, T. (2007). Assessing suitability for offender rehabilitation: Development and validation of the Treatment Readiness Questionnaire. *Criminal Justice and Behavior, 34,* 1427–1440. doi:10.1177/0093854807305827

Caspi, A., & Bem, D. (1990). Personality continuity and change across the life course. In L. Pervin (Ed.), *Handbook of personality: Theory and research* (pp. 549–575). New York, NY: Guilford Press.

Caspi, A., Bem, D. J., & Elder, G. H. (1989). Continuities and consequences of interactional styles across the life course. *Journal of Personality, 57,* 375–406. doi:10.1111/j.1467-6494.1989.tb00487.x

Caspi, A., Lynam, D. R., Moffitt, T. E., & Silva, P. A. (1993). Unraveling girls' delinquency: Biological, dispositional, and contextual contributions to adolescent misbehavior. *Developmental Psychology, 29,* 19–30. doi:10.1037/0012-1649.29.1.19

Caspi, A., Roberts, B. W., & Shiner, R. L. (2005). Personality development: Stability and change. *Annual Review of Psychology, 56*, 453–484. doi:10.1146/annurev.psych.55.090902.141913

Caspi, A., & Shiner, R. L. (2006). Personality development. In W. Damon & R. Lerner (Series Eds.) & N. Eisenberg (Vol. Ed.), *Handbook of child psychology: Vol. 3. Social, emotional, and personality development* (6th ed., pp. 300–365). Hoboken, NJ: Wiley.

Catchpole, R. E., & Gretton, H. M. (2003). The predictive validity of risk assessment with violent young offenders: A 1-year examination of criminal outcome. *Criminal Justice and Behavior, 30*, 688–708. doi:10.1177/0093854803256455

Cauffman, E., & Steinberg, L. (2000). (Im)maturity of judgment in adolescence: Why adolescents may be less culpable than adults. *Behavioral Sciences & the Law, 18*, 741–760. doi:10.1002/bsl.416

Cauffman, E., Steinberg, L., & Piquero, A. R. (2005). Psychological, neuropsychological and physiological correlates of serious antisocial behavior in adolescence: The role of self-control. *Criminology, 43*, 133–176. doi:10.1111/j.0011-1348.2005.00005.x

Cecil, C. A. M., Lysenko, L. J., Jaffee, S. R., Pingault, J.-B., Smith, R. G., Relton, C. L., . . . Barker, E. D. (2014). Environmental risk, oxytocin receptor gene (OXTR) methylation and youth callous–unemotional traits: A 13-year longitudinal study. *Molecular Psychiatry, 19*, 1071–1077. doi:10.1038/mp.2014.95

Chambers, W. J., Puig-Antich, J., Hirsch, M., Paez, P., Ambrosini, P. J., Tabrizi, M. A., & Davies, M. (1985). The assessment of affective disorders in children and adolescents by semistructured interview: Test–retest reliability of the Schedule for Affective Disorders and Schizophrenia for School Aged Children, present episode version. *Archives of General Psychiatry, 42*, 696–702.

Champion, D. J., & Mays, G. L. (1991). *Transferring juveniles to criminal courts: Trends and implications for criminal justice.* New York, NY: Praeger.

Chanda, M. L., & Levitin, D. J. (2013). The neurochemistry of music. *Trends in Cognitive Sciences, 17*, 179–193.

Chang, L. (2003). Variable effects of children's aggression, social withdrawal, and prosocial leadership as functions of teacher beliefs and behaviors. *Child Development, 74*, 535–548. doi:10.1111/1467-8624.7402014

Chapman, J. F. (2012). The juvenile forensic court clinic in theory and practice. In E. Grigorenko (Ed.), *Handbook of juvenile forensic psychology and psychiatry* (pp. 201–214). New York, NY: Springer. doi:10.1007/978-1-4614-0905-2_13

Chen, D. R., & Salekin, R. T. (2012). Transfer to adult court: Enhancing clinical forensic evaluations and informing policy. In E. L. Grigorenko (Ed.), *Handbook of juvenile forensic psychology and psychiatry* (pp. 105–125). New York, NY: Springer Science + Business Media.

Chen, X., Li, D., Li, Z., Li, B., & Liu, M. (2000). Sociable and prosocial dimensions of social competence in Chinese children: Common and unique contributions to social, academic, and psychological adjustment. *Developmental Psychology, 36*, 302–314. doi:10.1037/0012-1649.36.3.302

Chen, X., Liu, M., Rubin, K. H., Cen, G., Gao, X., & Li, D. (2002). Sociability and prosocial orientation as predictors of youth adjustment: A seven-year longitudinal study in a Chinese sample. *International Journal of Behavioral Development, 26*, 128–136. doi:10.1080/01650250042000690

Childs, A., Fite, P. J., Moore, T. M., Lochman, J. E., & Pardini, D. A. (2014). Bidirectional associations between parenting behavior and child callous–unemotional traits: Does parental depression moderate this link? *Journal of Abnormal Child Psychology, 42*, 1141–1151.

Chu, C. M., & Ogloff, J. (2012). Sentencing of adolescent offenders in Victoria: A review of empirical evidence and practice. *Psychiatry, Psychology and Law, 19*, 325–344. doi:10.1080/13218719.2011.565716

Clark, L. A., & Watson, D. (1995). Construct validity: Basic issues in objective scale development. *Psychological Assessment, 7*, 309–319. doi:10.1037/1040-3590.7.3.309

Clark, L. A., Watson, D., & Mineka, S. (1994). Temperament, personality, and the mood and anxiety disorders. *Journal of Abnormal Psychology, 103*, 103–116. doi:10.1037/0021-843X.103.1.103

Cleckley, H. (1941). *The mask of sanity*. St. Louis, MO: Mosby.

Cloninger, C. R., Svrakic, D. M., & Przybeck, T. R. (1993). A psychobiological model of temperament and character. *Archives of General Psychiatry, 50*, 975–990. doi:10.1001/archpsyc.1993.01820240059008

Coghill, D., & Sonuga-Barke, E. J. S. (2012). Annual research review: Categories versus dimensions in the classification and conceptualization of child and adolescent mental disorders—Implications of recent empirical study. *Journal of Child Psychology and Psychiatry, 53*, 469–489. doi:10.1111/j.1469-7610.2011.02511.x

Columbia DISC Development Group. (1999). *NIMH Diagnostic Interview Schedule for Children*. Unpublished report, Columbia University/New York State Psychiatric Unit, New York, NY.

Comer, J. S., & Barlow, D. H. (2014). The occasional case against broad dissemination and implementation: Retaining a role for specialty care in the delivery of psychological treatments. *American Psychologist, 69*, 1–18. doi:10.1037/a0033582

Committee on Ethical Guidelines for Forensic Psychologists. (1991). Specialty guidelines for forensic psychologists. *Law and Human Behavior, 15*, 655–665. doi:10.1007/BF01065858

Conklin, A., & Westen, D. (2001). Thematic Apperception Test. In W. I. Dorfman & M. Herson (Eds.), *Understanding psychological assessment* (pp. 107–133). Dordrecht, the Netherlands: Kluwer Academic. doi:10.1007/978-1-4615-1185-4_6

Conners, C. K. (2008). *Conners 3rd edition (Conners 3)*. San Antonio, TX: The Psychological Corporation.

Conti, R. P. (2004). Malingered ADHD in adolescents diagnosed with conduct disorder: A brief note. *Psychological Reports, 94*, 987–988. doi:10.2466/pr0.94.3.987-988

Costa, P. T., & McCrae, R. R. (1992a). The five-factor model of personality and its relevance to personality disorders. *Journal of Personality Disorders, 6*, 343–359.

Costa, P. T., & McCrae, R. R. (1992b). *NEO–PI–R professional manual*. Odessa, FL: Psychological Assessment Resources, Inc.

Costa, P. T., & McCrae, R. R. (1992c). Normal personality assessment in clinical practice: The NEO Personality Inventory. *Psychological Assessment, 4*, 5–13.

Cottle, C. C., Lee, R. J., & Heilbrun, K. (2001). The prediction of criminal recidivism in juveniles: A meta-analysis. *Criminal Justice and Behavior, 28*, 367–394. doi:10.1177/0093854801028003005

Cronbach, L. J., & Meehl, P. E. (1955). Construct validity in psychological tests. *Psychological Bulletin, 52*, 281–302.

Cunningham, M. D. (2010). *Evaluation for capital sentencing*. New York, NY: Oxford University Press.

Currie, M. R., Wood, C. E., Williams, B., & Bates, G. W. (2012). Aggression Replacement Training (ART) in Australia: A longitudinal youth justice evaluation. *Psychiatry, Psychology and Law, 19*, 577–604. doi:10.1080/13218719.2011.615807

Curtis, N. M., Ronan, K. R., Heiblum, N., & Crellin, K. (2009). Dissemination and effectiveness of multisystemic treatment in New Zealand: A benchmarking study. *Journal of Family Psychology, 23*, 119–129. doi:10.1037/a0014974

Damasio, A. (1994). *Descartes' error: Emotion, reason, and the human brain*. New York, NY: Penguin Books.

Davidson, R. J., Lewis, D. A., Alloy, L. B., Amaral, D. G., Bush, G., Cohen, J. D., . . . Peterson, B. S. (2002). Neural and behavioral substrates of mood and mood regulation. *Biological Psychiatry, 52*, 478–502.

Davidson, R. J., Putnam, K. M., & Larson, C. L. (2000, July 28). Dysfunction in the neural circuitry of emotion regulation—A possible prelude to violence. *Science, 289*, 591–594.

Deater-Deckard, K. (2014). Family matters: Intergenerational and interpersonal processes of executive function and attentive behavior. *Current Directions in Psychological Science, 23*, 230–236. doi:10.1177/0963721414531597

Decety, J., Chen, C., Harenski, C., & Kiehl, K. A. (2013). An fMRI study of affective perspective taking in individuals with psychopathy: Imagining another in pain does not evoke empathy. *Frontiers in Human Neuroscience, 7*, 489. doi:10.3389/fnhum.2013.00489

De Clercq, B., & De Fruyt, F. (2003). Personality disorder symptoms in adolescence: A five-factor model perspective. *Journal of Personality Disorders, 17*, 269–292. doi:10.1521/pedi.17.4.269.23972

De Fruyt, F., Bartels, M., Van Leeuwen, K. G., De Clercq, B., Decuyper, M., & Mervielde, I. (2006). Five types of personality continuity in childhood and adolescence. *Journal of Personality and Social Psychology, 91*, 538–552. doi:10.1037/0022-3514.91.3.538

De Fruyt, F., Mervielde, I., Hoekstra, H., & Rolland, J. (2000). Assessing adolescents' personality with the NEO–PI–R. *Assessment, 7*, 329–345. doi:10.1177/107319110000700403

DeLisi, M., Neppl, T. K., Lohman, B. J., Vaughn, M. G., & Shook, J. J. (2013). Early starters: Which type of criminal onset matters most for delinquent careers? *Journal of Criminal Justice, 41*, 12–17. doi:10.1016/j.jcrimjus.2012.10.002

De Los Reyes, A., & Kazdin, A. E. (2005). Informant discrepancies in the assessment of childhood psychopathology: A critical review, theoretical framework, and recommendations for further study. *Psychological Bulletin, 131*, 483–509. doi:10.1037/0033-2909.131.4.483

DiCataldo, F., & Grisso, T. (1995). A typology of juvenile offenders based on the judgments of juvenile court professionals. *Criminal Justice and Behavior, 22*, 246–262. doi:10.1177/0093854895022003004

Digman, J. M. (1963). Principal dimensions of child personality as inferred from teacher's judgments. *Child Development, 34*, 43–60.

Digman, J. M. (1990). Personality structure: Emergence of the five-factor model. *Annual Review of Psychology, 41*, 417–440. doi:10.1146/annurev.ps.41.020190.002221

Digman, J. M., & Inouye, J. (1986). Further specification of the five robust factors of personality. *Journal of Personality and Social Psychology, 50*, 116–123. doi:10.1037/0022-3514.50.1.116

DiIulio, J. J., Jr. (1995, November 27). The coming of the super-predators. *The Weekly Standard*, 23–28.

DiIulio, J. J., Jr. (1996, Spring). My Black crime problem, and ours. *City Journal* (New York, NY), 25. Retrieved from http://www.city-journal.org/html/6_2_my_black.html

Dishion, T. J. (2012). Juvenile forensic psychology and psychiatry: The movement toward data-based innovations. In E. Grigorenko (Ed.), *Handbook of juvenile forensic psychology and psychiatry* (pp. 579–584). New York, NY: Springer.

Dishion, T. J., & Kavanagh, K. (2003). *Intervening in adolescent problem behavior: A family-centered approach*. New York, NY: Guilford Press.

Dmitrieva, J., Monahan, K. C., Cauffman, E., & Steinberg, L. (2012). Arrested development: The effects of incarceration on the development of psychosocial maturity. *Development and Psychopathology, 24*, 1073–1090. doi:10.1017/S0954579412000545

Dodge, K. A., Lansford, J. E., Burks, V. S., Bates, J. E., Pettit, G. S., Fontaine, R., & Price, J. M. (2003). Peer rejection and social information-processing factors in the development of aggressive behavior problems in children. *Child Development, 74*, 374–393. doi:10.1111/1467-8624.7402004

Dolan, M. C., & Rennie, C. E. (2008). The Structured Assessment of Violence Risk in Youth as a predictor of recidivism in a United Kingdom cohort of adolescent offenders with conduct disorder. *Psychological Assessment, 20,* 35–46. doi:10.1037/1040-3590.20.1.35

Douglas, K. S., Guy, L. S., & Hart, S. D. (2009). Psychosis as a risk factor for violence to others: A meta-analysis. *Psychological Bulletin, 135,* 679–706.

Douglas, K. S., Hart, S. D., Webster, C. D., & Belfrage, H. (2013). *HCR-20V3: Assessing risk of violence—User guide.* Burnaby, British Columbia, Canada: Mental Health, Law, and Policy Institute, Simon Fraser University.

Douglas, K. S., & Skeem, J. L. (2005). Violence risk assessment: Getting specific about being dynamic. *Psychology, Public Policy, and Law, 11,* 347–383.

Draganski, B., Gaser, C., Kempermann, G., Kuhn, H. G., Winkler, J., Büchel, C., & May, A. (2006). Temporal and spatial dynamics of brain structure changes during extensive learning. *Journal of Neuroscience, 26,* 6314–6317.

Draganski, B., Kherif, F., Klöppel, S., Cook, P. A., Alexander, D. C., Parker, G. J. M., . . . Frackowiak, R. S. J. (2008). Evidence for segregated and integrative connectivity patterns in the human basal ganglia. *Journal of Neuroscience, 28,* 7143–7152.

Earley, R. L. (2010). Social eavesdropping and the evolution of conditional cooperation and cheating strategies. *Philosophical Transactions of the Royal Society of London B, 365,* 2675–2686.

Earley, R. L., Edwards, J. T., Aseem, O., Felton, K., Blumer, L. S., Karom, M., & Grober, M. S. (2006). Social interactions tune aggression and stress responsiveness in a territorial cichlid fish (*Archocentrus nigrofasciatus*). *Physiology & Behavior, 88,* 353–363.

Earley, R. L., & Hsu, Y. (2008). Reciprocity between endocrine state and contest behavior in the killifish, *Kryptolebias marmoratus. Hormones and Behavior, 53,* 442–451.

Eckholm, E. (2014, January). Juveniles facing lifelong terms despite rulings. *The New York Times.* Retrieved from http://mobile.nytimes.com/2014/01/20/us/juveniles-facing-lifelong-terms-despite-rulings.html?referrer=

Eisenberg, N., Fabes, R. A., Guthrie, I. K., & Reiser, M. (2000). Dispositional emotionality and regulation: Their role in predicting quality of social functioning. *Journal of Personality and Social Psychology, 78,* 136–157. doi:10.1037/0022-3514.78.1.136

Eisenberg, N., Pidada, S., & Liew, J. (2001). The relations of regulation and negative emotionality to Indonesian children's social functioning. *Child Development, 72,* 1747–1763. doi:10.1111/1467-8624.00376

Elbert, T., Pantev, C., Weinbruch, C., Rockstroh, B., & Taub, E. (1995, October 20). Increased cortical representation of the fingers of the left hand in string players. *Science, 270,* 305–307.

Erikson, E. H. (1950). Growth and crises of the "healthy personality." In M. E. Senn (Ed.), *Symposium on the Healthy Personality* (pp. 91–146). Oxford, England: Josiah Macy, Jr. Foundation.

Erikson, E. H. (1959). Identity and the life cycle: Selected papers. *Psychological Issues, 1*, 11–171.

Erikson, E. H. (1963). *Childhood and society*. New York, NY: Norton.

Erikson, E. H. (1968). *Identity: Youth and crisis*. Oxford, England: Norton.

Evans, G. W., & Cassells, R. C. (2014). Childhood poverty, cumulative risk exposure, and mental health in emerging adults. *Clinical Psychological Science, 2*, 287–296. doi:10.1177/2167702613501496

Ewing, C. P. (1990). Juveniles or adults? Forensic assessment of juveniles considered for trial in criminal court. *Forensic Reports, 3*, 3–13.

Eyal, A., Vincent, G. M., Harenski, C. L., Calhoun, V. D., Sinnott-Armstrong, W., Gazzaniga, M. S., & Kiehl, K. A. (2007). Neuroprediction of future rearrest. *Proceedings of the National Academy of Sciences of the United States of America, 110*, 6223–6228.

Eyde, L. D., Robertson, G. J., Krug, S. E., Moreland, K. L., Robertson, A. G., Shewan, C. M., & Primoff, E. S. (1993). *Responsible test use: Case studies for assessing human behavior*. Washington, DC: American Psychological Association.

Eysenck, H. (1997). Personality and experimental psychology: The unification of psychology and the possibility of a paradigm. *Journal of Personality and Social Psychology, 73*, 1224–1237. doi:10.1037/0022-3514.73.6.1224

Eysenck, S. B. G. (1963). *Junior Eysenck Personality Inventory*. San Diego, CA: Educational and Industrial Testing Service and Human Services.

Eysenck, S. B. G., Makaremi, A., & Barrett, P. T. (1994). A cross-cultural study of personality—Iranian and English children. *Personality and Individual Differences, 16*, 203–210.

Fabry, J. J., Bertinetti, J., & Guzman-Cavazos, L. (2011). Characteristics of juvenile offenders with invalid and valid MMPI–A profiles. *Psychological Reports, 108*, 908–918. doi:10.2466/03.09.16.28.PR0.108.3.908-918

Fagan, J. (2008). Juvenile crime and criminal justice: Resolving border disputes. *The Future of Children, 18*, 81–118. doi:10.1353/foc.0.0014

Fagan, J., & Zimring, F. E. (2000). *The changing borders of juvenile justice: Transfer of adolescents to criminal court*. Chicago, IL: University of Chicago Press.

Farrington, D. P., Ullrich, S., & Salekin, R. T. (2010). Environmental influences on child and adolescent psychopathy. In R. T. Salekin & D. R. Lynam (Eds.), *Handbook of child and adolescent psychopathy* (pp. 202–230). New York, NY: Guilford Press.

Faust, D., Hart, K., & Guilmette, T. J. (1988). Pediatric malingering: The capacity of children to fake believable deficits on neuropsychological testing. *Journal of Consulting and Clinical Psychology, 56*, 578–582.

Fein, R. A., Appelbaum, K., Barnum, R., & Baxter, P. (1991). The Designated Forensic Professional Program: A state government–university partnership to improve forensic mental health services. *Journal of Mental Health Administration, 18*, 223–230. doi:10.1007/BF02518593

Feld, B. C. (1997). Abolish the juvenile court: Youthfulness, criminal responsibility, and sentencing policy. *Journal of Criminal Law and Criminology, 88*, 68–136. doi:10.2307/1144075

Feld, B. C. (1999). *Bad kids: Race and the transformation of the juvenile court.* New York, NY: Oxford University Press.

Ferrari, J. R., & Pychyl, T. A. (2012). "If I wait, my partner will do it": The role of conscientiousness as a mediator in the relation of academic procrastination and perceived social loafing. *North American Journal of Psychology, 14*, 13–24.

Field, C. A., Adinoff, B., Harris, T., Ball, S. A., & Carroll, K. M. (2009). Construct, concurrent and predictive validity of the URICA: Data from two multi-site clinical trials. *Drug and Alcohol Dependence, 101*, 115–123. doi:10.1016/j.drugalcdep.2008.12.003

Fields, S. (1996, October 17). The super-predator. *Washington Times*, p. A23.

Fischer, K. W., Stein, Z., & Heikkinen, K. (2009). Narrow assessments misrepresent develop and misguide policy: Comment on Steinberg, Cauffman, Graham, and Banich (2009). *American Psychologist, 64*, 595–600. doi:10.1037/a0017105

Floyd, F. J., & Widaman, K. F. (1995). Factor analysis in the development and refinement of clinical assessment instruments. *Psychological Assessment, 7*, 286–299. doi:10.1037/1040-3590.7.3.286

Fontaine, N. M., McCrory, E. P., Boivin, M., Moffitt, T. E., & Viding, E. (2011). Predictors and outcomes of joint trajectories of callous–unemotional traits and conduct problems in childhood. *Journal of Abnormal Psychology, 120*, 730–742. doi:10.1037/a0022620

Forth, A. E., & Book, A. S. (2010). Psychopathic traits in children and adolescents: The relationship with antisocial behaviors and aggression. In R. T. Salekin & D. R. Lynam (Eds.), *Handbook of child and adolescent psychopathy* (pp. 251–283). New York, NY: Guilford Press.

Forth, A. E., & Burke, H. C. (1998). Psychopathy in adolescence: Assessment, violence, and adolescent precursors. In D. J. Cooke, A. E. Forth, & R. D. Hare (Eds.), *Psychopathy: Theory, research, and implications for society* (pp. 205–229). Dordrecht, The Netherlands: Kluwer.

Forth, A. E., Kosson, D. S., & Hare, R. D. (2003). *Hare Psychopathy Checklist: Youth Version.* Toronto, Ontario, Canada: Multi-Health Systems.

Foster, S. L., & Cone, J. D. (1995). Validity issues in clinical assessment. *Psychological Assessment, 7*, 248–260. doi:10.1037/1040-3590.7.3.248

Frank, J. D. (1959). The dynamics of the psychotherapeutic relationship. *Psychiatry, 22*, 17–39.

Franklin, K. (2013, May 31). Forensic implications of the *DSM–5:* Courts cling to DSM as "bible." *Psychology Today.* Retrieved from http://www.psychologytoday.com/blog/witness/201305/forensic-implications-the-dsm-5-part-ii-ii

Fredrickson, B. L. (2001). The role of positive emotions in positive psychology: The broaden-and-build theory of positive emotions. *American Psychologist, 56*, 218–226.

Freud, S. (2011). *Three essays on the theory of sexuality*. Eastford, CT: Martino Fine Books. (Original work published 1905)

Frick, P. J., Cornell, A., Barry, C., Bodin, S., & Dane, H. (2003). Callous–unemotional traits and conduct problems in the prediction of conduct problem severity, aggression, and self-report of delinquency. *Journal of Abnormal Child Psychology*, *31*, 457–470. doi:10.1023/A:1023899703866

Frick, P. J., & Hare, R. D. (2001). *The Antisocial Process Screening Device*. Toronto, Ontario, Canada: Multi-Health Systems.

Frick, P. J., & Moffitt, T. E. (2010). *A proposal to the DSM–5 childhood disorders and the ADHD and disruptive behavior disorders work groups to include a specifier to the diagnosis of conduct disorder based on the presence of callous–unemotional traits.* Washington, DC: American Psychiatric Association.

Frick, P. J., & Scheffield Morris, A. (2004). Temperament and developmental pathways to conduct problems. *Journal of Clinical Child and Adolescent Psychology*, *33*, 54–68. doi:10.1207/S15374424JCCP3301_6

Fried, C. S., & Reppucci, N. D. (2001). Criminal decision making: The development of adolescent judgment, criminal responsibility, and culpability. *Law and Human Behavior*, *25*, 45–61. doi:10.1023/A:1005639909226

Funder, D. C., Parke, R. D., Tomlinson-Keasey, C., & Widaman, K. (Eds.). (1993). *Studying lives through time: Personality and development*. Washington, DC: American Psychological Association. doi:10.1037/10127-000

Gadow, K. D., & Sprafkin, J. (2002). *Child Symptom Inventory—4 screening and norms manual*. Stony Brook, NY: Checkmate Plus.

Gallagher, K. C. (2002). Does child temperament moderate the influence of parenting on adjustment? *Developmental Review*, *22*, 623–643. doi:10.1016/S0273-2297(02)00503-8

Garb, H. N. (2000). On empirically based decision making in clinical practice. *Prevention & Treatment*, *3*, 1–6. doi:10.1037/1522-3736.3.1.329c

Gardner, M., & Steinberg, L. (2005). Peer influence on risk taking, risk preference, and risky decision making in adolescence and adulthood: An experimental study. *Developmental Psychology*, *41*, 625–635.

Garfield, S. L. (1994). Research on client variables in psychotherapy. In S. L. Garfield & A. E. Bergin (Eds.), *Handbook of psychotherapy and behavior change* (3rd ed., pp. 190–228). New York, NY: Wiley.

Gazelle, H., & Ladd, G. W. (2003). Anxious solitude and peer exclusion: A diathesis–stress model of internalizing trajectories in childhood. *Child Development*, *74*, 257–278. doi:10.1111/1467-8624.00534

Gest, S. D. (1997). Behavioral inhibition: Stability and associations with adaptation from childhood to early adulthood. *Journal of Personality and Social Psychology*, *72*, 467–475. doi:10.1037/0022-3514.72.2.467

Giedd, J. N. (2004). Structural magnetic resonance imaging of the adolescent brain. In R. E. Dahl & L. P. Spear (Eds.), *Annals of the New York Academy of Sciences:*

Vol. 1021. *Adolescent brain development: Vulnerabilities and opportunities* (pp. 77–85). New York, NY: New York Academy of Sciences. doi:10.1196/annals.1308.009

Gillen, C., MacDougall, E., Forth, A. E., & Salekin, R. T. (2014). *The validity and reliability of the Risk–Sophistication–Treatment Inventory—Abbreviated (RSTI–A): A measure designed for juvenile evaluations.* Manuscript submitted for publication.

Glenn, A. L., & Raine, A. (2014). Neurocriminology: Implications for the punishment, prediction and prevention of criminal behavior. *Neuroscience, 15,* 54–63.

Gogtay, N., Giedd, J. N., Lusk, L., Hayashi, K. M., Greenstein, D., Vaiuzis, A. C., . . . Thompson, P. M. (2004). Dynamic mapping of human cortical development during childhood through early adolescence. *Proceedings of the National Academy of Sciences of the United States of America, 101,* 8174–8179. doi:10.1073/pnas.0402680101

Goldberg, J. H. (2007). Worldview of high-risk juvenile delinquents: Relationship to decisions to shoot. *Criminal Justice and Behavior, 34,* 846–861.

Goldsmith, H. H., Buss, A., Plomin, R., Rothbart, M. K., Thomas, A., Chess, S., . . . McCall, R. B. (1987). Roundtable: What is temperament? *Child Development, 58,* 505–529. doi:10.2307/1130527

Graham v. State of Florida, 560 U.S. 48 (2010).

Gray, J. A. (1970). The psychophysiological basis of introversion–extraversion. *Behaviour Research and Therapy, 8,* 249–266. doi:10.1016/0005-7967(70)90069-0

Gray, J. A. (1987). *The psychology of fear and stress.* New York, NY: Cambridge University Press.

Graziano, W. G. (2003). Personality development: An introduction toward process approaches to long-term stability and change in persons. *Journal of Personality, 71,* 893–904. doi:10.1111/1467-6494.7106001

Graziano, W. G., & Eisenberg, N. (1997). Agreeableness: A dimension of personality. In R. Hogan, J. Johnson, & S. Briggs (Eds.), *Handbook of personality psychology* (pp. 795–824). San Diego, CA: Academic Press. doi:10.1016/B978-012134645-4/50031-7

Graziano, W. G., Jensen-Campbell, L. A., & Finch, J. F. (1997). The self as a mediator between personality and adjustment. *Journal of Personality and Social Psychology, 73,* 392–404. doi:10.1037/0022-3514.73.2.392

Graziano, W. G., & Ward, D. (1992). Probing the Big Five in adolescence: Personality and adjustment during a developmental transition. *Journal of Personality, 60,* 425–439. doi:10.1111/j.1467-6494.1992.tb00979.x

Green, P., Allen, L. M., & Astner, K. (1996). *The Word Memory Test: A manual for the oral and computerized forms.* Durham, NC: CogniSyst.

Greenberger, E., Campbell, P., Sorensen, A. B., & O'Connor, J. O. (1971). *Toward the measurement of psychosocial maturity.* Baltimore, MD: Johns Hopkins University Press.

Greenberger, E., Josselson, R., Knerr, C., & Knerr, B. (1975). The measurement and structure of psychosocial maturity. *Journal of Youth and Adolescence, 4,* 127–143. doi:10.1007/BF01537437

Greenberger, E., & Sorensen, A. (1974). Toward a concept of psychosocial maturity. *Journal of Youth and Adolescence, 3,* 329–358.

Greenberger, E., Steinberg, L. D., Vaux, A., & McAuliffe, S. (1980). Adolescents who work: Effects of part-time employment on family and peer relations. *Journal of Youth and Adolescence, 9,* 189–202.

Greenfeld, D. (1987). Feigned psychosis in a 14-year-old girl. *Hospital & Community Psychiatry, 38,* 73–75.

Greenwood, P. (2008). Prevention and intervention programs for juvenile offenders. *The Future of Children, 18,* 185–210.

Gretton, H. M., McBride, M., Hare, R. D., O'Shaughnessy, R., & Kumka, G. (2001). Psychopathy and recidivism in adolescent sex offenders. *Criminal Justice and Behavior, 28,* 427–449. doi:10.1177/0093854801028003403

Griffin, P., Torbet, P., & Szymanski, L. (1998). *Trying juveniles as adults in criminal court: An analysis of state transfer provisions.* Washington, DC: Office of Juvenile Justice and Delinquency Prevention.

Grigorenko, E. L. (2012). At the junction of personality theories: Working with juvenile offenders. In E. L. Grigorenko (Ed.), *Handbook of juvenile forensic psychology and psychiatry* (pp. 253–279). New York, NY: Springer. doi:10.1007/978-1-4614-0905-2_17

Grisso, T. (2000). Forensic clinical evaluations related to waiver of jurisdiction. In J. Fagan & F. E. Zimring (Eds.), *The changing borders of juvenile justice: Transfer of adolescents to the criminal court* (pp. 321–352). Chicago, IL: University of Chicago Press.

Grisso, T. (2002). Using what we know about child maltreatment and delinquency. *Children's Services, 5,* 299–305. doi:10.1207/S15326918CS0504_6

Grisso, T. (2003a). *Evaluating competencies: Forensic assessments and instruments* (2nd ed.). New York, NY: Kluwer Academic/Plenum.

Grisso, T. (2003b). Forensic evaluation in delinquency cases. In A. M. Goldstein (Ed.), *Handbook of psychology: Forensic psychology* (Vol. 11, pp. 315–334). Hoboken, NJ: Wiley. doi:10.1002/0471264385.wei1117

Grisso, T. (2013). *Forensic evaluation of juveniles.* Sarasota, FL: Professional Resource Press. (Original work published 1998)

Grisso, T., & Quinlan, J. (2005). Juvenile court clinical services: A national description. *Juvenile & Family Court Journal, 56,* 9–20. doi:10.1111/j.1755-6988.2005.tb00175.x

Grisso, T. E., & Schwartz, R. G. (2000). *Youth on trial: A developmental perspective on juvenile justice.* Chicago, IL: University of Chicago Press.

Grisso, T., Steinberg, L., Woolard, J., Cauffman, E., Scott, E., Graham, S., . . . Schwartz, R. (2003). Juveniles' competence to stand trial: A comparison of adolescents' and adults' capacities as trial defendants. *Law and Human Behavior, 27,* 333–363. doi:10.1023/A:1024065015717

Grisso, T., Tomkins, A., & Casey, P. (1988). Psychosocial concepts in juvenile law. *Law and Human Behavior, 12*, 403–437. doi:10.1007/BF01044626

Grisso, T., & Vierling, L. (1978). Minors' consent to treatment: A developmental perspective. *Professional Psychology: Research and Practice, 9*, 412–427. doi:10.1037/0735-7028.9.3.412

Grisso, T., & Vincent, G. M. (2005a). The context for mental health screening and assessment. In T. Grisso, G. M. Vincent, & D. Seagrave (Eds.), *Mental health screening and assessment in juvenile justice* (pp. 44–70). New York, NY: Guilford Press.

Grisso, T., & Vincent, G. M. (2005b). The empirical limits of forensic mental health assessment. *Law and Human Behavior, 29*, 1–5. doi:10.1007/s10979-005-1396-0

Grotevant, H. D. (1998). Adolescent development in family contexts. In N. Eisenberg (Ed.), *Handbook of child psychology: Vol. 3. Social, emotional, and personality development* (5th ed., pp. 1097–1149). Hoboken, NJ: Wiley.

Hagekull, B., & Bohlin, G. (2003). Early temperament and attachment as predictors of the five factor model of personality. *Attachment & Human Development, 5*, 2–18. doi:10.1080/1461673031000078643

Hall, G. S. (1904). *Adolescence: Its psychology and its relations to physiology, anthropology, sociology, sex, crime, religion, and education (Vols. 1–2)*. New York, NY: Appleton.

Halverson, C. F., Havill, V. L., Deal, J., Baker, S. R., Victor, J. B., Pavlopoulos, V., . . . Wen, L. (2003). Personality structure as derived from parental ratings of free descriptions of children: The Inventory of Child Individual Differences. *Journal of Personality, 71*, 995–1026. doi:10.1111/1467-6494.7106005

Halverson, C. F., Kohnstamm, G. A., & Martin, R. P. (Eds.). (1994). *The developing structure of temperament and personality from infancy to adulthood*. Hillsdale, NJ: Erlbaum.

Hamilton, M. (1967). Development of a rating scale for primary depressive illness. *British Journal of Social and Clinical Psychology, 6*, 278–296.

Hampson, S. E., Edmonds, G. W., Goldberg, L. R., Dubankoski, J. P., & Hillier, T. A. (2013). Childhood conscientiousness relates to objectively measured adult physical health four decades later. *Health Psychology, 32*, 925–928. doi:10.1037/a0031655

Hanson, J. L., Chung, M. K., Avants, B. B., Shirtcliff, E. A., Gee, J. C., Davidson, R. J., & Pollak, S. D. (2010). Early stress is associated with alterations in the orbitofrontal cortex: A tensor-based morphometry investigation of brain structure and behavioral risk. *The Journal of Neuroscience, 30*, 7466–7472.

Hare, R. D. (1991). *Hare Psychopathy Checklist—Revised: Technical manual*. Toronto, Ontario, Canada: Multi-Health Systems.

Harris, G. T., & Rice, M. E. (2006). Treatment of psychopathy: A review of empirical findings. In C. J. Patrick (Ed.), *Handbook of psychopathy* (pp. 555–572). New York, NY: Guilford Press.

Harris, P. W., & Jones, P. R. (1999). Differentiating delinquent youths for program planning and evaluation. *Criminal Justice and Behavior, 26*, 403–434. doi:10.1177/0093854899026004001

Hathaway, S. R., & McKinley, J. C. (1943). *Manual for the Minnesota Multiphasic Personality Inventory.* New York, NY: The Psychological Corporation.

Hawes, D. J., & Dadds, M. R. (2005). The treatment of conduct problems in children with callous–unemotional traits. *Journal of Consulting and Clinical Psychology, 73*, 737–741. doi:10.1037/0022-006X.73.4.737

Hawes, D. J., Price, M. J., & Dadds, M. R. (2014). Callous–unemotional traits and the treatment of conduct problems in childhood and adolescence: A comprehensive review. *Clinical Child and Family Psychology Review, 17*, 248–267. doi:10.1007/s10567-014-0167-1

Hawes, S. W., Mulvey, E. P., Schubert, C. A., & Pardini, D. A. (2014). Structural coherence and temporal stability of psychopathic personality features during emerging adulthood. *Journal of Abnormal Psychology, 123*, 623–633.

Hawley, P. H. (2003). Prosocial and coercive configurations of resource control in early adolescence: A case for the well-adapted Machiavellian. *Merrill–Palmer Quarterly, 49*, 279–309. doi:10.1353/mpq.2003.0013

Haynes, S. N., Richard, D. C. S., & Kubany, E. S. (1995). Content validity in psychological assessment: A functional approach to concepts and methods. *Psychological Assessment, 7*, 238–247. doi:10.1037/1040-3590.7.3.238

Heaven, P. L., Ciarrochi, J., & Vialle, W. (2007). Conscientiousness and Eysenckian psychoticism as predictors of school grades: A one-year long longitudinal study. *Personality and Individual Differences, 42*, 535–546. doi:10.1016/j.paid.2006.07.028

Hecker, T., & Steinberg, L. (2002). Psychological evaluation at juvenile court disposition. *Professional Psychology: Research and Practice, 33*, 300–306. doi:10.1037/0735-7028.33.3.300

Heilbrun, K., Grisso, T., & Goldstein, A. (2008). *Foundations of forensic mental health assessment* (Vol. 1). New York, NY: Oxford University Press.

Heilbrun, K., Leheny, C., Thomas, L., & Huneycutt, D. (1997). A national survey of U.S. statutes on juvenile transfer: Implications for policy and practice. *Behavioral Sciences & the Law, 15*, 125–149. doi:10.1002/(SICI)1099-0798(199721)15:2<125::AID-BSL265>3.0.CO;2-R

Heilbrun, K., Rogers, R., & Otto, R. (2002). Forensic assessment: Current status and future directions. In J. P. Ogloff (Ed.), *Taking psychology and law into the twenty-first century* (pp. 119–146). New York, NY: Kluwer Academic/Plenum.

Hemphill, J. F. (2003). Interpreting the magnitude of correlation coefficients. *American Psychologist, 58*, 78–79.

Henry, B., Caspi, A., Moffitt, T. E., Harrington, H., & Silva, P. A. (1999). Staying in school protects boys with poor self-regulation in childhood from later crime: A longitudinal study. *International Journal of Behavioral Development, 23*, 1049–1073. doi:10.1080/016502599383667

Henry, B., Caspi, A., Moffitt, T. E., & Silva, P. A. (1996). Temperamental and familial predictors of violent and nonviolent criminal convictions: Age 3 to age 18. *Developmental Psychology, 32*, 614–623. doi:10.1037/0012-1649.32.4.614

Herholz, S. C., & Zatorre, R. J. (2012). Musical training as a framework for brain plasticity: Behavior, function, and structure. *Neuron, 76*, 486–500.

Herjanic, B., & Reich, W. (1982). Development of a psychiatric interview for children: Agreement between child and parent on individual symptoms. *Journal of Abnormal Child Psychology, 10*, 307–324.

Hill, P. L., Turiano, N. A., Mroczek, D. K., & Roberts, B. W. (2012). Examining concurrent and longitudinal relations between personality traits and social well-being in adulthood. *Social Psychological and Personality Science, 3*, 698–705. doi:10.1177/1948550611433888

Hipwell, A. E., Stepp, S., Feng, X., Burke, J., Battista, D. R., Loeber, R., & Keenan, K. (2011). Impact of oppositional defiant disorder dimensions on the temporal ordering of conduct problems and depression across childhood and adolescence in girls. *Journal of Child Psychology and Psychiatry, 52*, 1099–1108.

Hodges, K., Kline, J., Fitch, P., McKnew, D., & Cytryn, L. (1981). The Child Assessment Schedule: A diagnostic interview for research and clinical use. *Catalog of Selected Documents in Psychology, 17*, 56.

Hodges, K., Kline, J., Stern, L., Cytryn, L., & McKnew, D. (1982). The development of the Child Assessment Schedule interview for research and clinical use. *Journal of Abnormal Child Psychology, 10*, 173–189.

Hodgson v. State of Minnesota, 497 U.S. 417 (1990).

Hoffman, M. L. (1977). Personality and social development. *Annual Review of Psychology, 28*, 295–321. doi:10.1146/annurev.ps.28.020177.001455

Hoge, R. D. (2002). Standardized instruments for assessing risk and need in youthful offenders. *Criminal Justice and Behavior, 29*, 380–396. doi:10.1177/0093854802029004003

Hoge, R. D. (2005). Youth Level of Service/Case Management Inventory. In T. Grisso, G. Vincent, & D. Seagrave (Eds.), *Mental health screening and assessment in juvenile justice* (pp. 283–294). New York, NY: Guilford Press.

Hoge, R. D. (2012). Forensic assessments of juveniles: Practice and legal considerations. *Criminal Justice and Behavior, 39*, 1255–1270. doi:10.1177/0093854812444024

Hoge, R. D., & Andrews, D. A. (2002). *Youth Level of Service/Case Management Inventory*. Toronto, Ontario, Canada: Multi-Health Systems.

Hoge, R. D., & Andrews, D. A. (2010). *Youth Level of Service/Case Management Inventory 2.0*. Toronto, Ontario, Canada: Multi-Health Systems.

Hoge, R. D., Andrews, D. A., & Leschied, A. W. (1995). Investigations of variables associated with probation and custody dispositions in a sample of juveniles. *Journal of Clinical Child Psychology, 24*, 279–286.

Hoge, R. D., Andrews, D. A., & Leschied, A. W. (1996). An investigation of risk and protective factors in a sample of youthful offenders. *Journal of Child Psychology and Psychiatry and Allied Disciplines, 37*, 419–424.

Holmqvist, R., Hill, T., & Lang, A. (2009). Effects of aggression replacement training in young offender institutions. *International Journal of Offender Therapy and Comparative Criminology, 53*, 74–92. doi:10.1177/0306624X07310452

Homant, R. J. (2010). Risky altruism as a predictor of criminal victimization. *Criminal Justice and Behavior, 37*, 1195–1216. doi:10.1177/0093854810378841

Huey, S. J., & Weisz, J. R. (1997). Ego control, ego resiliency, and the five-factor model as predictors of behavioral and emotional problems in clinic-referred children and adolescents. *Journal of Abnormal Psychology, 106*, 404–415. doi:10.1037/0021-843X.106.3.404

Huizinga, D., Esbensen, F., & Weiher, A. W. (1991). Are there multiple paths to delinquency? *The Journal of Criminal Law & Criminology, 82*, 1–36.

In re Gault, 387 U.S. 1. (1967).

Insel, T. (2013, April 29). Transforming diagnosis [Web log post]. Retrieved from http://www.nimh.nih.gov/about/director/2013/transforming-diagnosis.shtml

Iselin, A.-M. R., DeCoster, J., & Salekin, R. T. (2009). Maturity in adolescent and young adult offenders: The role of cognitive control. *Law and Human Behavior, 33*, 455–469. doi:10.1007/s10979-008-9160-x

Iselin, A-M. R., & Salekin, R. T. (2014). *The Risk–Sophistication–Treatment Inventory Self-Report manual.* Manuscript in preparation.

Israel, S., Moffitt, T. E., Belsky, D. W., Hancox, R. J., Poulton, R., Roberts, B., . . . Caspi, A. (2014). Translating personality psychology to help personalize medicine for young adult patients. *Journal of Personality and Social Psychology, 106*, 484–498.

Izzo, R. L., & Ross, R. R. (1990). Meta-analysis of rehabilitation programs for juvenile delinquents: A brief report. *Criminal Justice and Behavior, 17*, 134–142. doi:10.1177/0093854890017001008

Jaffee, S., Caspi, A., Moffitt, T. E., Belsky, J., & Silva, P. (2001). Why are children born to teen mothers at risk for adverse outcomes in young adulthood? Results from a 20-year longitudinal study. *Development and Psychopathology, 13*, 377–397.

Jahn, A. L., Fox, A. S., Abercrombie, H. C., Shelton, S. E., Oakes, T. R., Davidson, R. J., & Kalin, N. H. (2010). Subgenual prefrontal cortex activity predicts individual differences in hypothalamic–pituitary–adrenal activity across different contexts. *Biological Psychiatry, 67*, 175–181.

James, C., Stams, G. J. M., Asscher, J. J., De Roo, A. K., & der Laan, P. H. (2013). Aftercare programs for reducing recidivism among juvenile and young adult offenders: A meta-analytic review. *Clinical Psychology Review, 33*, 263–274. doi:10.1016/j.cpr.2012.10.013

Jang, K. L., McCrae, P. T., Angleitner, A., Riemann, R., & Livesley, J. W. (1998). Heritability of the facet level traits in a cross-cultural twin sample: Support for a hierarchical model of personality. *Journal of Personality and Social Psychology, 74*, 1556–1565. doi:10.1037/0022-3514.74.6.1556

Javaras, K. N., Schaefer, S. M., van Reekum, C. M., Lapate, R. C., Greischar, L. L., Bachhuber, D. R., & Davidson, R. J. (2012). Conscientiousness predicts greater recovery from negative emotion. *Emotion, 12*, 875–881. doi:10.1037/a0028105

Jensen-Campbell, L. A., Gleason, K. A., Adams, R., & Malcolm, K. T. (2003). Interpersonal conflict, Agreeableness, and personality development. *Journal of Personality, 71*, 1059–1086. doi:10.1111/1467-6494.7106007

Jesness, C. F. (1988). The Jesness Inventory Classification System. *Criminal Justice and Behavior, 15*, 78–91. doi:10.1177/0093854888015001007

Jesness, C. F., & Wedge, R. F. (1984). Validity of a revised Jesness Inventory I-Level Classification with delinquents. *Journal of Consulting and Clinical Psychology, 52*, 997–1010. doi:10.1037/0022-006X.52.6.997

Jesness, C. F., & Wedge, R. F. (1985). *Jesness Inventory Classification System: Supplementary manual.* Palo Alto, CA: Consulting Psychologists Press.

John, O. P., Caspi, A., Robins, R. W., Moffitt, T. E., & Stouthamer-Loeber, M. (1994). The "Little Five": Exploring the nomological network of the five-factor model of personality in adolescent boys. *Child Development, 65*, 160–178. doi:10.2307/1131373

Jones, R. M., Akers, J. F., & White, J. M. (1994). Revised classification criteria for the Extended Objective Measure of Ego Identity Status (EOMEIS). *Journal of Adolescence, 17*, 533–549. doi:10.1006/jado.1994.1047

Jones, S. E., Miller, J. D., & Lynam, D. R. (2011). Personality, antisocial behavior, and aggression: A meta-analytic review. *Journal of Criminal Justice, 39*, 329–337. doi:10.1016/j.jcrimjus.2011.03.004

Jordan, K. L., & Myers, D. L. (2007). The decertification of transferred youth: Examining the determinants of reverse waiver. *Youth Violence and Juvenile Justice, 5*, 188–206. doi:10.1177/1541204006295150

Jordan, M. (2008). *Readiness for change as a predictor of treatment effectiveness: An application of the transtheoretical model* (Unpublished doctoral dissertation). University of North Texas, Denton.

Jouriles, E. N., McDonald, R., Mueller, V., & Rosenfield, D. (2014). Interparental conflict, community violence, and child problems: Making sense of counterintuitive findings. *American Journal of Orthopsychiatry, 84*, 275–283.

Judge, T. A., Higgins, C. A., Thoresen, C. J., & Barrick, M. R. (1999). The Big Five personality traits, general mental ability, and career success across the life span. *Personnel Psychology, 52*, 621–652. doi:10.1111/j.1744-6570.1999.tb00174.x

Kagan, J., Snidman, N., Zentner, M., & Peterson, E. (1999). Infant temperament and anxious symptoms in school age children. *Development and Psychopathology, 11*, 209–224. doi:10.1017/S0954579499002023

Kalogerakis, M. (1992a). Disposition. In *Handbook of psychiatric practice in the juvenile court* (pp. 71–77). Washington, DC: American Psychiatric Association.

Kalogerakis, M. (1992b). Violent juveniles. In *Handbook of psychiatric practice in the juvenile court* (pp. 111–119). Washington, DC: American Psychiatric Association.

Kanacri, B., Rosa, V., & Di Guinta, L. (2012). The mediational role of values in linking personality traits to civic engagement in Italian youth. *Journal of Prevention & Intervention in the Community, 40*, 8–21. doi:10.1080/10852352.2012.633064

Kang, T., Wood, J., Eno Louden, J., & Ricks, E. (2014, March). *Prevalence of psychological disorders in a predominantly Hispanic sample of first-time juvenile offenders*. Paper presented at the annual conference of the American Psychology Law Society, New Orleans, LA.

Karson, M., & Nadkarni, L. (2013). *Principles of forensic report writing*. Washington, DC: American Psychological Association. doi:10.1037/14182-000

Kaufman, A. S., & Kaufman, N. L. (2002). *Kaufman Brief Intelligence Test, Second Edition*. San Antonio, TX: The Psychological Corporation.

Kaufman, D. M., Birmaher, B., Brent, D., Rao, U., Flynn, C., Moreci, P., . . . Ryan, N. (1997). Schedule for Affective Disorders and Schizophrenia for School-Age Children—Present and Lifetime Version (K-SADS–PL). *Journal of the American Academy of Child & Adolescent Psychiatry, 36*, 980–988.

Kazdin, A. E. (2000). Adolescent development, mental disorders, and decision making of delinquent youths. In T. Grisso & R. G. Schwartz (Eds.), *Youth on trial: A developmental perspective on juvenile justice* (pp. 33–65). Chicago, IL: University of Chicago Press.

Kazdin, A. E. (2006). Arbitrary metrics: Implications for identifying evidence-based treatments. *American Psychologist, 61*, 42–49.

Kazdin, A. E. (2010). *The Kazdin method for parenting the defiant child: With no pills, no therapy, and no contest of wills*. New York, NY: Houghton-Mifflin.

Kazdin, A. E., & Blase, S. L. (2011). Rebooting psychotherapy research and practice to reduce the burden of mental illness. *Perspectives on Psychological Science, 6*, 21–37. doi:10.1177/1745691610393527

Kazdin, A. E., & Rabbitt, S. (2013). Novel models for delivering mental health services and reducing the burdens of mental illness. *Clinical Psychological Science, 1*, 170–191.

Kearney, C. A., & Beasley, J. F. (1994). The clinical treatment of school refusal behavior: A survey of referral and practice characteristics. *Psychology in the Schools, 31*, 128–132. doi:10.1002/1520-6807(199404)31:2<128::AID-PITS2310310207>3.0.CO;2-5

Kent v. United States, 383 U.S. 541 (1966).

Kern, M. L., Duckworth, A. L., Urzua, S. S., Loeber, R., Stouthamer-Loeber, M., & Lynam, D. R. (2013). Do as you're told! Facets of agreeableness and early adult outcomes for inner-city boys. *Journal of Research in Personality, 47*, 795–799. doi:10.1016/j.jrp.2013.08.008

Kernberg, P. F., Weiner, A. S., & Bardenstein, K. K. (2000). *Personality disorders in children and adolescents*. New York, NY: Basic Books.

King, D. C., Abram, K. M., Romero, E. G., Washburn, J. J., Welty, L. J., & Teplin, L. A. (2011). Childhood maltreatment and psychiatric disorders among detained youths. *Psychiatric Services, 62*, 1430–1438. doi:10.1176/appi.ps.004412010

Kirshner, B., Pozzoboni, K., & Jones, H. (2011). Learning how to manage bias: A case study of youth participatory action research. *Applied Developmental Science, 15*, 140–155. doi:10.1080/10888691.2011.587720

Klietz, S. J., Borduin, C. M., & Schaeffer, C. M. (2010). Cost–benefit analysis of multisystemic therapy with serious and violent juvenile offenders. *Journal of Family Psychology, 24*, 657–666. doi:10.1037/a0020838

Klimstra, T. A., Luyckx, K., Branje, S., Teppers, E., Goossens, L., & Meeus, W. J. (2013). Personality traits, interpersonal identity, and relationship stability: Longitudinal linkages in late adolescence and youth adulthood. *Journal of Youth and Adolescence, 42*, 1661–1673. doi:10.1007/s10964-012-9862-8

Kochanska, G., Gross, J. N., Lin, M., & Nichols, K. E. (2002). Guilt in young children: Development, determinants, and relations with a broader system of standards. *Child Development, 73*, 461–482. doi:10.1111/1467-8624.00418

Kochanska, G., & Knaack, A. (2003). Effortful control as a personality characteristic of young children: Antecedents, correlates, and consequences. *Journal of Personality, 71*, 1087–1112. doi:10.1111/1467-6494.7106008

Koenig, A. L., Cicchetti, D., & Rogosch, F. A. (2004). Moral development: The association between maltreatment and young children's prosocial behaviors and moral transgressions. *Social Development, 13*, 87–106. doi:10.1111/j.1467-9507.2004.00258.x

Kohlberg, L. (1981). *Stages and aging in moral development*. San Francisco, CA: Harper & Row.

Kohnstamm, G. A., Halverson, C. F., Mervielde, I., & Havill, V. (1998). *Parental descriptions of child personality: Developmental antecedents of the Big Five?* Mahwah, NJ: Erlbaum.

Kok, B. E., Coffey, K. A., Cohn, M. A., Catalino, L. I., Vacharkulksemsuk, T., Algoe, S. B., . . . Fredrickson, B. L. (2013). How positive emotions build physical health: Perceived positive social connections account for the upward spiral between positive emotions and vagal tone. *Psychological Science, 24*, 1123–1132.

Kokko, K., & Pulkkinen, L. (2000). Aggression in childhood and long-term unemployment in adulthood: A cycle of maladaptation and some protective factors. *Developmental Psychology, 36*, 463–472. doi:10.1037/0012-1649.36.4.463

Koprowski, G. (1996, October 23). The rise of the teen super-predator. *Washington Times*, p. A17.

Krettenauer, T., Colasante, T., Buchmann, M., & Malti, T. (2014). The development of moral emotions and decision-making from adolescence to early adulthood: A 6-year longitudinal study. *Journal of Youth and Adolescence, 43*, 583–596.

Krueger, R. F. (1999). Personality traits in late adolescence predict mental disorders in early adulthood: A prospective–epidemiological study. *Journal of Personality, 67*, 39–65. doi:10.1111/1467-6494.00047

Krueger, R. F., Markon, K. E., Patrick, C. J., Benning, S. D., & Kramer, M. D. (2007). Linking antisocial behavior, substance use, and personality: An integrative quantitative model of the adult externalizing spectrum. *Journal of Abnormal Psychology, 116*, 645–666. doi:10.1037/0021-843X.116.4.645

Krueger, R. F., McGue, M., & Iacono, W. G. (2001). The higher-order structure of common *DSM* mental disorders: Internalization, externalization, and their connections to personality. *Personality and Individual Differences, 30,* 1245–1259. doi:10.1016/S0191-8869(00)00106-9

Krueger, R. F., & South, S. C. (2009). Externalizing disorders: Cluster 5 of the proposed meta-structure for the *DSM–V* and *ICD–11*. *Psychological Medicine, 39,* 2061–2070. doi:10.1017/S0033291709990328

Krueger, R. F., & Tackett, J. L. (2007). Behavior genetic designs. In R. W. Robins, R. Fraley, & R. F. Krueger (Eds.), *Handbook of research methods in personality psychology* (pp. 62–78). New York, NY: Guilford Press.

Kruh, I. P., & Brodsky, S. L. (1997). Clinical evaluations for transfer of juveniles to criminal court: Current practices and future research. *Behavioral Sciences & the Law, 15,* 151–165. doi:10.1002/(SICI)1099-0798(199721)15:2<151::AID-BSL267>3.0.CO;2-U

Kubak, F., & Salekin, R. T. (2009). Psychopathy and anxiety in children and adolescents: New insights and developmental pathways to offending. *Journal of Psychopathology and Behavioral Assessment, 31,* 271–284.

Kumsta, R., Sonuga-Barke, E., & Rutter, M. (2012). Adolescent callous–unemotional traits and conduct disorder in adoptees exposed to severe early deprivation. *The British Journal of Psychiatry, 200,* 197–201. doi:10.1192/bjp.bp.110.089441

Lacourse, E., Baillargeon, R., Dupéré, V., Vitaro, F., Romano, E., & Tremblay, R. (2010). Two-year predictive validity of conduct disorder subtypes in early adolescence: A latent class analysis of a Canadian longitudinal sample. *Journal of Child Psychology and Psychiatry, 51,* 1386–1394. doi:10.1111/j.1469-7610.2010.02291.x

Lahey, B. B. (2009). Public health significance of neuroticism. *American Psychologist, 64,* 241–256.

Lahey, B. B. (2014). What we need to know about callous–unemotional traits: Comment on Frick, Ray, Thornton, and Kahn (2014). *Psychological Bulletin, 140,* 58–63.

Lahey, B. B., Moffitt, T. E., & Caspi, A. (2003). *Causes of conduct disorder and juvenile delinquency.* New York, NY: Guilford Press.

Lahey, B. B., Van Hulle, C. A., Singh, A. L., Waldman, I. D., & Rahouz, P. J. (2011). Higher-order genetic and environmental structure of prevalent forms of child and adolescent psychopathology. *Archives of General Psychiatry, 68,* 181–189. doi:10.1001/archgenpsychiatry.2010.192

Lamb, M. E., Chuang, S. S., Wessels, H., Broberg, A. G., & Hwang, C. P. (2002). Emergence and construct validation of the Big Five factors in early childhood: A longitudinal analysis of their ontogeny in Sweden. *Child Development, 73,* 1517–1524. doi:10.1111/1467-8624.00487

Landenberger, N. A., & Lipsey, M. W. (2005). The positive effects of cognitive-behavioral programs for offenders: A meta-analysis of factors associated with effective treatment. *Journal of Experimental Criminology, 1,* 451–476. doi:10.1007/s11292-005-3541-7

Larchar, D., & Gruber, C. P. (1995). *Personality Inventory for Youth.* Torrance, CA: WPS.

Laursen, B., Hafen, C. A., Rubin, K. H., Booth-LaForce, C., & Rose-Krasnor, L. (2010). The distinctive difficulties of disagreeable youth. *Merrill–Palmer Quarterly, 56,* 80–103. doi:10.1353/mpq.0.0040

Laursen, B., Pulkkinen, L., & Adams, R. (2002). The antecedents and correlates of Agreeableness in adulthood. *Developmental Psychology, 38,* 591–603. doi:10.1037/0012-1649.38.4.591

LeGrand, S., & Martin, R. C. (2001). Juvenile male sexual offenders: The quality of motivation system of assessment and treatment issues. *Journal of Child Sexual Abuse, 10,* 23–49.

Leichsenring, F., & Rabung, S. (2008). Effectiveness of long-term psychodynamic psychotherapy. *Journal of the American Medical Association, 300,* 1551–1565. doi:10.1001/jama.300.13.1551

Leigh, J., Westen, D., Barends, A., Mendel, M. J., & Byers, S. (1992). The assessment of complexity of representations of people using TAT and interview data. *Journal of Personality, 60,* 809–834. doi:10.1111/j.1467-6494.1992.tb00275.x

Leistico, A.-M. R., & Salekin, R. T. (2003). Testing the reliability and validity of the Risk, Sophistication–Maturity, and Treatment Amenability Inventory (RST–I): An assessment tool for juvenile offenders. *International Journal of Forensic Mental Health, 2,* 101–117. doi:10.1080/14999013.2003.10471182

Leistico, A.-M. R., Salekin, R. T., DeCoster, J., & Rogers, R. (2008). A large-scale meta-analysis relating the Hare measures of psychopathy to antisocial conduct. *Law and Human Behavior, 32,* 28–45. doi:10.1007/s10979-007-9096-6

Lengua, L. J. (2002). The contribution of emotionality and self-regulation to the understanding of children's responses to multiple risk. *Child Development, 73,* 144–161. doi:10.1111/1467-8624.00397

Leuner, B., Caponiti, J. M., & Gould, E. (2012). Oxytocin stimulates adult neurogenesis even under conditions of stress and elevated glucocorticoids. *Hippocampus, 22,* 861–868.

Leuner, B., Glasper, E. R., & Gould, E. (2010). Parenting and plasticity. *Trends in Neurosciences, 33,* 465–473.

Leuner, B., & Gould, E. (2010a). Dendritic growth in medial prefrontal cortex and cognitive flexibility are enhanced during the postpartum period. *Journal of Neuroscience, 30,* 13499–13503.

Leuner, B., & Gould, E. (2010b). Structural plasticity and hippocampus function. *Annual Review of Psychology, 61,* 111–140. doi:10.1146/annurev.psych.093008.100359

Leuner, B., Gould, E., & Shors, T. J. (2006). Is there a link between adult neurogenesis and learning? *Hippocampus, 16,* 216–224. doi:10.1002/hipo.20153

Lewis, M. (1993). The development of deception. In M. Lewis & C. Saarni (Eds.), *Lying and deception in everyday life* (pp. 90–105). New York, NY: Guilford Press.

Limber, S. P. (2011). Development, evaluation, and future directions of the Olweus Bullying Prevention Program. *Journal of School Violence, 10*, 71–87. doi:10.108 0/15388220.2010.519375

Lipsey, M. W. (2009). The primary factors that characterize effective interventions with juvenile offenders: A meta-analytic review. *Victims & Offenders, 4*, 124–147. doi:10.1080/15564880802612573

Lipsey, M. W., & Derzon, J. H. (1998). Predictors of violent or serious delinquency in adolescence and early adulthood: A synthesis of longitudinal research. In R. Loeber & D. P. Farrington (Eds.), *Serious and violent juvenile offenders: Risk factors and successful interventions* (pp. 86–105). Thousand Oaks, CA: Sage Publications.

Litwack, T. R. (2002). Some questions for the field of violence risk assessment and forensic mental health: Or, "back to basics" revisited. *International Journal of Forensic Mental Health, 1*, 171–178. doi:10.1080/14999013.2002.10471171

Livsey, S. (2012). *Juvenile delinquency probation caseload, 2009.* Washington, DC: Office of Juvenile Justice and Delinquency Prevention. Retrieved from http://www.ojjdp.gov/pubs/239082.pdf

Lochman, J. E., Wells, K. C., Qu, L., & Chen, L. (2013). Three year follow-up of Coping Power intervention effects: Evidence of neighborhood moderation? *Prevention Science, 14*, 364–376.

Loeber, R. (1990). Development and risk factors of juvenile antisocial behavior and delinquency. *Clinical Psychology Review, 10*, 1–41. doi:10.1016/0272-7358(90)90105-J

Loeber, R. (1991). Antisocial behavior: More enduring than changeable? *Journal of the American Academy of Child & Adolescent Psychiatry, 30*, 393–397. doi:10.1097/00004583-199105000-00007

Loeber, R., & Farrington, D. (1998). Never too early, never too late: Risk factors and successful interventions for serious and violent juvenile offenders. *Studies on Crime & Crime Prevention, 7*, 7–30.

Loeber, R., & Hay, D. (1997). Key issues in the development of aggression and violence from childhood to early adulthood. *Annual Review of Psychology, 48*, 371–410.

Loeber, R., Menting, B., Lynam, D. R., Moffitt, T. E., Stouthamer-Loeber, M., Stallings, R., . . . Pardini, D. (2012). Findings from the Pittsburgh Youth Study: Cognitive impulsivity and intelligence as predictors of the age–crime curve. *Journal of the American Academy of Child & Adolescent Psychiatry, 51*, 1136–1149.

Loeber, R., & Stouthamer-Loeber, M. (1998). Development of juvenile aggression and violence: Some common misconceptions and controversies. *American Psychologist, 53*, 242–259. doi:10.1037/0003-066X.53.2.242

Loeber, R., Stouthamer-Loeber, M., & Green, S. M. (1991). Age of onset of problem behavior in boys, and later disruptive and delinquent behaviors. *Criminal Behavior and Mental Health, 1*, 229–246.

Loehlin, J. C. (1992). *Genes and environment in personality development*. Newbury Park, CA: Sage.

Lucenko, B. A., He, L., Mancuso, D., & Felver, B. (2011). *Effects of functional family parole on rearrest and employment for youth in Washington State: Executive summary*. Retrieved from http://www.dshs.wa.gov/pdf/ms/rda/research/2/24.pdf

Luthar, S. S. (1991). Vulnerability and resilience: A study of high risk adolescents. *Child Development, 62*, 600–616. doi:10.2307/1131134

Lykken, D. T. (1995). *The antisocial personalities*. Mahwah, NJ: Erlbaum.

Lynam, D. R. (2012). Assessment of maladaptive variants of five-factor model traits. *Journal of Personality, 80*, 1593–1613. doi:10.1111/j.1467-6494.2012.00775.x

Lynam, D. R., Caspi, A., Moffitt, T. E., Loeber, R., & Stouthamer-Loeber, M. (2007). Longitudinal evidence that psychopathy scores in early adolescence predict adult psychopathy. *Journal of Abnormal Psychology, 116*, 155–165. doi:10.1037/0021-843X.116.1.155

Lynam, D. R., Caspi, A., Moffitt, T. E., Wikström, P. H., Loeber, R., & Novak, S. (2000). The interaction between impulsivity and neighborhood context on offending: The effects of impulsivity are stronger in poorer neighborhoods. *Journal of Abnormal Psychology, 109*, 563–574. doi:10.1037/0021-843X.109.4.563

Lynam, D. R., & Gudonis, L. (2005). The development of psychopathy. *Annual Review of Clinical Psychology, 1*, 381–407. doi:10.1146/annurev.clinpsy.1.102803.144019

Manders, W. A., Deković, M., Asscher, J. J., van der Laan, P. H., & Prins, P. J. M. (2013). Psychopathy as predictor and moderator of multisystemic therapy outcomes among adolescents treated for antisocial behavior. *Journal of Abnormal Child Psychology, 41*, 1121–1132. doi:10.1007/s10802-013-9749-5

Mann, L., Harmoni, R., & Power, C. (1989). Adolescent decision-making: The development of competence. *Journal of Adolescence, 12*, 265–278. doi:10.1016/0140-1971(89)90077-8

Marcia, J. E. (1966). Development and validation of ego identity status. *Journal of Personality and Social Psychology, 3*, 551–558. doi:10.1037/h0023281

Marcia, J. E. (1980). Identity in adolescence. In J. Adelson (Ed.), *Handbook of adolescent psychology* (pp. 159–187). New York, NY: Wiley.

Marcia, J. E. (1994). The empirical study of ego identity. In H. A. Bosma, T. L. G. Graafsma, H. D. Grotevant, & D. J. de Levita (Eds.), *Identity and development: An interdisciplinary approach* (pp. 67–80). Thousand Oaks, CA: Sage.

Marczyk, G. R., Heilbrun, K., Lander, T., & DeMatteo, D. (2003). Predicting juvenile recidivism with the PCL:YV, MAYSI, and YLS/CMI. *International Journal of Forensic Mental Health, 2*, 7–18. doi:10.1080/14999013.2003.10471175

Markey, P. M., Markey, C. N., & Tinsley, B. J. (2004). Children's behavioral manifestations of the five-factor model of personality. *Personality and Social Psychology Bulletin, 30*, 423–432. doi:10.1177/0146167203261886

Markon, K. E., Krueger, R. F., & Watson, D. (2005). Delineating the structure of normal and abnormal personality: An integrative hierarchical approach. *Journal of Personality and Social Psychology, 88*, 139–157. doi:10.1037/0022-3514.88.1.139

Martin, R. C. (1989). *The Quality of Motivation Questionnaire.* Lee's Summit, MO: RCM Enterprises.

Martin, R. P., Wisenbaker, J., & Huttunen, M. (1994). Review of factor analytic studies of temperament measures based on the Thomas–Chess structural model: Implications for the Big Five. In C. F. Halverson, G. A. Kohnstamm, & R. P. Martin (Eds.), *The developing structure of temperament and personality from infancy to adulthood* (pp. 157–172). Hillsdale, NJ: Erlbaum.

Massetti, G. M., Pelham, W. E., Chacko, A., Walker, K., Arnold, F., Keenan, J., . . . Burrows-MacLean, L. (2003, November). Situational variability of ADHD, ODD, and CD: Psychometric properties of the DBD interview and rating scale. Poster presented at the 37th annual convention of the Association for Advancement of Behavior Therapy, Boston, MA.

Massetti, G. M., Pelham, W. E., & Gnagy, E. M. (2005, June). Situational variability of ADHD, ODD, and CD: Psychometric properties of the DBD interview and rating scale for an ADHD sample. Poster presented at the annual meeting of the International Society for Research in Child and Adolescent Psychopathology, New York, NY.

Masten, A. S., Coatsworth, J. D., Neemann, J., Gest, S. D., Tellegen, A., & Garmezy, N. (1995). The structure and coherence of competence from childhood through adolescence. *Child Development, 66*, 1635–1659. doi:10.2307/1131901

Matarazzo, J. D. (1992). Psychological testing and assessment ion the 21st century. *American Psychologist, 47*, 1007–1018.

May, J., Osmond, K., & Billick, S. (2014). Juvenile delinquency treatment and prevention: A literature review. *Psychiatric Quarterly, 85*, 295–301.

Maziade, M., Caron, C., Cote, R., Merette, C., Bernier, H., Laplante, B., . . . Thivierge, J. (1990). Psychiatric status of adolescents who had extreme temperaments at age 7. *The American Journal of Psychiatry, 147*, 1531–1536.

McCann, J. T. (1998). *Malingering and deception in adolescents: Assessing credibility in clinical and forensic settings.* Washington, DC: American Psychological Association.

McCarthy, F. B. (1977). The role of the concept of responsibility in juvenile delinquency proceedings. *University of Michigan Journal of Law Reform, 10*, 181–219. Retrieved from http://heinonline.org/HOL/LandingPage?handle=hein.journals/umijlr10&div=14&id=&page=

McConnaughy, E. A., Prochaska, J. O., & Velicer, W. F. (1983). Stages of change in psychotherapy: Measurement and sample profiles. *Psychotherapy: Theory, Research & Practice, 20*, 368–375. doi:10.1037/h0090198

McCrae, R. R., & Costa, P. T. (1992). Discriminant validity of NEO–PI–R facet scales. *Educational and Psychological Measurement, 52*, 229–237.

McCrae, R. R., & Costa, P. T. (1996). Toward a new generation of personality theories: Theoretical contexts for the five-factor model. In J. S. Wiggins (Ed.), *The* five-factor model of personality: Theoretical perspectives (pp. 51–87). New York, NY: Guilford Press.

McCrae, R. R., & Costa, P. T. (1997). Personality trait structure as a human universal. *American Psychologist, 52,* 509–516. doi:10.1037/0003-066X.52.5.509

McCrae, R. R., Costa, P. T., Terracciano, A., Parker, W. D., Mills, C. J., De Fruyt, F., & Mervielde, I. (2002). Personality trait development from age 12 to age 18: Longitudinal, cross-sectional, and cross-cultural analyses. *Journal of Personality and Social Psychology, 83,* 1456–1468. doi:10.1037/0022-3514.83.6.1456

McMahon, R. J., & Forehand, R. L. (2003). *Helping the noncompliant child: Family-based treatment for oppositional behavior* (2nd ed.). New York, NY: Guilford Press.

McNulty, J. K., & Fincham, F. D. (2012). Beyond positive psychology? Toward a contextual view of psychological processes and well-being. *American Psychologist, 67,* 101–110.

Meade, B., & Steiner, B. (2010). The total effects of boot camps that house juveniles: A systematic review of the evidence. *Journal of Criminal Justice, 38,* 841–853. doi:10.1016/j.jcrimjus.2010.06.007

Mealey, L. (1995). The sociobiology of sociopathy: An integrated evolutionary model. *Behavioral and Brain Sciences, 18,* 523–599. doi:10.1017/S0140525X00039595

Meeus, W., van de Schoot, R., Keijsers, L., Schwartz, S. J., & Branje, S. (2010). On the progression and stability of adolescent identity formation: A five wave longitudinal study in early-to-middle and middle-to-late adolescence. *Child Development, 81,* 1565–1581. doi:10.1111/j.1467-8624.2010.01492.x

Megargee, E. I. (1984). A new classification system for criminal offenders: VI. Differences among the types on the Adjective Checklist. *Criminal Justice and Behavior, 11,* 349–376. doi:10.1177/0093854884011003007

Megargee, E. I., & Bohn, M. J., Jr. (1979). *Classifying criminal offenders: A new system based on the MMPI.* Beverly Hills, CA: Sage.

Melton, G. B., Petrila, J., Poythress, N. G., & Slobogin, C. (1987). *Psychological evaluations for the courts: A handbook for mental health professionals and lawyers.* New York, NY: Guilford Press.

Melton, G. B., Petrila, J., Poythress, N. G., & Slobogin, C. (1997). *Psychological evaluations for the courts: A handbook for mental health professionals and lawyers* (2nd ed.). New York, NY: Guilford Press.

Meng, A., Segal, R., & Boden, E. (2013). American juvenile justice system: History in the making. *International Journal of Adolescent Medicine and Health, 25,* 275–278. doi:10.1515/ijamh-2013-0062

Mervielde, I., De Clercq, B., De Fruyt, F., & Van Leeuwen, K. (2005). Temperament, personality and developmental psychopathology as childhood antecedents of personality disorders. *Journal of Personality Disorders, 19,* 171–201. doi:10.1521/pedi.19.2.171.62627

Miller, J. (1998, Winter). Riding the crime wave: Why words we use matter so much. *Nieman Reports.* Retrieved from http://www.nieman.harvard.edu/reports/article/102294/Riding-the-Crime-Wave.aspx

Miller, R. C. (1958). *Personality patterns among delinquent behavior types*. Oxford, England: Catholic University of America Press.

Miller, W. R., & Rollnick, S. (2012). *Motivational Interviewing: Helping people change*. New York, NY: Guilford Press.

Miller v. State of Alabama, 567 U.S. (2012).

Millon, T., with Millon, C., & Davis, R. (1993). *The Millon Adolescent Clinical Inventory*. San Antonio, TX: The Psychological Corporation.

Millon, T., Tringone, T., Millon, C., & Grossman, S. (2005). *Millon Preadolescent Clinical Inventory*. San Antonio, TX: The Psychological Corporation.

Moffitt, T. E. (1993). Adolescent-limited and life-course persistent antisocial behavior: A developmental taxonomy. *Psychological Review, 100,* 674–701. doi:10.1037/0033-295X.100.4.674

Moffitt, T. E. (2003). Life-course persistent and adolescent-limited antisocial behavior: A 10-year research review and research agenda. In B. B. Lahey, T. E. Moffitt, & A. Caspi (Eds.), *Causes of conduct disorder and juvenile delinquency* (pp. 49–75). New York, NY: Guilford Press.

Moffitt, T. E. (2007). A review of the research on the taxonomy of life course persistent versus adolescent-limited antisocial behavior. In D. J. Flannery, A. T. Vazsonyi, & I. D. Waldman (Eds.), *The Cambridge handbook of violent behavior and aggression* (pp. 43–74). Cambridge, England: Cambridge University Press.

Moffitt, T. E., Caspi, A., Belsky, J., & Silva, P. A. (1992). Childhood experience and the onset of menarche: A test of a sociobiological model. *Child Development, 63,* 47–58.

Moffitt, T. E., Caspi, A., Rutter, M., & Silva, P. A. (2001). *Sex differences in antisocial behavior: Conduct disorder, delinquency, and violence in the Dunedin Longitudinal Study*. Cambridge, England: Cambridge University Press. doi:10.1017/CBO9780511490057

Monahan, J., & Walker, L. (1988). Social science research in law: A new paradigm. *American Psychologist, 43,* 465–472. doi:10.1037/0003-066X.43.6.465

Moreno, S., & Bidelman, G. M. (2014). Examining neural plasticity and cognitive benefit through the unique lens of musical training. *Hearing Research, 308,* 84–97.

Morey, L. C. (2007). *Personality Assessment Inventory—Adolescent*. Lutz, FL: Psychological Assessment Resources.

Mulvey, E. (1984). Judging amenability to treatment in juvenile offenders: Theory and practice. In N. D. Reppucci, L. A. Weithorn, E. P. Mulvey, & J. Monahan (Eds.), *Children, mental health, and the law* (pp. 195–210). Beverly Hills, CA: Sage.

Mulvey, E. P., & Iselin, A.-M. R. (2008). Improving professional judgments of risk and amenability in juvenile justice. *The Future of Children, 18,* 35–57. doi:10.1353/foc.0.0012

Muris, P., Schmidt, H., Merckelbach, H., & Schouten, E. (2001). The structure of negative emotions in adolescents. *Journal of Abnormal Child Psychology, 29,* 331–337. doi:10.1023/A:1010361913186

Murray, H. A. (1937). *Thematic Apperception Test manual*. Cambridge, MA: Harvard University Press.

Murray, J., Loeber, R., & Pardini, D. (2012). Parental involvement in the criminal justice system and the development of youth theft, marijuana use, depression, and poor academic performance. *Criminology, 50,* 255–302. doi:10.1111/j.1745-9125.2011.00257.x

Murrie, D. C., Boccaccini, M. T., McCoy, W., & Cornell, D. G. (2007). Diagnostic labeling in juvenile court: How do descriptions of psychopathy and conduct disorder influence judges? *Journal of Clinical Child and Adolescent Psychology, 36,* 228–241. doi:10.1080/15374410701279602

Nagin, D., & Tremblay, R. E. (1999). Trajectories of boys' physical aggression, opposition, and hyperactivity on the path to physically violent and nonviolent juvenile delinquency. *Child Development, 70,* 1181–1196. doi:10.1111/1467-8624.00086

Nagy, T. F. (2011). *Essential ethics for psychologists: A primer for understanding and mastering core issues*. Washington, DC: American Psychological Association.

National Council of Juvenile and Family Court Judges. (2005). *Juvenile delinquency guidelines: Improving court practice in juvenile delinquency cases*. Retrieved from http://www.ncjfcj.org/resource-library/publications/juvenile-delinquency-guidelines-improving-court-practice-juvenile

National Institute of Mental Health. (1991). *NIMH Diagnostic Interview Schedule for Children, Version 2.3*. Rockville, MD: Author.

Newman, D. L., Caspi, A., Moffitt, T. E., & Silva, P. A. (1997). Antecedents of adult interpersonal functioning: Effects of individual differences in age 3 temperament. *Developmental Psychology, 33,* 206–217. doi:10.1037/0012-1649.33.2.206

Niarhos, F. J., & Routh, D. K. (1992). The role of clinical assessment in the juvenile court: Predictors of juvenile dispositions and recidivism. *Journal of Clinical Child Psychology, 21,* 151–159. doi:10.1207/s15374424jccp2102_7

Nigg, J. T. (2006). Temperament and developmental psychopathology. *Journal of Child Psychology and Psychiatry, 47,* 395–422. doi:10.1111/j.1469-7610.2006.01612.x

Nugent, W., & Ely, G. (2010). The effects of aggression replacement training on periodicities in antisocial behavior in a short-term shelter for adolescents. *Journal of the Society for Social Work and Research, 1,* 140–158. doi:10.5243/jsswr.2010.11

Odgers, C. L., Caspi, A., Nagin, D. S., Piquero, A. R., Slutske, W. S., Milne, B. J., . . . Moffitt, T. E. (2008). Is it important to prevent early exposure to drugs and alcohol among adolescents? *Psychological Science, 19,* 1037–1044.

Odgers, C. L., Moffitt, T. E., Broadbent, J. M., Dickson, N., Hancox, R. J., Harrington, H., . . . Caspi, A. (2008). Female and male antisocial trajectories: From childhood origins to adult outcomes. *Development and Psychopathology, 20,* 673–716.

Odgers, C. L., Moffitt, T. E., Tach, L. M., Sampson, R. J., Taylor, A., Matthews, C. L., & Caspi, A. (2009). The protective effects of neighborhood collective efficacy on British children growing up in deprivation: A developmental analysis. *Developmental Psychology, 45,* 942–957.

Odgers, C. L., Reppucci, N. D., & Moretti, M. M. (2005). Nipping psychopathy in the bud: An examination of the convergent, predictive, and theoretical utility of the PCL–YV among adolescent girls. *Behavioral Sciences & the Law, 23,* 743–763. doi:10.1002/bsl.664

Oldenettel, D., & Wordes, M. (2000). *The community assessment centers concept.* Washington, DC: Office of Juvenile Justice and Delinquency Prevention.

Olson, S. L., Schilling, E. M., & Bates, J. E. (1999). Measurement of impulsivity: Construct coherence, longitudinal stability, and relationship with externalizing problems in middle childhood and adolescence. *Journal of Abnormal Child Psychology, 27,* 151–165. doi:10.1023/A:1021915615677

Olver, M. E., Stockdale, K. C., & Wong, S. P. (2012). Short and long-term prediction of recidivism using the Youth Level of Service/Case Management Inventory in a sample of serious young offenders. *Law and Human Behavior, 36,* 331–344. doi:10.1037/h0093927

Olweus, D., & Limber, S. P. (2010a). Bullying in school: Evaluation and dissemination of the Olweus Bullying Prevention Program. *American Journal of Orthopsychiatry, 80,* 124–134. doi:10.1111/j.1939-0025.2010.01015.x

Olweus, D., & Limber, S. P. (2010b). The Olweus Bullying Prevention Program: Implementation and evaluation over two decades. In S. R. Jimerson, S. M. Swearer, & D. L. Espelage (Eds.), *Handbook of bullying in schools: An international perspective* (pp. 377–401). New York, NY: Routledge.

Orvaschel, H., Puig-Antich, J., Chambers, W., Tabrizi, M. A., & Johnson, R. (1982). Retrospective assessment of child psychopathology with the Kiddie-SADS-E. *Journal of the American Academy of Child Psychiatry, 21,* 392–397.

Otto, R. K., DeMier, R., & Boccaccini, M. (2014). *Forensic reports and testimony: A guide to effective communication for psychologists and psychiatrists.* Hoboken, NJ: Wiley.

Oudekerk, B. A., Burgers, D. E., & Reppucci, N. D. (2014). Romantic partner deviance and the continuity of violence from adolescence to adulthood among offending girls. *Journal of Research on Adolescence, 24,* 27–39. doi:10.1111/j.1532-7795.2012.00823.x

Page, G. L., & Scalora, M. J. (2004). The utility of locus of control for assessing juvenile amenability to treatment. *Aggression and Violent Behavior, 9,* 523–534. doi:10.1016/S1359-1789(03)00047-8

Pardini, D. A., & Fite, P. J. (2010). Symptoms of conduct disorder, oppositional defiant disorder, attention-deficit/hyperactivity disorder, and callous–unemotional traits as unique predictors of psychosocial maladjustment in boys: Advancing an evidence base for *DSM–V. Journal of the American Academy of Child & Adolescent Psychiatry, 49,* 1134–1144.

Pardini, D. A., Fite, P. J., & Burke, J. D. (2008). Bidirectional associations between parenting practices and conduct problems in boys from childhood to adolescence: The moderating effect of age and African-American ethnicity. *Journal of Abnormal Child Psychology, 36,* 647–662.

Pardini, D. A., Lochman, J. E., & Powell, N. (2007). The development of callous–unemotional traits and antisocial behavior in children: Are there shared and/or unique predictors? *Journal of Clinical Child and Adolescent Psychology, 36,* 319–333.

Park, G. H. (2011). *The role of extracurricular activity in positive youth development* (Unpublished doctoral dissertation). Temple University, Philadelphia, PA.

Patterson, G. R. (1975). *Families: Applications of social learning to family life.* Champaign, IL: Research Press.

Patterson, G. R. (1976). The aggressive child: Victim and architect of a coercive system. In E. J. Mash, L. A. Hamerlynck, & L. C. Handy (Eds.), *Behavior modification and families* (pp. 267–316). New York, NY: Brunner/Mazel.

Patterson, G. R. (1997). Performance models for parenting: A social interaction perspective. In J. E. Grusec & L. Kuczynski (Eds.), *Parenting of children's internalization of values: A handbook of contemporary theory* (pp. 193–226). Hoboken, NJ: Wiley.

Paus, T. (2005). Mapping brain maturation and cognitive development during adolescence. *Trends in Cognitive Sciences, 9,* 60–68. doi:10.1016/j.tics.2004.12.008

Paus, T., Leonard, G., Lerner, J. V., Lerner, R. M., Perron, M., Pike, G. B., . . . Steinberg, L. (2008). Morphological properties of the action–observation cortical network in adolescents with low and high resistance to peer influence. *Social Neuroscience, 3,* 303–316. doi:10.1080/17470910701563558

Penney, S. R., Lee, Z., & Moretti, M. M. (2010). Gender differences in risk factors for violence: An examination of the predictive validity of the Structured Assessment of Violence Risk in Youth. *Aggressive Behavior, 36,* 390–404. doi:10.1002/ab.20352

Penney, S. R., & Moretti, M. M. (2005). The transfer of juveniles to adult court in Canada and the United States: Confused agendas and compromised assessment procedures. *International Journal of Forensic Mental Health, 4,* 19–37. doi:10.1080/14999013.2005.10471210

Perry, N. W. (1995). Children's comprehension of truths, lies, and false beliefs. In T. Ney (Ed.), *True and false allegations of child sexual abuse: Assessment and case management* (pp. 73–98). New York, NY: Brunner/Mazel.

Peskin, J. (1992). Ruse and representations: On children's ability to conceal information. *Developmental Psychology, 28,* 84–89. doi:10.1037/0012-1649.28.1.84

Pessiglione, M., Schmidt, L., Draganski, B., Kalisch, R., Lau, H., Dolan, R. J., & Frith, C. D. (2007, May 11). How the brain translates money into force: A neuroimaging study of subliminal motivation. *Science, 316,* 904–906.

Petrosino, A., Turpin-Petrosino, C., & Buehler, J. (2002). Scared Straight and other juvenile awareness programs for preventing juvenile delinquency. *Cochrane Database of Systematic Reviews, 2,* CD002796.

Petrosino, A., Turpin-Petrosino, C., & Finckenauer, J. O. (2000). Well-meaning programs can have harmful effects! Lessons from experiments such as Scared Straight. *Crime & Delinquency, 46,* 354–379. doi:10.1177/0011128700046003006

Phillippi, S. Jr., Below, L., & Cuffie, D. (2010). Evidence-based practice for juvenile justice reform in Louisiana. *Louisiana State University School of Public Health and Louisiana Models for Change in Juvenile Justice, 20*, 1–2.

Piaget, J. (1929). *The child's conception of the world* (J. Tomlinson, Trans). New York, NY: Harcourt Brace. (Original work published 1926)

Piaget, J. (1952). *The origins of intelligence in children* (M. Cook, Trans.). New York, NY: International Universities Press. (Original work published 1933)

Piaget, J. (1983). Piaget's theory (G. Cellerier & J. Langer, Trans.). In P. H. Mussen (Series Ed.) & W. Kessen (Volume Ed.), *Handbook of child psychology: History, theory, and methods* (4th ed., Vol. 1, pp. 103–126). New York, NY: Wiley. (Original work published 1970)

Piehler, T. F., Bloomquist, M. L., August, G. J., Gewirtz, A. H., Lee, S. S., & Lee, W. S. (2014). Executive functioning as a mediator of conduct problems prevention in children of homeless families residing in temporary supportive housing: A parallel process latent growth modeling approach. *Journal of Abnormal Child Psychology, 42*, 681–692.

Polak, A., & Harris, P. L. (1999). Deception by young children following noncompliance. *Developmental Psychology, 35*, 561–568. doi:10.1037/0012-1649.35.2.561

Provorse, D., & Sarata, B. (1989). The social psychology of juvenile court judges in rural communities. *Journal of Rural Community Psychology, 10*, 3–15.

Putnam, S. P., Sanson, A. V., & Rothbart, M. K. (2002). Child temperament and parenting. In M. H. Bornstein (Ed.), *Handbook of parenting: Vol. 1. Children and parenting* (2nd ed., pp. 255–277). Mahwah, NJ: Erlbaum.

Puzzanchera, C. (2003). *Delinquency cases waived to criminal court, 1990–1999.* Washington, DC: Office of Juvenile Justice and Delinquency Prevention. Retrieved from https://www.ncjrs.gov/pdffiles1/ojjdp/fs200304.pdf

Puzzanchera, C. (2013a). *Juvenile arrests 2010.* Washington, DC: Office of Juvenile Justice and Delinquency Prevention. Retrieved from http://www.ncjj.org/Publication/Juvenile-Arrests-2010.aspx

Puzzanchera, C. (2013b). *Juvenile arrests 2011.* Washington, DC: Office of Juvenile Justice and Delinquency Prevention. Retrieved from http://www.ojjdp.gov/pubs/244476.pdf

Quay, H. C. (1964). Dimensions of personality in delinquent boys as inferred from the factor analysis of case history data. *Child Development, 35*, 479–484.

Quay, H. C. (1966). Personality patterns in preadolescent delinquent boys. *Educational and Psychological Measurement, 26*, 99–110.

Quay, H. C. (1987). *Handbook of juvenile delinquency.* Oxford, England: Wiley.

Raine, A., Reynolds, C., Venables, P. H., Mednick, S. A., & Farrington, D. P. (1998). Fearlessness, stimulation-seeking, and large body size at age 3 years as early predispositions to childhood aggression at age 11 years. *Archives of General Psychiatry, 55*, 745–751. doi:10.1001/archpsyc.55.8.745

Rains, G. D. (2002). *Principles of human neuropsychology*. New York, NY: McGraw-Hill.

Raskin, D. C., & Esplin, P. W. (1991). Statement validity assessment: Interview procedures and content analysis of children's statements of sexual abuse. *Behavioral Assessment, 13*, 265–291.

Raven, J. C. (1996). *Raven's Standard Progressive Matrices*. San Antonio, TX: The Psychological Corporation.

Redding, R. (2010, June). Juvenile transfer laws: An effective deterrent to delinquency? *Juvenile Justice Bulletin*. Washington, DC: Office of Juvenile Justice and Delinquency Prevention.

Reich, W., & Todd, R. D. (2002). *The Missouri Assessment of Genetics Interview for Children*. Unpublished structured interview.

Reichard, R. J., Riggio, R. E., Guerin, D. W., Oliver, P. H., Gottfried, A. W., & Gottfried, A. E. (2011). A longitudinal analysis of relationships between adolescent personality and intelligence with adult leader emergence and transformational leadership. *The Leadership Quarterly, 22*, 471–481. doi:10.1016/j.leaqua.2011.04.005

Rennie, C., & Dolan, M. (2010). Predictive validity of the youth level of service/case management inventory in custody sample in England. *The Journal of Forensic Psychiatry & Psychology, 21*, 407–425. doi:10.1080/14789940903452311

Rettig, R. P. (1980). Considering the use and usefulness of juvenile detention: Operationalizing social theory. *Adolescence, 15*, 443–459.

Reynolds, C. R., & Kamphaus, R. W. (2004). *Behavioral Assessment System for Children, Second Edition*. San Antonio, TX: The Psychological Corporation.

Reynolds, W. M. (1998). *Adolescent Psychopathology Scale*. Lutz, FL: Psychological Assessment Resources, Inc.

Rhoades, B., Campbell, L., & Bumbarger, B. (2011). *Evidence-based intervention programs: 2010 outcomes summary*. Report prepared for the Pennsylvania Commission on Crime and Delinquency. Retrieved from http://www.fftllc.com/documents/2010%20Evidence-based%20Intervention%20Outcome%20Summary_9-16-11.pdf

Richers, J. E., & Cicchetti, D. (1993). Mark Twain meets *DSM–III–R*: Conduct disorder, development, and the concept of harmful dysfunction. *Development and Psychopathology, 5*, 5–29. doi:10.1017/S0954579400004235

Roberts, B. W., & DelVecchio, W. F. (2000). The rank-order consistency of personality traits from childhood to old age: A quantitative review of longitudinal studies. *Psychological Bulletin, 126*, 3–25. doi:10.1037/0033-2909.126.1.3

Roberts, B. W., Walton, K. E., & Viechtbauer, W. (2006). Patterns of mean-level change in personality traits across the life course: A meta-analysis of longitudinal studies. *Psychological Bulletin, 132*, 1–25. doi:10.1037/0033-2909.132.1.1

Robin, A. L., & Foster, S. L. (1989). *Negotiating parent–adolescent conflict: A behavioral–family systems approach*. New York, NY: Guilford Press.

Rogers, R. (1997). *Clinical assessment of malingering an deception* (2nd ed.). New York, NY: Guilford Press.

Rogers, R. (2001). *Handbook of diagnostic and structured interviewing*. New York, NY: Guilford Press.

Rogers, R. (2008). *Clinical assessment of malingering and deception* (3rd ed.). New York, NY: Guilford Press.

Rogers, R., Bagby, R. M., & Dickens, S. E. (1992). *Structured Interview of Reported Symptoms professional manual*. Odessa, FL: Psychological Assessment Resources.

Rogers, R., & Ewing, C. P. (1989). Ultimate opinion proscriptions: A cosmetic fix and a plea for empiricism. *Law and Human Behavior, 13,* 357–374.

Rogers, R., & Ewing, C. P. (2003). The prohibition of ultimate opinions: A misguided enterprise. *Journal of Forensic Psychology Practice, 3,* 65–75.

Rogers, R., Hinds, J. D., & Sewell, K. W. (1996). Feigning psychopathology among adolescent offenders: Validation of the SIRS, MMPI–A, and SIMS. *Journal of Personality Assessment, 67,* 244–257.

Roper v. Simmons, 543 U.S. 551 (2005).

Rorschach, H. (1951). *Psychodiagnostics*. New York, NY: Grune & Stratton. (Original work published 1921)

Rosenfeld, B., & Penrod, S. D. (2011). *Research methods in forensic psychology*. Hoboken, NJ: Wiley.

Rothbart, M. K., Ahadi, S. A., & Evans, D. E. (2000). Temperament and personality: Origins and outcomes. *Journal of Personality and Social Psychology, 78,* 122–135. doi:10.1037/0022-3514.78.1.122

Rothbart, M. K., Ahadi, S. A., Hershey, K. L., & Fisher, P. (2001). Investigations of temperament at three to seven years: The Children's Behavior Questionnaire. *Child Development, 72,* 1394–1408. doi:10.1111/1467-8624.00355

Rothbart, M. K., & Bates, J. E. (1998). Temperament. In W. Damon (Series Ed.) & N. Eisenberg (Vol. Ed.), *Handbook of child psychology: Vol. 3. Social, emotional, and personality development* (5th ed., pp. 105–176). New York, NY: Wiley.

Rothbart, M. K., & Derryberry, D. (2002). Temperament in children. In C. von Hofsten & L. Backman (Eds.), *Psychology at the turn of the millennium: Vol. 2. Social, developmental, and clinical perspectives* (pp. 17–35). New York, NY: Taylor & Francis.

Rubin, K. H., Bukowski, W., & Parker, J. G. (1998). Peer interactions, relationships, and groups. In W. Damon (Series Ed.) & N. Eisenberg (Vol. Ed.), *Handbook of child psychology: Vol. 3. Social, emotional, and personality development* (5th ed., pp. 619–700). New York, NY: Wiley.

Rubin, K. H., Burgess, K. B., Dwyer, K. M., & Hastings, P. D. (2003). Predicting preschoolers' externalizing behaviors from toddler temperament, conflict, and maternal negativity. *Developmental Psychology, 39,* 164–176. doi:10.1037/0012-1649.39.1.164

Ruffman, T., Olson, D. R., Ash, T., & Keenan, T. (1993). The ABCs of deception: Do young children understand deception in the same way as adults? *Developmental Psychology, 29,* 74–87. doi:10.1037/0012-1649.29.1.74

Rutter, M. (2000). Resilience reconsidered: Conceptual considerations, empirical findings, and policy implications. In J. P. Shonkoff & S. J. Meisels (Eds.), *Handbook of early childhood intervention* (pp. 651–682). Cambridge, England: Cambridge University Press. doi:10.1017/CBO9780511529320.030

Rutter, M. (2003). Critical paths from risk indicator to causal mechanism. In B. B. Lahey, T. E. Moffitt, & A. Caspi (Eds.), *Causes of conduct disorder and juvenile delinquency* (pp. 3–24). New York, NY: Guilford Press.

Ryan, R. M., Plant, R. W., & O'Malley, S. (1995). Initial motivations for alcohol treatment: Relations with patient characteristics, treatment involvement, and dropout. *Addictive Behaviors, 20,* 279–297. doi:10.1016/0306-4603(94)00072-7

Sacks, H., & Reader, W. D. (1992). *Handbook of psychiatric practice in the juvenile court.* Arlington, VA: American Psychiatric Association.

Salekin, K. L., Ogloff, J. R. P., Ley, R., & Salekin, R. T. (2002). The Overcontrolled Hostility Scale: An evaluation of its applicability with an adolescent population. *Criminal Justice and Behavior, 29,* 718–733. doi:10.1177/009385402237924

Salekin, R. T. (1998). [Miami Juvenile Detention Center Project]. Unpublished raw data.

Salekin, R. T. (2002a). Clinical evaluation of youth considered for transfer to adult criminal court: Refining practice and directions for science. *Journal of Forensic Psychology Practice, 2,* 55–72. doi:10.1300/J158v02n01_03

Salekin, R. T. (2002b). Juvenile waiver to adult court: How can developmental and child psychology inform policy decision making. In B. Bottoms, M. B. Kovera, & B. McAuliff (Eds.), *Children and the law: Social science and U.S. law* (pp. 203–232). Cambridge, England: Cambridge University Press.

Salekin, R. T. (2002c). Psychopathy and therapeutic pessimism: Clinical lore or clinical reality? *Clinical Psychology Review, 22,* 79–112. doi:10.1016/S0272-7358(01)00083-6

Salekin, R. T. (2004). *Risk–Sophistication–Treatment Inventory (RST-I).* Lutz, FL: Psychological Assessment Resources.

Salekin, R. T. (2006). Psychopathy in children and adolescents: Key issues in conceptualization and assessment. In C. J. Patrick (Ed.), *Handbook of psychopathy* (pp. 389–414). New York, NY: Guilford Press.

Salekin, R. T. (2008). Psychopathy and recidivism from mid-adolescence to young adulthood: Cumulating legal problems and limiting life opportunities. *Journal of Abnormal Psychology, 117,* 386–395. doi:10.1037/0021-843X.117.2.386

Salekin, R. T. (2010). Treatment of child and adolescent psychopathy: Focusing on change. In R. T. Salekin & D. R. Lynam (Eds.), *Handbook of child and adolescent psychopathy* (pp. 343–373). New York, NY: Guilford Press.

Salekin, R. T. (2014). *The Risk–Sophistication–Treatment Inventory Self-Report.* Manual in preparation.

Salekin, R. T., Barker, E. D., Ang, X., & MacDougall, E. (2012). Indexing adolescent psychopathy: Commentary on Dawson, McCuish, Hart, and Corrado. *International Journal of Forensic Mental Health, 11,* 80–86. doi:10.1080/14999013.2012.676150

Salekin, R. T., & Debus, S. A. (2008). Child and adolescent psychopathy. In R. Jackson (Ed.), *Learning forensic evaluations* (pp. 347–383). New York, NY: Routledge.

Salekin, R. T., & Grimes, R. D. (2008). Clinical forensic evaluations for juvenile transfer to adult criminal court. In R. Jackson (Ed.), *Learning forensic assessment* (pp. 313–346). New York, NY: Routledge.

Salekin, R. T., Jarrett, M. A., & Adams, E W. (2013). Assessment and measurement of change considerations in psychotherapy research. In J. S. Comer & P. C. Kendall (Eds.), *The Oxford handbook of research strategies for clinical psychology* (pp. 103–119). New York, NY: Oxford University Press.

Salekin, R. T., Kubak, F. A., & Lee, Z. (2008). Deception in children and adolescents. In R. Rogers (Ed.), *Clinical assessment of malingering and deception* (3rd ed., pp. 343–364). New York, NY: Guilford Press.

Salekin, R. T., Lee, Z., Schrum-Dillard, C. L., & Kubak, F. A. (2010). Child psychopathy and protective factors: IQ and motivation to change. *Psychology, Public Policy, and Law, 16,* 158–176. doi:10.1037/a0019233

Salekin, R. T., Leistico, A.-M. R., Trobst, K. K., Schrum, C. L., & Lochman, J. E. (2005). Adolescent psychopathy and personality theory—The Interpersonal Circumplex: Expanding evidence of a nomological net. *Journal of Abnormal Child Psychology, 33,* 445–460. doi:10.1007/s10802-005-5726-Y

Salekin, R. T., Lester, W. S., & Sellers, M.-K. (2012). Psychopathy in youth and mental sets: Incremental versus entity theories of intelligence. *Law and Human Behavior, 36,* 283–292. doi:10.1037/h0093971

Salekin, R. T., & Lynam, D. R. (2010a). Child and adolescent psychopathy: An introduction. In R. T. Salekin & D. R. Lynam (Eds.), *Handbook of child and adolescent psychopathy* (pp. 1–11). New York, NY: Guilford Press.

Salekin, R. T., & Lynam, D. R. (2010b). *Handbook of child and adolescent psychopathy.* New York, NY: Guilford Press.

Salekin, R. T., Rogers, R., & Machin, D. (2001). Psychopathy in youth: Pursuing diagnostic clarity. *Journal of Youth and Adolescence, 30,* 173–195. doi:10.1023/A:1010393708227

Salekin, R. T., Rogers, R., & Ustad, K. L. (2001). Juvenile waiver to adult criminal courts: Prototypes for dangerousness, sophistication—maturity, and amenability to treatment. *Psychology, Public Policy, and Law, 7*, 381–408. doi:10.1037/1076-8971.7.2.381

Salekin, R. T., Rosenbaum, J., & Lee, Z. (2008). Child and adolescent psychopathy: Stability and change. *Psychiatry, Psychology and Law, 15*, 224–236. doi:10.1080/13218710802014519

Salekin, R. T., Tippey, J. G., & Allen, A. D. (2012). Treatment of conduct problem youth with interpersonal callous traits using mental models: Measurement of risk and change. *Behavioral Sciences & the Law, 30*, 470–486. doi:10.1002/bsl.2025

Salekin, R. T., Worley, C., & Grimes, R. D. (2010). Treatment of psychopathy: A review and brief introduction to the mental model approach for psychopathy. *Behavioral Sciences & the Law, 28*, 235–266. doi:10.1002/bsl.928

Salekin, R., Yff, R., Neumann, C., Leistico, A., & Zalot, A. (2002). Juvenile transfer to adult courts: A look at the prototypes for dangerousness sophistication–maturity and amenability to treatment through a legal lens. *Psychology, Public Policy, and Law, 8*, 373–410. doi:10.1037/1076-8971.8.4.373

Salekin, R. T., Ziegler, T. A., Larrea, M. A., Anthony, V. L., & Bennett, A. (2003). Predicting dangerousness with the MACI Psychopathy Scale. *Journal of Personality Assessment, 80*, 154–163. doi:10.1207/S15327752JPA8002_04

Salihovic, S., Kerr, M., Özdemir, M., & Pakalniskiene, V. (2012). Directions of effects between adolescent psychopathic traits and parental behavior. *Journal of Abnormal Child Psychology, 40*, 957–969.

Samuel, D. B., & Gore, W. L. (2012). Maladaptive variants of conscientiousness and agreeableness. *Journal of Personality, 80*, 1669–1696. doi:10.1111/j.1467-6494.2012.00770.x

Sanborn, J. B., Jr. (1994). Certification to criminal court: The important policy questions of how, when, and why. *Crime & Delinquency, 40*, 262–281. doi:10.1177/0011128794040002007

Sarata, B., & Provorse, D. (1989). Should there be a psychology of delinquency? *PsycCRITIQUES, 34*, 234–235. doi:10.1037/027759

Sattler, J. M. (1998). *Clinical and forensic interviewing of children and families: Guidelines for the mental health, education, pediatric, and child maltreatment fields.* San Diego, CA: Sattler Publishing.

Sattler, J. M., & Hoge, R. D. (2006). *Assessment of children: Behavioral, social, and clinical foundations* (5th ed.). San Diego, CA: Sattler Publishing.

Saudino, K. J., & Cherny, S. S. (2001). Sources of continuity and change in observed temperament. In R. N. Emde & J. K. Hewitt (Eds.), *Infancy to early childhood: Genetic and environmental influences on developmental change* (pp. 89–110). New York, NY: Oxford University Press.

Saudino, K. J., & Plomin, R. (1996). Personality and behavior genetics: Where have we been and where are we going? *Journal of Research in Personality, 30*, 335–347. doi:10.1006/jrpe.1996.0023

Sautter, J. A., Brown, T. A., Littvay, L., Sautter, A. C., & Bearnes, B. (2008). Attitude and divergence in business students: An examination of personality differences in business and non-business students. *Electronic Journal of Business Ethics and Organization Studies*, *13*, 70–78.

Savitsky, J. C., & Karras, D. (1984). Competency to stand trial among adolescents. *Adolescence*, *19*, 349–358.

Sawyer, A. M., & Borduin, C. M. (2011). Effects of MST through midlife: A 21.9-year follow up to a randomized clinical trial with serious and violent juvenile offenders. *Journal of Consulting and Clinical Psychology*, *79*, 643–652. doi:10.1037/a0024862

Scalia, J. (dissenting). *Roper v. Simmons*, 543 U.S. 551 (2005).

Schetky, D., & Benedek, E. (1980). *Child psychiatry and the law*. New York, NY: Brunner/Mazel.

Schetky, D., & Benedek, E. (1992). *Clinical handbook of child psychiatry and the law*. Baltimore, MD: Williams & Wilkins.

Schetky, D., & Benedek, E. (2002). *Principles and practice of child and adolescent forensic psychiatry*. Washington, DC: American Psychiatric Publishing.

Schmidt, F., Hoge, R. D., & Gomes, L. (2005). Reliability and validity analyses of the Youth Level of Service/Case Management Inventory. *Criminal Justice & Behavior*, *32*, 329–344. doi:10.1177/0093854804274373

Schroeder, B. A., Messina, A., Schroeder, D., Good, K., Barto, S., Saylor, J., & Masiello, M. (2012). The implementation of a statewide bullying prevention program: Preliminary findings from the field and the importance of coalitions. *Health Promotion Practice*, *13*, 489–495. doi:10.1177/1524839910386887

Schweizer, S., Grahn, J., Hampshire, A., Mobbs, D., & Dalgleish, T. (2013). Training the emotional brain: Improving affective control through emotional working memory training. *The Journal of Neuroscience*, *33*, 5301–5311. doi:10.1523/JNEUROSCI.2593-12.2013

Scott, E. S., & Steinberg, L. (2008). *Rethinking juvenile justice*. Cambridge, MA: Harvard University Press.

Seagrave, D., & Grisso, T. (2002). Adolescent development and the measurement of juvenile psychopathy. *Law and Human Behavior*, *26*, 219–239.

Seibert, L. A., Miller, J. D., Few, L. R., Zeichner, A., & Lynam, D. R. (2011). An examination of the structure of self-report psychopathy measures and their relations with general traits and externalizing behaviors. *Personality Disorders*, *2*, 193–208. doi:10.1037/a0019232

Seligman, M. E. P., Rashid, T., & Parks, A. C. (2006). Positive psychotherapy. *American Psychologist*, *61*, 774–788. doi:10.1037/0003-066X.61.8.774

Sexton, T., & Turner, C. W. (2010). The effectiveness of functional family therapy for youth with behavioral problems in a community practice setting. *Journal of Family Psychology*, *24*, 339–348. doi:10.1037/a0019406

Shedler, J. (2010). The efficacy of psychodynamic psychotherapy. *American Psychologist, 65,* 98–109. doi:10.1037/a0018378

Shiner, R. L. (1998). How shall we speak of children's personalities in middle childhood?: A preliminary taxonomy. *Psychological Bulletin, 124,* 308–332. doi:10.1037/0033-2909.124.3.308

Shiner, R. L. (2000). Linking childhood personality with adaptation: Evidence for continuity and change across time into late adolescence. *Journal of Personality and Social Psychology, 78,* 310–325. doi:10.1037/0022-3514.78.2.310

Shiner, R. L. (2006). Temperament and personality in childhood. In D. K. Mroczek & T. D. Little (Eds.), *Handbook of personality development* (pp. 213–230). Mahwah, NJ: Erlbaum.

Shiner, R., & Caspi, A. (2003). Personality differences in childhood and adolescence: Measurement, development, and consequences. *Journal of Child Psychology and Psychiatry, 44,* 2–32. doi:10.1111/1469-7610.00101

Shiner, R. L., & Masten, A. S. (2002). Transactional links between personality and adaptation from childhood through adulthood. *Journal of Research in Personality, 36,* 580–588. doi:10.1016/S0092-6566(02)00508-1

Shiner, R. L., & Masten, A. S. (2008). Personality in childhood: A bridge from early temperament to adult outcomes. *European Journal of Developmental Science, 2,* 158–175.

Shiner, R. L., Masten, A. S., & Roberts, J. M. (2003). Childhood personality foreshadows adult personality and life outcomes two decades later. *Journal of Personality, 71,* 1145–1170. doi:10.1111/1467-6494.7106010

Shiner, R. L., Masten, A. S., & Tellegen, A. (2002). A developmental perspective on personality in emerging adulthood: Childhood antecedents and concurrent adaptation. *Journal of Personality and Social Psychology, 83,* 1165–1177. doi:10.1037/0022-3514.83.5.1165

Shook, J. J., Vaughn, M., Goodkind, S., & Johnson, H. (2011). An empirical portrait of youthful offenders who sell drugs. *Journal of Criminal Justice, 39,* 224–231. doi:10.1016/j.jcrimjus.2011.02.014

Silverman, W. K., & Albano, A. M. (1996). *The Anxiety Disorders Interview Schedule for DSM–IV—Child and Parent Versions.* London, England: Oxford University Press.

Silverthorn, P., & Frick, P. J. (1999). Developmental pathways to antisocial behavior: The delayed-onset pathway in girls. *Development and Psychopathology, 11,* 101–126.

Slobogin, C. (1999). Treating kids right: Deconstructing and reconstructing the amenability to treatment concept. *Contemporary Legal Issues, 10,* 299–333.

Slotboom, A.-M., Havill, V. L., Pavlopoulos, V., & De Fruyt, F. (1998). Developmental changes in personality descriptions of children: A cross-national comparison of parental descriptions of children. In G. A. Kohnstamm, C. F. Halverson, I. Mervielde, & V. L. Havill (Eds.), *Parental descriptions of child personality: Developmental antecedents of the Big Five?* (pp. 127–153). Mahwah, NJ: Erlbaum.

Smith, G. P. (1992). *Structured Inventory of Malingered Symptomatology*. Lutz, FL: Psychological Assessment Resources.

Smith, G. P., & Burger, G. K. (1997). Detection of malingering: Validation of the Structured Inventory of Malingered Symptomatology (SIMS). *Journal of the American Academy of Psychiatry and the Law, 25*, 183–189.

Smith, M. L., & Glass, G. V. (1978). Meta-analysis of psychotherapy outcome studies. *American Psychologist, 32*, 752–760.

Snyder, H. N., & Sickmund, M. (2006). *Juvenile offenders and victims: 2006 National report*. Washington, DC: U.S. Department of Justice, Office of Justice Programs, Office of Juvenile Justice and Delinquency Prevention.

Sodian, B. (1991). The development of deception in young children. *British Journal of Developmental Psychology, 9*, 173–188. doi:10.1111/j.2044-835X.1991.tb00869.x

Spice, A., Viljoen, J. L., Gretton, H. M., & Roesch, R. (2010). Psychological assessment for adult sentencing of juvenile offenders: An evaluation of the RSTI and the SAVRY. *International Journal of Forensic Mental Health, 9*, 124–137. doi:10.1080/14999013.2010.501846

Sroufe, L. A., Carlson, E. A., Levy, A. K., & Egeland, B. (1999). Implications of attachment theory for developmental psychopathology. *Development and Psychopathology, 11*, 1–13. doi:10.1017/S0954579499001923

Stein, L. A. R., Graham, J. R., & Williams, C. L. (1995). Detecting fake-bad MMPI–A profiles. *Journal of Personality Assessment, 65*, 415–427. doi:10.1207/s15327752jpa6503_3

Steinberg, L., Albert, D., Cauffman, E., Banich, M., Graham, S., & Woolard, J. (2008). Age differences in sensation seeking and impulsivity as indexed by behavior and self-report: Evidence for a dual systems model. *Developmental Psychology, 44*, 1764–1778. doi:10.1037/a0012955

Steinberg, L., & Cauffman, E. (1996). Maturity of judgment in adolescence: Psychosocial factors in adolescent decision making. *Law and Human Behavior, 20*, 249–272.

Steinberg, L., & Cauffman, E. (1999). A developmental perspective on serious juvenile crime: When should juveniles be treated as adults? *Federal Probation, 63*, 52–57.

Steinberg, L., & Cauffman, E. (2000). A developmental perspective on judicial boundary. In J. Fagan & F. E. Zimring (Eds.), *The changing borders of juvenile justice: Transfer of adolescents to criminal court* (pp. 379–406). Chicago, IL: University of Chicago Press.

Steinberg, L., Greenberger, E., Jacobi, M., & Garduque, L. (1981). Early work experience: A partial antidote for adolescent egotism. *Journal of Youth and Adolescence, 10*, 141–157. doi:10.1007/BF02091741

Steinberg, L., & Scott, E. S. (2003). Less guilty by reason of adolescence: Developmental immaturity, diminished responsibility, and the juvenile death penalty. *American Psychologist, 58*, 1009–1018. doi:10.1037/0003-066X.58.12.1009

Steinberg, R. (2008). *Suicidal and aggressive behavior in latency-age children: Measures of aggression, annihilation anxiety and quality of object relations* (Unpublished doctoral dissertation). Long Island University, Brooklyn, NY.

Steller, M., & Koehnken, G. (1989). Criteria-based statement analysis. In D. C. Raskin (Ed.), *Psychological methods in criminal investigation and evidence* (pp. 217–245). New York, NY: Springer.

Stepp, S. D., Burke, J. D., Hipwell, A. E., & Loeber, R. (2012). Trajectories of attention deficit hyperactivity disorder and oppositional defiant disorder symptoms as precursors of borderline personality disorder symptoms in adolescent girls. *Journal of Abnormal Child Psychology, 40*, 7–20.

Sternberg, R. J. (2000). Implicit theories of intelligence as exemplar stories of success: Why intelligence test validity is in the eye of the beholder. *Psychology, Public Policy, and Law, 6*, 159–167. doi:10.1037/1076-8971.6.1.159

Stoolmiller, M. (2001). Synergistic interaction of child manageability problems and parent-discipline tactics in predicting future growth in externalizing behavior for boys. *Developmental Psychology, 37*, 814–825. doi:10.1037/0012-1649.37.6.814

Stouthamer-Loeber, M. (1986). Lying as a problem behavior in children: A review. *Clinical Psychology Review, 6*, 267–289.

Stouthamer-Loeber, M., & Loeber, R. (1986). Boys who lie. *Journal of Abnormal Child Psychology, 14*, 551–564.

Strasburger, L. H. (1989). The juvenile transfer hearing and the forensic psychiatrist. In R. Rosner (Ed.), *Juvenile psychiatry and the law* (pp. 391–403). New York, NY: Plenum Press. doi:10.1007/978-1-4684-5526-7_23

Strathman, A., Gleicher, F., Boninger, D. S., & Edwards, C. S. (1994). The consideration of future consequences: Weighing immediate and distant outcomes of behavior. *Journal of Personality and Social Psychology, 66*, 742–752. doi:10.1037/0022-3514.66.4.742

Strauss, S. S., & Clarke, B. A. (1992). Decision-making patterns in adolescent mothers. *Image: The Journal of Nursing Scholarship, 24*, 69–74. doi:10.1111/j.1547-5069.1992.tb00702.x

Stringaris, A., & Goodman, R. (2009a). Longitudinal outcome of youth oppositionality: Irritable, headstrong, and hurtful behaviors have distinctive predictions. *Journal of the American Academy of Child & Adolescent Psychiatry, 48*, 404–412.

Stringaris, A., & Goodman, R. (2009b). Three dimensions of oppositionality in youth. *Journal of Child Psychology and Psychiatry, 50*, 216–223.

Stringaris, A., Maughan, B., & Goodman, R. (2010). What is a disruptive disorder? Temperamental antecedents of oppositional defiant disorder: Findings from the Avon Longitudinal Study. *Journal of the American Academy of Child & Adolescent Psychiatry, 49*, 474–483.

Svansdottir, E., van den Broek, K. C., Karlsson, H. D., Olason, D. T., Thorgilsson, H., & Denollet, J. (2013). The distressed (Type D) and five-factor models of personality in young, healthy adults and their association with emotional inhibition and distress. *Personality and Individual Differences, 55,* 123–128. doi:10.1016/j.paid.2013.02.008

Swanson, J., Borum, R., Swartz, M., & Monahan, J. (1996). Psychotic symptoms and disorders and the risk of violent behaviour in the community. *Criminal Behaviour and Mental Health, 6,* 309–329. doi:10.1002/cbm.118

Tackett, J. L. (2006). Evaluating models of the personality–psychopathology relationship in children and adolescents. *Clinical Psychology Review, 26,* 584–599. doi:10.1016/j.cpr.2006.04.003

Tackett, J. L. (2007). Investigating personality–psychopathology relationships in childhood: Highlighting aggressive versus non-aggressive antisocial behaviors. *Dissertation Abstracts International: Section B: The Sciences and Engineering, 67*(11), 6747.

Talwar, V., Gordon, H. M., & Lee, K. (2007). Lying in the elementary school years: Verbal deception and its relation to second-order belief understanding. *Developmental Psychology, 43,* 804–810.

Talwar, V., & Lee, K. (2002). Development of lying to conceal a transgression: Children's control of expressive behavior during verbal deception. *International Journal of Behavioral Development, 26,* 436–444.

Tanenhaus, D. S. (2000). The evolution of transfer out of the juvenile court. In J. Fagan & F. E. Zimring (Eds.), *The changing borders of juvenile justice: Transfer of adolescents to the criminal court* (pp. 13–43). Chicago, IL: University of Chicago Press.

Tarasoff v. Regents of the University of California, 17 Cal. 3d 425, 551 P.2d 334, 131 Cal. Rptr. 14 (Cal. 1976).

Tellegen, A. (1985). Structures of mood and personality and their relevance to assessing anxiety, with an emphasis on self-report. In A. Tuma & J. D. Maser (Eds.), *Anxiety and the anxiety disorders* (pp. 681–706). Hillsdale, NJ: Erlbaum.

Teplin, L. A., Abram, K. M., McClelland, G. M., Dulcan, M. K., & Mericle, A. A. (2002). Psychiatric disorders in youth in juvenile detention. *Archives of General Psychiatry, 59,* 1133–1143. doi:10.1001/archpsyc.59.12.1133

Teplin, L. A., Welty, L. J., Abram, K. M., Dulcan, M. K., & Washburn, J. J. (2012). Prevalence and persistence of psychiatric disorders in youth after detention: A prospective longitudinal study. *Archives of General Psychiatry, 69,* 1031–1043.

Thomas, A., & Chess, S. (1977). *Temperament and development.* New York, NY: Brunner/Mazel.

Thomas, A., Chess, S., & Birch, H. (1968). *Temperament and behavior disorders in children.* New York, NY: New York University Press.

Thomas, A., Chess, S., Birch, H., Hertzig, M., & Korn, S. (1963). *Behavioral individuality in early childhood.* New York, NY: New York University Press.

Tobin, R. M., Graziano, W. G., Vanman, E. J., & Tassinary, L. G. (2000). Personality, emotional experience, and efforts to control emotions. *Journal of Personality and Social Psychology, 79*, 656–669. doi:10.1037/0022-3514.79.4.656

Todd, R. D., Joyner, C., Heath, A. C., Neuman, R. J., & Reich, W. (2003). Reliability and stability of a semistructured *DSM–IV* interview designed for family studies. *Journal of the American Academy of Child & Adolescent Psychiatry, 42*, 1460–1468.

Tombaugh, T. N. (1996). *Test of Memory Malingering*. San Antonio, TX: The Psychological Corporation.

Trapnell, P. D., & Wiggins, J. S. (1990). Extension of the Interpersonal Adjective Scales to include the Big Five dimensions of personality. *Journal of Personality and Social Psychology, 59*, 781–790. doi:10.1037/0022-3514.59.4.781

Trotter, C., & Evans, P. (2012). An analysis of supervision skills in youth probation. *Australian and New Zealand Journal of Criminology, 45*, 255–273. doi:10.1177/0004865812443678

Turner, S. M., DeMers, S. T., Fox, H., & Reed, G. (2001). APA's guidelines for test user qualifications: An executive summary. *American Psychologist, 56*, 1099–1113. doi:10.1037/0003-066X.56.12.1099

Tyler, J., Darville, R., & Stalnaker, K. (2001). Juvenile boot camps: A descriptive analysis of program diversity and effectiveness. *The Social Science Journal, 38*, 445–460. doi:10.1016/S0362-3319(01)00130-6

Uliaszek, A. A., Zinbarg, R. E., Mineka, S., Craske, M. G., Sutton, J. M., Griffith, J. W., & Hammen, C. (2010). The role of Neuroticism and Extraversion in the stress–anxiety and stress–depression relationships. *Anxiety, Stress, & Coping, 23*, 363–381. doi:10.1080/10615800903377264

Umamaheswar, J. (2013). Bringing hope and change: A study of youth probation officers in Toronto. *International Journal of Offender Therapy and Comparative Criminology, 57*, 1158–1182. doi:10.1177/0306624X12445986

Vanhalst, J., Klimstra, T. A., Luyckx, K., Scholte, R. J., Engels, R. E., & Goossens, L. (2012). The interplay of loneliness and depressive symptoms across adolescence: Exploring the role of personality traits. *Journal of Youth and Adolescence, 41*, 776–787. doi:10.1007/s10964-011-9726-7

van Reekum, C. M., Urry, H. L., Johnstone, T., Thurow, M. E., Frye, C. J., Jackson, C. A., . . . Davidson, R. J. (2007). Individual differences in amygdala and ventromedial prefrontal cortex activity are associated with evaluation speed and psychological well-being. *Journal of Cognitive Neuroscience, 19*, 237–248.

Van Voorhis, P. (1994). *Psychological classification of the adult male prison inmate*. Albany: State University of New York Press.

Vaughan, S. C. (1997). *The talking cure: The science behind psychotherapy*. New York, NY: Henry Holt.

Vaughn, M. G., & DeLisi, M. (2008). Were Wolfgang's chronic offenders psychopaths? On the convergent validity between psychopathy and career criminality. *Journal of Criminal Justice, 36*, 33–42. doi:10.1016/j.jcrimjus.2007.12.008

Vaughn, M. G., Howard, M. O., & DeLisi, M. (2008). Psychopathic personality traits and delinquent careers: An empirical examination. *International Journal of Law and Psychiatry, 31*, 407–416. doi:10.1016/j.ijlp.2008.08.001

Vernham, Z., Vrij, A., Mann, S., Leal, S., & Hillman, J. (2014). Collective interviewing: Eliciting cues to deceit using a turn-taking approach. *Psychology, Public Policy, and Law, 20*, 309–324.

Vincent, G. M., Chapman, J., & Cook, N. E. (2011). Risk-needs assessment in juvenile justice: Predictive validity of the SAVRY, racial differences, and the contribution of needs factors. *Criminal Justice and Behavior, 38*, 42–62.

Vitacco, M. J., & Salekin, R. T. (2013). Adolescent psychopathy and the law. In K. A. Kiehl & W. P. Sinnott-Armstrong (Eds.), *Handbook on psychopathy and law* (pp. 78–89). New York, NY: Oxford University Press.

Vitacco, M. J., Salekin, R. T., & Rogers, R. (2010). Forensic issues for child and adolescent psychopathy. In R. T. Salekin & D. R. Lynam (Eds.), *Handbook of child and adolescent psychopathy* (pp. 374–397). New York, NY: Guilford Press.

Vrij, A., Mann, S., Jundi, S., Hillman, J., & Hope, L. (2014). Detection of concealment in an information-gathering interview. *Applied Cognitive Psychology.* Advance online publication. doi:10.1002/acp.3051

Vygotsky, L. S. (1986). *Thought and language.* (A. Kozulin, Trans.). Cambridge, MA: MIT Press. (Original work published 1934)

Walker, J. V. III, & Lampropoulos, G. K. (2014). A comparison of self-help (homework) activities for mood enhancement: Results from a brief randomized controlled trial. *Journal of Psychotherapy Integration, 24*, 46–64. doi:10.1037/a0036145

Walper, S., Kruse, J., Noack, P., & Schwarz, B. (2004). Parental separation and adolescents' felt insecurity with mothers: Effects of financial hardship, interparental conflict, and maternal parenting in East and West Germany. *Marriage & Family Review, 36*, 115–145. doi:10.1300/J002v36n03_07

Ward, T., Day, A., Howells, K., & Birgden, A. (2004). The multifactor offender readiness model. *Aggression and Violent Behavior, 9*, 645–673. doi:10.1016/j.avb.2003.08.001

Warren, J. R. (1966). Birth order and social behavior. *Psychological Bulletin, 65*, 38–49. doi:10.1037/h0022739

Warren, M. Q. (1971). Classification of offenders as an aid to efficient management and effective treatment. *Journal of Criminal Law, Criminology, and Police Science, 62*, 239–258. doi:10.2307/1141881

Washburn, J. J., Romero, E. G., Welty, L. J., Abram, K. M., Teplin, L. A., McClelland, G. M., & Paskar, L. D. (2007). Development of antisocial personality disorder in detained youths: The predictive value of mental disorders. *Journal of Consulting and Clinical Psychology, 75*, 221–231. doi:10.1037/0022-006X.75.2.221

Wasserman, G. A., McReynolds, L. S., Lucas, C. P., Fisher, P., & Santos, L. (2002). The voice DISC–IV with incarcerated male youths: Prevalence of disorder. *Journal of the American Academy of Child & Adolescent Psychiatry, 41*, 314–321. doi:10.1097/00004583-200203000-00011

Wasserman, G. A., McReynolds, L. S., Whited, A. L., Keating, J. M., Musabegovic, H., & Huo, Y. (2008). Juvenile probation officers' mental health decision making. *Administration and Policy in Mental Health and Mental Health Services Research, 35*, 410–422. doi:10.1007/s10488-008-0183-x

Watson, D., & Clark, L. (1993). Behavioral disinhibition versus constraint: A dispositional perspective. In D. M. Wegner & J. W. Pennebaker (Eds.), *Handbook of mental control* (pp. 506–527). Englewood Cliffs, NJ: Prentice Hall.

Wechsler, D. (2004). *Wechsler Intelligence Scale for Children—Fourth Edition*. London, England: Pearson Assessments.

Weinberger, D. A., & Schwartz, G E. (1990). Distress and restraint as superordinate dimensions of self-reported adjustment: A typological perspective. *Journal of Personality, 58*, 381–417.

Weisz, J. R., & Hawley, K. M. (2002). Developmental factors in the treatment of adolescents. *Journal of Consulting and Clinical Psychology, 70*, 21–43. doi:10.1037/0022-006X.70.1.21

Weisz, J. R., & Kazdin, A. E. (Eds.). (2010). *Evidence-based psychotherapies for children and adolescents* (2nd ed.). New York, NY: Guilford Press.

Weiten, W. (2013). *Psychology: Themes and variations* (9th ed.). Belmont, CA: Thomson Wadsworth.

Weller, E. B., Weller, R. A., Fristad, M. A., Rooney, M. T., & Schecter, J. (2000). Children's Interview for Psychiatric Syndromes (ChIPS). *Journal of the American Academy of Child & Adolescent Psychiatry, 39*, 76–84. doi:10.1097/00004583-200001000-00019

West, H. C., & Sabol, W. J. (2009). *Prison inmates at mid-year-2008: Statistical tables*. Washington, DC: U.S. Department of Justice, Office of Justice Programs, Bureau of Justice Statistics.

Westen, D., Klepser, J., Ruffins, S. A., Silverman, M., Lifton, N., & Boekamp, J. (1991). Object relations in childhood and adolescence: The development of working representations. *Journal of Consulting and Clinical Psychology, 59*, 400–409. doi:10.1037/0022-006X.59.3.400

Westen, D., Novotny, C. M., & Thompson-Brenner, H. (2004). The empirical status of empirically supported psychotherapies: Assumptions, findings, and reporting in controlled clinical trials. *Psychological Bulletin, 130*, 631–663.

Whelan, Y. M., Stringaris, A., Maughan, B., & Barker, E. D. (2013). Developmental continuity of oppositional defiant disorder subdimensions at ages 8, 10, and 13 years and their distinct psychiatric outcomes at age 16 years. *Journal of the American Academy of Child & Adolescent Psychiatry, 52*, 961–969. doi:10.1016/j.jaac.2013.06.013

Widiger, T. A., Lynam, D. R., Miller, J. D., & Oltmanns, T. F. (2012). Measures to assess maladaptive variants of the five-factor model. *Journal of Personality Assessment, 94*, 450–455. doi:10.1080/00223891.2012.677887

Wiggins, J. S., Trapnell, P., & Phillips, N. (1988). Psychometric and geometric characteristics of the Revised Interpersonal Adjective Scale (IAS–R). *Multivariate Behavioral Research, 23,* 517–530.

Wiggins, J. S., & Trobst, K. K. (2002). The Interpersonal Adjectives Scales: Big Five version (IASR–B5). In B. de Raad & M. Perugini (Eds.), *Big Five assessment* (pp. 264–276). Ashland, OH: Hogrefe & Huber.

Wilkinson, G. S., & Robertson, G. J. (2006). *Wide Range Achievement Test 4 professional manual.* Lutz, FL: Psychological Assessment Resources.

Wille, B., De Fruyt, F., & De Clercq, B. (2013). Expanding and reconceptualizing aberrant personality at work: Validity of five-factor model aberrant personality tendencies to predict career outcomes. *Personnel Psychology, 66,* 173–223. doi:10.1111/peps.12016

Wilson, J. J., & Howell, J. C. (1995). Comprehensive strategy for serious, violent, and chronic juvenile offenders. In J. C. Howell, B. Krisberg, J. D. Hawkins, & J. J. Wilson (Eds.), *A sourcebook: Serious, violent, and chronic juvenile offenders* (pp. 36–47). Thousand Oaks, CA: Sage.

Wilson, S. J., Lipsey, M. W., & Derzon, J. H. (2003). The effects of school-based intervention programs on aggressive behavior: A meta-analysis. *Journal of Consulting and Clinical Psychology, 71,* 136–149.

Witt, P. H. (2003). Transfer of juveniles to adult court: The case of H. H. *Psychology, Public Policy, and Law, 9,* 361–380. doi:10.1037/1076-8971.9.3-4.361

Witt, P. H., & Dyer, F. J. (1997). Juveniles transfer cases: Risk assessment and risk management. *The Journal of Psychiatry & Law, 25,* 581–614.

Woodcock, R. W., McGrew, K. S., & Mather, N. (2001). *Woodcock–Johnson III Tests of Cognitive Abilities.* Itasca, IL: Riverside.

Woolard, J. L., Fondacaro, M. R., & Slobogin, C. (2001). Informing juvenile justice policy: Directions for behavioral science research. *Law and Human Behavior, 25,* 13–24. doi:10.1023/A:1005635808317

Woolard, J. L., Odgers, C., Lanza-Kaduce, L., & Daglis, H. (2005). Juveniles within adult correctional settings: Legal pathways and developmental considerations. *International Journal of Forensic Mental Health, 4,* 1–18. doi:10.1080/14999013.2005.10471209

World Health Organization. (2012). *International classification of diseases* (11th ed.). Geneva, Switzerland: Author.

Wright, J., Beaver, K., DeLisi, M., & Vaughn, M. (2008). Evidence of negligible parenting influences on self-control, delinquent peers, and delinquency in a sample of twins. *Justice Quarterly, 25,* 544–569.

Wu, J., Zhang, J., Ding, X., Li, R., & Zhou, C. (2013). The effects of music on brain functional networks: A network analysis. *Neuroscience, 250,* 49–59.

Yamagata, S., Ando, J., Yoshimura, K., Ostendorf, F., Rainer, R., Spinath, F., & Livesley, W. J. (2006). Is the genetic structure of human personality universal?

A cross-cultural twin study from North America, Europe, and Asia. *Journal of Personality and Social Psychology, 90,* 987–998. doi:10.1037/0022-3514.90.6.987

Yates, B. D., Nordquist, C. R., & Schultz-Ross, A. R. (1996). Feigned psychiatric symptoms in the emergency room. *Psychiatric Services, 47,* 998–1000.

Yuille, J. C. (1988). The systematic assessment of children's testimony. *Canadian Psychology, 29,* 247–262.

Zahn, M. A., Hawkins, S. R., Chiancone, J., & Whitworth, A. (2008). *Girls study group: Understanding and responding to girls' delinquency.* Washington, DC: U.S. Department of Justice.

Zahner, G. E. (1991). The feasibility of conducting structured diagnostic interviews with preadolescents: A community field trial of the DISC. *Journal of the American Academy of Child & Adolescent Psychiatry, 30,* 659–668. doi:10.1097/00004583-199107000-00020

Zalot, A. A. (2002a). *How do dangerousness, sophistication–maturity, and amenability to treatment influence the juvenile transfer decision?* (Unpublished honors thesis). University of Alabama, Tuscaloosa.

Zalot, A. A. (2002b). [Taylor Hardin Secure Medical Facility Project]. Unpublished raw data.

Zimbardo, P. G., & Boyd, J. N. (1999). Putting time in perspective: A valid, reliable individual-differences metric. *Journal of Personality and Social Psychology, 77,* 1271–1288.

Zimring, F. E. (1998). *American youth violence.* New York, NY: Oxford University Press.

INDEX

ABOUT THE AUTHOR

Randall T. Salekin, PhD, is a professor and the director of the Disruptive Behavior Clinic (DBC) at the University of Alabama. He also serves as the Associate Director of the Center for the Prevention of Youth Behavior Problems. Dr. Salekin is an expert in the assessment and treatment of young people with disruptive behavior disorders who are referred from the community or the juvenile court. He provides assessment, treatment, and general consultation recommendations. Dr. Salekin is the author of the Risk–Sophistication–Treatment Inventory (RSTI), one of the primary measures for assessing youth who have come into contact with the law. His research focuses on understanding the causes and correlates of disruptive behavior in children, including youth with interpersonal callousness (limited prosocial emotion). In addition, his research and practice focus on the treatment of conduct problems in young people with interpersonal callous traits. Dr. Salekin's assessment and treatment efforts have been found to be both innovative and effective for youth with oppositional defiant disorders, conduct disorders, and limited prosocial emotion. Dr. Salekin is the author of numerous research publications, the *Handbook of Child and Adolescent Psychopathy*, and has received both national and international recognition for his work.